Forfar On This Day

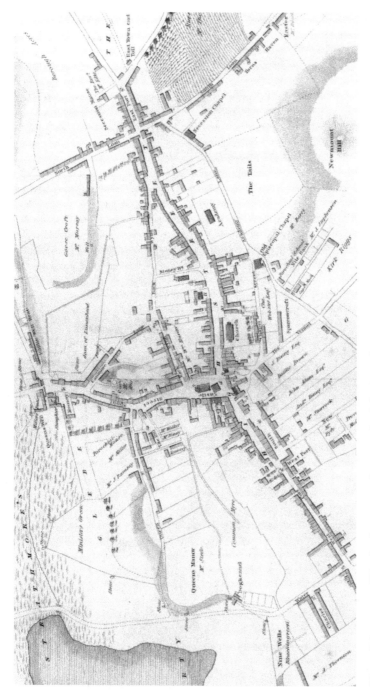

Plan of the town of Forfar from actual survey by John Wood, 1822

Forfar On This Day

David W. Potter

Kennedy & Boyd
an imprint of
Zeticula Ltd,
Unit 13,
196 Rose Street,
Edinburgh,
EH2 4AT,
Scotland.

http://www.kennedyandboyd.co.uk
admin@kennedyandboyd.co.uk

First published 2021

Hardback ISBN 978-1-84921-219-9
Paperback ISBN 978-1-84921-220-5

Acknowledgements

The author would like to gratefully acknowledge the sources of the photographs in this book.

These have been found in a variety of books, booklets and websites, e.g. the "Portrait Gallery of Forfar Notables", the numerous "Kirn Poke" books of the late Ernest Mann and "A Historical Walk Ower Bummie" by the same gentleman, "Old Forfar" by Fiona Scharlau, "A Forfar Loon in Bygone Days" by Bill Harvey, "St James's Forfar – The Story of A Congregation" by Rev John F Kirk and "Across The Years-Episcopacy in Forfar" by Edward Luscombe. George Dempster of Dunnichen is from "Portrait Gallery of Forfar Notables", drawn by John Young.

Thanks also to Jim Nicol for the image of Lang Strang.

The town plans of Forfar in 1827 and 1832, and advertisements, are reproduced with the permission of the National Library of Scotland.

He would also like to acknowledge the help and co-operation of Forfar Athletic FC and Strathmore CC for the use of photographs of their respective sports, the family of John Killacky for the photograph of the great cyclist, and the Scottish Political Archive, University of Stirling, for the leaflet featuring Douglas Young.

Aileen Elliott of the Forfar And District Historical Society has also proved to be very helpful and co-operative.

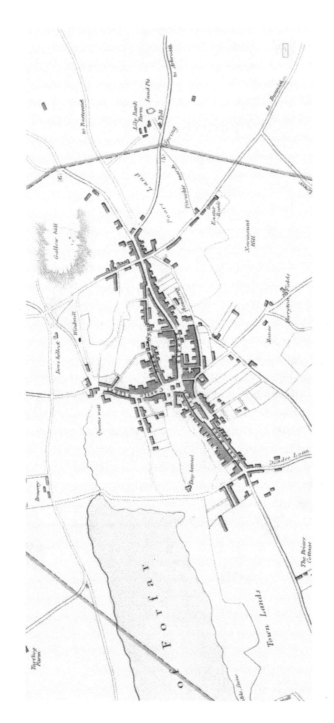

Forfar in 1831. This plan, published in 1832, shows buildings noticeably generalised.

Contents

Baxter the Bridie,
Forfar Athletic's mascot

W. Shepherd, Advertisement from 1847

Introduction

"Bonnie Munross will be a' moss
Brechin a bra burgh toon
But Farfar will be Farfar still
Fin Dundee's a dug doun"

It was my privilege to be born and brought up in Forfar, and although it is now many years since I last lived there, it is nevertheless not something that one shakes off very easily. Forfar has its own distinctive accent, its own culture and its way of life. And although you can leave Forfar, Forfar will never leave you. You remain a loon — or the female equivalent.

It is a small town. It is small enough for everyone to know almost everyone else in the town. Whether this is a good thing or not, I forbear to say, but let us just say that you are not likely to be ignored, certainly not for long! Forfar people like to know everything that goes on. Your sins will find be found out sooner there than anywhere else, but you will also be helped quicker than anywhere else. The community will look after you.

This history of this town is a vast and diverse study. This book will not claim to be a history of the town. What it does claim to do is to give readers an excerpt, a sample of what life was like on any given day of the year. There is no hierarchy in what has been chosen — world wars are interspersed with Church socials and cycling events, the affairs of Forfar Athletic and Strathmore Cricket club, tennis and golf — but they all have something to do with the town. I hope some sort of picture will emerge of what the town has been like in the past and what it can be like in the future.

The town cannot be seen in isolation, and one of the interesting things about Forfar history is how it intertwines with national history. It is pompous to claim that Forfar is a microcosm of the world, but there are elements of truth there nevertheless, and this is why what happens in the town must be seen against the backdrop of what is happening in the world.

Occasionally, I was surprised with some of the things that I discovered. The 1889 "lock out" for example is worthy of deeper study, and my deeply held belief that the Church automatically sided uncompromisingly with factory owners in the 19th century in the same way as it had sided with the landowners against the tenants half a century previously was thoroughly shattered. Even the press took the side of the workers!

I have tried to reflect everything in the town. This is not always possible, and naturally I am attracted to the aspects of the town's life that I am interested in. The reader will probably guess that I am interested in football, cricket, politics and the Great War. So I am, but my main interest remains the town that I was born and brought up in and which I still love. Many long years have now passed since I last lived in Forfar, but this only intensifies the affection I retain for the place.

My thanks are due to *The Forfar Dispatch*, *The Forfar Herald*, *The Courier* and many other newspapers, the Forfar and District Historical Society, and many other people who over the years have told me stories about the town that we love. In addition, tribute must be paid to the many Forfarians, alive and dead, who have unwittingly perhaps contributed to this book just by the odd remark about something that once happened!

List of Illustrations

January

January 1 1900

New Year's Day (New Century's Day in this case, although the pedants might claim that New Century's Day should be 1901) was celebrated in Forfar with more than its usual extravagance this year.

There had been an upturn in the jute trade (thanks to the need for the wrapping of military equipment in jute for transport to South Africa for the Boer War) and wages had been increased.

The Forfar Herald sees good and bad in all this. It was nice to see the town so prosperous with so many Forfarians back home to see their relatives and money being spent in such profusion in the local shops on Saturday December 30, but Hogmanay itself, even though it was the Sabbath, saw far too many "young men, evidently with a disregard for the Sabbath, wandering about our streets in a state of intoxication, jostling decent people and singing popular songs".

And as 12 o'clock approached a large crowd "chiefly of the rough class already described" assembled in the neighbourhood of the Cross, in spite of the bad weather. As the steeple clock struck the hour, greetings were exchanged and "the bottle" was very much in evidence and "healths were pledged to an extent that must have been injurious to the health of not a few".

And then the "first footing" began. Some young Forfar men were far away of course in South Africa, where news wasn't always good, and their health was drunk to as well. On New Year's Day itself, the weather was much improved, the Band played at 12.00 noon, various institutions gave their annual treat to local children, and Forfar Athletic played Bo-ness at Station Park, unfortunately losing 4-5 in a thrilling game.

January 2 1952

Today at his house in Willowbrae, Brechin Road, Alec Troup died.

He had been ill for some time with cancer of the throat, and in some ways his death was considered to be a merciful release. He was only 56.

Not only was he one of the best football players of his day, he was also a total gentleman, much loved by all who had played for him or against him and was also a well-known figure in the town in spite of his modest demeanour. He had made his debut in senior football at Station Park on New Year's Day 1914 and had made an instant impact in a 6-0 thrashing of Arbroath.

Alex Troup,
Forfar's greatest
football player

The First World War had got in the way of his career, but after serving in the Royal Engineers, Alec had played for Dundee before moving to Everton in 1923 where he provided the ammunition for the great William Ralph Dean commonly known as "Dixie". He returned to Dundee for a few seasons in 1930 before he retired.

He played five times for Scotland, and might have played oftener had his career not coincided with that of Alan Morton of Rangers.

He had been brought up in Queen Street, then lived for a while in West High Street before moving to the Brechin Road. When he retired from football he ran a Gentleman's Clothes Shop in Castle Street.

His funeral a few days later was well attended by so many of those who had played with him for Forfar, Dundee, Everton and Scotland.

The Muckle Inn, originally meant to be the Railway
Hotel for the first railway station.

January 3 1839

Today, the Arbroath to Forfar Railway was opened to the public.

There had been a few trial runs last week containing passengers, but today was the official opening. The first train, pulled by a locomotive called *Victoria* (in honour of the new Queen), left Arbroath Station (Almerlecloss Depot) at 8.30 in the morning and in "rather less than an hour", arrived in Forfar (Playfield Station) where hundreds of people were waiting to see the new phenomenon of the age.

At 10.30 am the train began its return journey where it stopped at Clocksbriggs, Auldbar Road, Guthrie, Friockheim and Leysmill on its journey to Arbroath. The train had three first class carriages, one second class and two third class.

The journey was repeated in the afternoon, and the Chairman of the Company Mr Lindsay Carnegie provided a meal for some of the VIPs on board the train. Railways had been around for about ten years now, and it was clear that Forfar was ahead of most of the United Kingdom in having a railway and a station.

Most business men saw the possibilities of being able to send goods to large cities and busy seas ports with all speed, many others were just curious and saved up their pennies in order to afford a ride on a train someday, but there were still a few who felt that such noisy contraptions were contrary to the will of God who provided horses for the purpose of pulling goods.

They were certainly very noisy and frightening to people whose only noise that they were familiar with hitherto was the clattering of a loom. But the "gridiron" was the thing of the future, and it would revolutionise transport for the rest of the century and beyond.

In Forfar there were plans to build a huge hotel across from the station. It would be called the "Muckle Inn", but by the time it was built, the station had moved, and it became a dwelling house.

January 4 1926

Today the Registrar Mr John F Craik produced his statistics for last year and set them in context with the previous years.

The population of the town was still increasing with 192 births and 177 deaths. Both of those figures are down on the years of the early 1920s.

The "baby boom" of the first few years after the war had passed — a phenomenon caused by soldiers coming home from the war and deciding to get married and start a family, or soldiers already married deciding to resume their family — and the death rate had fallen as well now that the Spanish flu and its aftermath (it lingered for a few years after its peak in 1918 and 1919) had finally gone.

The deaths in 1925 showed 16 deaths of babies under a year, which was high but well under the national average, and most people in Forfar died over the age of 70. The birth rate contained "rather too many" who were born out of wedlock.

Marriages had dropped in 1925 to 70 from 83 in 1924 and the 90s before that, but the marriage rate was one of those things which sometimes defied rational analysis. These figures did tend to prove that the quality of life in Forfar was quite good by the standard of the times and certainly a great deal better than some of the larger cities like Dundee or Glasgow, for example.

A factor in that was of course the quality of the air that one breathed. Jute factories and their "lums" were filthy, dirty things but Forfarians were never too far away from the fresher air of the countryside.

January 5 1908

Forfar people attended Church this morning with a smile on their face, following the news that broke late last night and was now spreading like wildfire round the town.

The Manor Linen and Jute Works, commonly known as Craik's, had been saved! A consortium of Forfar business men had managed to form a Limited Company and had bought the concern for £8,000.

Craik's had been in administration since last August but managed to continue trading and paying their workers until December 28. The doors had apparently been closed for the last time on that date, leading to a miserable and anxious New Year Holiday for the 300 people employed there.

But The Forfar Factory Workers Union had spearheaded a rescue attempt, sinking some of their own funds into the new company and persuading some influential and rich local people to join them. It did of course have massive popular support because everyone realised that if a firm the size of Craik's went out of business, the effect on the local economy could be catastrophic.

Craik's was the oldest and largest factory in town, having opened in March 1863 as a power loom factory. It was a family concern and for a while did very well. It was extended in 1870 as the market for jute took off, mainly because of the end of the American Civil War in 1865 which led to the United States extending westwards and needing jute for the covered wagons.

Last night's news meant that there was now a chance that the factory might begin to prosper again, but no-one was under any illusions that there was any guarantee of continued progress.

January 6 1948

Len Halstead, for so long the cricket professional at Lochside for Strathmore, has been appointed professional/groundsman at Meigle for the 1948 season.

A Yorkshire man, and now nearly 50, he had been the professional at Brechin for a year, then had returned to play as an amateur at Strathmore, thinking presumably that his days as a professional cricketer were over.

The Meigle job was clearly an opportunity that he did not want to turn down although he did keep on stating his love for the Forfar club. *The Forfar Dispatch* is of the opinion that it is his love of cricket that has kept him going for he is an admirable coach, a useful bowler, a batsman who can be relied upon to put on a score in a hurry or to offer stubborn resistance if required.

It is as a fielder that he is best remembered, and not least because of the size of his hands which were often described as shovels. For a small man, his huge hands were out of proportion to the rest of him, and the ball simply sank into his hands in the slips.

In point of fact, he had many years left in him and later became professional for Kirkcaldy. He was always a great character with Kirkcaldy, who played then at the Beveridge Park, and on one occasion had to share the ground with a German circus.

One day he claimed that an elephant had relieved itself on his wicket, and as he put it himself, "I had to go an fookin' remind them who won t'last fookin' war, and they'd better remove it toot fookin' sweet".

He died in Kirkcaldy in 1974.

January 7 1921

The sheer versatility of the Reid Hall Cinema as a place of entertainment is proved tonight.

Under the management of Mr Gayle and Mr Whitaker, there will be a film called "Maciste in Love". Then Miss Ellis Drake and Company will do a Sketch (by special request) called "My Husband", then the screen will be used again for the Serial — Episode Twelve of "The Woman In Grey".

And all this for seats ranging from 5 pence to the expensive ones at 1 shilling 10 pence! The Serial is the real attraction because last week's episode left everyone on the edge of their seats wondering what was going to happen next, and no doubt this week's will do likewise.

And then this Friday night, once the audience have gone home, the chairs removed and the floor swept, there will be a dance which starts at 10.30 pm and lasts until 3.00 am on the Saturday morning.

Then it will return to being a cinema in time for the Matinee at 2.30 pm for children for a "penny hie" (one and a half pence). Old Peter Reid, still held in blessed and revered memory in the town, would never have understood what the cinema was all about, but his munificence to the town he loved had no better example than this.

The cinema is clearly the big thing in the entertainment industry these days with even gossip of how there might be "talkie" films soon, and even some in colour! But would "talkie" films do the piano player out of a job?

January 8 1931

The Forfar Dispatch takes stock at the start of the year.

It is by no means sanguine about the prospects for 1931 in the jute trade or any other trade. The jute trade has been in recession since 1929, and although it is famous for its resilience and ability to bounce back, this recession is worldwide and far deeper rooted than previous recessions in the 1890s, 1911/12 or 1920/21.

Some factories in Dundee have closed altogether. Fortunately that has not yet happened in Forfar, but there have been several occasions of workers being laid off, and a great deal of "short time" working. 1,088 people (about one tenth of the town's population) have claimed dole in 1930, and although some were blatant fraudsters and were denied any dole, the total amount paid out was a staggering £26,672.

The problem about all this, of course, is that as so many people work in jute, any recession is liable to hit everything in the town, including shops, hotels and pubs. Agriculture was also in a perilous state in the area, but mixed bathing is now allowed in the town Baths, and both the Old Kirk and St James's Kirk now have the electric light.

Football is still going strong, as indeed are the two cinemas which have had the good sense not to price themselves out of the market. Not only that, but 19 more people were born in Forfar than died, and Forfar people celebrated the New Year in traditional fashion, and the Loch has been frozen for a few weeks which has encouraged skating and the "roaring game" of curling. Hope always springs eternal!

January 9 1919

Today four German Prisoners of War from Eassie Camp appeared at Forfar Sheriff Court.

The Procurator Fiscal Mr Thomas Hart explained that they were on a charge of killing and stealing a sheep from Castleton Farm belonging to Mr Thomas Wedderspoon. They had broken camp on December 5, killed a sheep, skinned it, buried the entrails and took the carcase back to the camp.

Speaking through a non-commissioned German officer who was acting as an interpreter, the four Germans pleaded guilty, tendering as an excuse the shortage of rations in their camp. The Commandant of the camp, for his part, stated that the accused all had adequate rations.

Sheriff Gordon stated that even if there had been some excuse in this respect, this was a very serious matter and he sentenced each of the four Germans to three months imprisonment. Probably a similar sentence would have been handed out had it been four locals who committed this crime, but it does seem a little hard on the Germans who were far from home.

Repatriation to face justice in Germany might have been a better option — for what good was three months in prison in Scotland going to do to anyone? — but the circumstances of early 1919 were hardly conducive to any spirit of reconciliation or forgiveness.

"Hang The Kaiser" "Make Germany Pay" and "No Mercy For The Hun" were the slogans of the day both in Forfar and every other place. The van conveying the prisoners to and from court was jeered at and spat upon by the angry Forfar populace.

January 10 1856

The Courier is perplexed and dismayed about what happened today at Forfar Police Station.

There was a boy in custody by the name of Peter Morris, about 12 years old, who had been caught breaking into a bothy in Aberlemno with intent to steal. He had told the police that he was a Dundonian, his mother had died and he was on the run from his abusive, drunken father and was looking for his uncle who lived in either Arbroath or Forfar.

He had broken into the bothy with two others (who had escaped) because he was starving. This story was listened to with a great deal of sympathy and the boy was being held pending further investigation. Today however a respectable looking man appeared at Forfar Police Station and asked if a John McKenzie was in custody.

The answer was in the negative but then the Sergeant began to wonder whether "Peter Morris" was in fact "John McKenzie". Mr McKenzie was taken to the cell to see the boy and immediately identified him as his son. He lived in a respectable house in Dundee, his mother was alive and well, and there was little that could be done to contain this boy.

He had taken up with bad company, and had left his home in Dundee some time ago "on a plundering excursion". He had no uncle either in Arbroath or Forfar.

This story, with certain aspects which remind one of Charles Dickens and "Oliver Twist" is one which causes the writer of *The Courier* to despair. No-one seems to know what happened to the boy in later years.

January 11 1926

1926 is the year made infamous by the General Strike in early May, and tonight we got an early indication in the attitude expressed by Sir Robert Hutchison MP in a visit to the Meffan Hall for a meeting presided over by Provost Lowson and sadly attended by only a few people.

Robert Hutchison
MP 1924-31

Hutchison was a Liberal, but one of the Liberals who tended to support the Government in these complicated days of the 1920s. The main thrust of his speech was that the subsidy to the coalmining industry would have to be withdrawn on the grounds that it was "a pernicious form of state responsibility".

It was an odd attitude for a man from Kirkcaldy to have, and of course it was this very withdrawal of the subsidy which gave the owners the opportunity to close the pits in May and precipitate the General Strike.

On other matters, Sir Robert was charming, expressing delight that Forfar Athletic were now top of the Third Division of the Scottish League.

There was an air of mystery when a lady from the Women's Citizens Association delivered to him a written question in an envelope; Sir Robert read it and replied that he would write a reply to it!

In a public meeting, this seemed rather strange behaviour from both parties and naturally excited some interest. It was assumed that it might have something to do with the availability or otherwise of contraceptive advice to young women, one of the issues of the 1920s that everyone was obsessed about but no-one dared to mention in public!

January 12 1921

The Lowson Memorial Church tonight met to choose its new Minister to replace Mr Millar, the one previous incumbent since the Church had been built just before the Great War.

The Minister was chosen in a very open and fair way, for a short leet had been drawn up and each man on the short leet had preached to the Congregation last December, and then tonight a vote was taken.

Rev William T Smellie,
Lowson Memorial Church,
early 1920s

The man with a clear majority over the other three candidates was Reverend William T Smellie, currently Assistant Minister at North Berwick. Mr Smellie had an obvious disadvantage in his surname, but was otherwise very well equipped to take on this Church which had to be regarded as one of the plum clerical jobs in Scotland.

The Lowson Memorial Church was new, rich, a fine building and with a large Congregation in a town which was reckoned to be one of the best in Scotland to live in.

Mr Smellie came from Barrhead, had graduated MA from Glasgow University in 1915 and had done two years of his Divinity course when he obtained a commission in the Argyll and Sutherland Highlanders.

In June 1918 he was invalided home with the effects of gas, but returned a couple of months later and was given the OBE in January 1919 for services rendered during the German Spring Offensive of spring 1918. He had clearly made a favourable impression on the Lowson Memorial Congregation when he preached to them, and everyone wished him all the best in his job.

January 13 1891

At a special meeting of the Forfar Factory Workers Union in the Drill Hall, chaired by the Honorary President Tommy Roy, it was agreed that the Union should support the railway workers currently in dispute with the large railway companies.

Roy argued that the railway workers were waging the very same battle as the jute workers themselves had waged a couple of years ago. Their demands had been modest and reasonable and the employers had over-reacted by sacking men and getting blacklegs and scabs to do their job — and Roy knew (sadly) that at least one Forfar man was working at Taybridge Station, Dundee doing the job of a man on strike.

Loud hissing was heard at this point because, Forfar being Forfar, everyone knew who the man was! But Roy said that it was the duty of all workers to stand together, and lately, the Press had begun to support at least some of the workers, and possibly more surprisingly "the pulpit" had shown a little support for reasonable pay claims.

This was certainly the case in Forfar, and Roy's speech was greeted with loud applause. The Union decided that £30 of their own funds should be sent to the railwaymen, and £20 to the furnacemen who were involved in another but related dispute.

The Forfar Herald which had supported the jute workers in their own dispute with the factory owners in 1889 applauded this move saying that the jute workers were themselves very aware that outside support played a huge part in persuading the factory owners to come to terms.

THOS. MUIR, SON, & PATTON

LIMITED,

Colliery Agents,

Coal, Lime, and Cement Merchants,

and Carting Contractors,

OLD AND NEW RAILWAY STATIONS,

FORFAR.

BEST ENGLISH & SCOTCH HOUSEHOLD COAL.
ENGLISH TREBLE AND WISHAW WASHED NUTS.
ENGLISH AND SCOTCH SMALL COAL.
STEAM CHEW COAL.

ROUND CHAR, ANTHRACITE or BLIND COAL, for MILLERS, BAKERS'
OVENS, GREENHOUSES, and HEATING APPARATUS.

BRIQUETTES.   ENGLISH AND SCOTCH COKES.

ENGLISH and SCOTCH LIME.

FIRECLAY GOODS, including Pipes, Traps, Fire, and Composition Bricks, RED BRICKS, and DRAIN TILES.

Orders by post receive prompt and careful attention.

Special Quotations for Quantities, and WAGON LOADS of any of
the above at Railway Stations and Sidings.

FRESH DRAFF WEEKLY.

PRINCIPAL OFFICE—OLD STATION, 35 VICTORIA STREET.

TELEPHONE No. 13.

Representative—GEORGE WISHART.

1900 Advertisement

16

January 14 1938

Today occurred a tragic fatal accident at the works of Moffat and Sons in Academy Street, commonly referred to as "the Hauchie" when James Buchan Gold, 28 Easterbank, had his arm caught in a machine and died early the following day in Dundee Royal Infirmary.

What happened was that he was working at a mangle, leaned forward to straighten a piece of jute and may have stumbled and caught his hand in the machine.

It was a very rare accident and the Sheriff asked at the enquiry if it was not normal practice to stop the machine in order to adjust the jute. The answer was no. The foreman Stewart Balfour of Watt Street said that this was the first time in forty years that he had experienced an accident of this nature.

Although the man's hand and arm were badly damaged and there was heavy loss of blood, that need not have caused the death. He died in fact of a pulmonary embolism after an operation at the Dundee Royal Infirmary, and quite a few doctors and others questioned whether an operation was necessary or wise at this stage.

The town was shocked by the news, for Buchan Gold was a well-known local football player currently playing for East End, to whom he had returned after a less than successful season playing senior football with Arbroath. His favourite position was inside left, and he is described as being of a "quiet and unassuming nature".

His funeral at the Forfar Cemetery, conducted by Rev DM Bell a few days later was attended by almost the whole town. He was due to be married shortly to a young Forfar lady.

January 15 1902

There is a major argument going on in the town today about where Forfar Athletic's imminent Scottish Cup tie against Queen's Park should be played.

Forfar had excelled themselves in the previous round beating Abercorn of Paisley and now they had a big reward. The draw was made as Forfar Athletic v Queen's Park, but it is widely believed — in fact it is known "for a fact" — that Queen's Park have made a substantial offer to buy the ground rights and to play the game at Hampden Park, the ground on which Scottish Cup finals and Scotland v England Internationals have been played in the past.

Queen's Park were of course lavishly rich, commonly looked upon as the "snobby" team of Glasgow which had refused to turn professional. In recent years they had lost out a little to other Glasgow teams, but they now had plans to build a new and huge stadium to dwarf Celtic Park and Ibrox.

Their existing stadium (which eventually was sold to Third Lanark and became Cathkin Park) was good enough however, and quite a few Forfar players and even supporters must have been tempted by the offer of a chance to go there.

Nevertheless, the counter argument was that many Forfar supporters could not have afforded a trip to Glasgow, and that they deserved a chance to see the famous Glasgow club (10 times winners of the Scottish Cup) at Station Park.

Letters appeared from supporters calling themselves "Blue and Black" and "Play Up, Athletic" in *The Forfar Herald* arguing this point, and in the end the game was played at Station Park on January 25. Unsurprisingly, Queen's Park won 4-1.

Peter Reid's Forfar Rock

19

January 16 1897

Today perished one of Forfar's greatest characters in ex-Provost Peter Reid, a man of whom no-one seemed to have a bad word to say.

He was 93, born on October 6 1803. He was of course famous for his Peter Reid rock with people reportedly coming from all over Scotland to buy some "Peter Reid".

The story was often told of a small girl coming into his shop at 51 Castle Street, not being aware that the man serving her was Peter Reid himself and asking for "a but o' Peter Reid".

"Aye, lassie, and futtin but o' me dae ye want?"

The Home Secretary himself was even quoted as saying that Peter Reid's rock was the best in the three kingdoms. He was never a poor man, his father having owned a wheelwright's business in Queen Street, and his confectionery business sent orders to all over the world to make him a very rich man indeed.

The difference between Peter Reid and other Victorian capitalists was that Peter poured all his money back into the town that he loved. It was probably not true to say that he died a poor man — he was still a man of moderate means — but he had donated three things to the town — the Reid Hall, the Reid Park and what was called the Convalescent Ward of Forfar Infirmary, the porch outside the Main Entrance.

In his early years he had been a Liberal and a supporter of the Anti-Corn Law League (he was very much one of the driving forces behind the erection of the Peel Monument in the new Burial Ground at Newmonthill in 1851) and he had also been a keen supporter of the North in the American Civil War, such had been his hatred of slavery.

Peter Reid with his staff

January 17 1814

Today saw one of Forfar's largest ever funerals as the famous botanist George Don was laid to rest in the graveyard of the Old Parish Church, not far from the huge steeple in the throes of construction and now nearing completion.

George Don,
famous botanist

The Caledonian Mercury tells us that he was the former Superintendent of the Royal Botanic Garden of Edinburgh. "The extraordinary merits of Mr George Don as a practical botanist are very generally known from the frequent and well deserved eulogies bestowed on him in Dr Smith's Flora Britannica and Sowerby's English Botany."

He was born on October 11 1764, son of Alexander Don, a Forfar shoemaker and Isabel Fairweather. At one point he was apprenticed to a watchmaker in Dunblane, but he never settled at that, being all too obsessed with insects and plants, a hobby that was rare in those days.

He travelled all over Scotland and England collecting flowers, and he made Forfar famous for the "Forfar Garden, situated on a bank which slopes down to the Lake (sic) of Forfar" to which flocked visitors from all parts of the country.

He comes across as a lovable and slightly unworldly eccentric who was never all that good at managing finances and was frequently in debt. But he had no enemies and it was said that the whole town turned out to his funeral. He had died of what seems to have been throat cancer, and was succeeded by his two sons, George and David, who both became botanists as well.

January 18 1906

Today was polling day in the General Election. In 1906, constituencies could choose to vote whenever they wanted to within a framework of about three weeks, and already in other parts of the country there had been a few surprising results with the Liberals doing better than expected. In fact it would be a Liberal landslide victory, and this was mirrored in Forfar with the Liberals, it was claimed, outnumbering the Conservatives by about 15 to 1.

The constituency was called Montrose Burghs and consisted of Montrose, Arbroath, Brechin, Kirriemuir and Forfar. The sitting candidate was John Morley, already earmarked for the job of Secretary of State for India.

He arrived today from Brechin at about 2.00 pm with ex-Provost McDougall to visit his Committee Rooms in West High Street and then attend the polling station. He was cheered all the way, but said that it was a rather cold day to stand and deliver an election speech, especially when he was so confident that he was going to win anyway!

His supporters were very voluble about the need for Free Trade in order to allow cheaper foreign food into the country. There were one or two polite protesters with placards about "Votes For Women", and Morley smiled and waved tolerantly at them.

He then departed in order to catch a train to Arbroath, the railway workers all being keen to shake his hand as he boarded the train.

That evening as the polls closed at 8.00 pm and the ballot boxes were rushed to Montrose for the count, great excitement prevailed especially when late at night the "wire" arrived from the Post Office to the Liberal Committee Rooms telling them that Morley had prevailed by 4416 to 1922 votes.

January 19 1921

A long debate took place tonight at the Town Council under the Chairmanship of Provost Moffat about electricity.

There was a clear need for it to be introduced to Forfar which at the moment relied almost exclusively on gas for lighting and heating, although coal played a part as well — a somewhat precarious part, it had to be said, given the ongoing labour problems in the coal mining industry.

The Grampian Electricity Scheme was the main subject of discussion and questions were asked if Forfar would get the most favourable supply and rate, and if the damage to the roads in the burgh would be made good by either the Grampian Company or the Government.

Answers to these questions were still awaited. It was also suggested that electricity could be supplied by a few more local firms on a smaller scale, but the general consensus was that electricity had to be supplied on a grand scale if it were to be at all profitable. No decision was taken at this point, but Councillor Whitton in particular was keen that it should be introduced as soon as possible even if it meant that we would have to pay higher taxes.

It was generally agreed that electricity was definitely the source of energy for the future, but as with all new things in Forfar, there was a certain fear and suspicion of this potential source of power.

As it turned out, it would be more than thirty years before electricity was totally installed in Forfar. Gas was generally adequate for the needs of the town in the 1920s.

January 20 1946

It is almost a daily occurrence at Forfar Station to see a happy reunion as the slow process of demobilisation continues.

Even some of those who have been in the Far East are now beginning to trickle home. Reunions are in the main happy, but there are a few with distressing physical wounds.

Some have suffered illness in faraway countries, but the main thing is that "the leddies are comin' back". Others, of course, are not coming home, and these days must be difficult for their wives and mothers.

There is also a flu epidemic in Forfar with large absences reported at local schools, as there had been in 1919, but this time the general opinion is that both the war casualties and the flu cases are "bed enough, but no' as bed as the lest time".

There is also the key difference that although the soldiers are coming back to rationing and a few shortages, there is no unemployment to speak of with jobs readily available and a new Government in place determined to build a better tomorrow.

But in the meantime, the return of the service personnel is a great event in town with every person having his or her story to tell, often exaggerated, sometimes economical with the truth, but the main thing is to be able to walk down East High Street and along Castle Street and to see the sights that so many of them despaired of every being able to see again.

"This is a bra' place!"

January 21 1956

As a general rule, Forfarians do not nurse any sort of grievance that "the world is against them", but today was an exception and one which 65 years later still arouses strong feelings.

It was a local derby against St Johnstone, who, crucially, were going for promotion. The referee, a late replacement, was the well-respected Willie Brittle of Glasgow. He was sometimes called "brutal Brittle" for his perceived inability to put up with any nonsense.

The game started well for Forfar. They survived St Johnstone's early onslaught and half way through the second half were 3-0 up with goals from Gilbert Crowe, Ian Stewart and Willie Dunn.

Not only that, but the snow had stopped, and a watery, winter sun had appeared. The blizzard in the first half had been considerable, but the pitch had been re-lined at half-time, and everything, with 12 minutes remaining and most St Johnstone supporters heading across the road for an early train home, looked hunky-dorey for a shock victory for Forfar.

But then, Mr Brittle, unaccountably and apparently influenced by St Johnstone manager Johnny Pattillo prancing about on the touchline, stopped the game and led the players off. The first reaction was sheer disbelief. The snow had stopped, there was not even an awful lot of it on the pitch, but Mr Brittle said "Sorry, gentlemen, I could not see the lines".

Forfar naturally claimed the points but the Scottish League, with its dismal innate propensity to side with the strong against the weak, ruled that the game had to be replayed in the spring, and yes, you've guessed it, St Johnstone won!

Forfar Cross. Proclamation of King Edward VII, 1901

January 22 1901

It was at 7.30 pm this Tuesday evening that "intelligence" reached Forfar that Queen Victoria had died at the age of 81 at Osborne House on the Isle of Wight.

The news had been expected for several days, and Provost McDougall "with characteristic forethought" had arranged for notices to be put up at key points of the town, and arranged for the Parish Church bell to be tolled.

A meeting of the Town Council was summoned immediately and all social events were immediately cancelled including the Burns Concert on Friday night January 25 by the Forfar Tonic Sol-Fa Society.

A meeting was arranged for tomorrow at noon for all prominent citizens to express their condolences, and tonight, as was the custom on such occasions, people met huddled in closes to discuss the solemn news.

The Town would be in mourning until the Funeral was held on Saturday February 2, and would show windows "retained on shutter". Some shopkeepers and even householders draped their doors in black.

As she had been Queen since 1837, there were very few Forfarians with any clear memories of living under any other Sovereign. She had never been to Forfar, but the royal train had passed through the Station now and again en route to Balmoral.

The Prince of Wales was the new King. He would be called Edward VII. People wondered how he would react to being the King. It was no secret that he had enjoyed a few "adventures" (with ladies) in the past, but it was devoutly to be hoped that he would be a good King, not least because the country was still involved in that South African war against the Boers.

January 23 1917

Bailie Esplin was in no forgiving mood this morning at the Police Court.

Two boys David Henderson, aged 12, and James Christie, aged 13, both of West High Street appeared today charged with stealing two tins of condensed milk from the Grove Dairy Company's shop in East High Street in early January.

The police reported how the two boys had come into the shop and asked for an empty box. While the shop assistant was fetching the box, two tins of condensed milk had disappeared from the counter and one of them was later found in the possession of one of the boys.

Both boys pleaded guilty. Christie was a first offender, apparently, and was admonished, but Henderson had been involved in a similar offence some time previously and had then been warned that he might be sent to what was then known as an "Industrial School", notoriously tough places where bad boys were taught a trade.

Bailie Esplin decided that Henderson should go to the Dale Industrial School in Arbroath until he reached the age of 16. This would be "residential", although one hopes that the boy would be allowed home at weekends.

Both his father and mother pleaded eloquently for him, but Bailie Esplin said that he was being "spoilt" at home and had failed to take heed of a previous warning.

It does seem a little harsh on a 13 year old, but then again, it was war time and condensed milk was a very important commodity. It would be interesting to know what happened to David Henderson.

January 24 1885

Burns Night was on a Sunday this year.

The Victorian society in Forfar could not countenance any Burns Supper or celebration on the day itself, but that did not prevent Forfar from celebrating the occasion on the day before or the day after.

Ayrshire being not dissimilar to Forfarshire in culture and way of life, Burns was always well celebrated in Forfar. On the Saturday, the Forfar Temperance Club held a tea soirée in the Good Templar Hall with Mr J Cuthbert in the Chair.

The hall was "crowded to excess" with men, women and children, and a good time was had by all. Temperance and Burns are not necessarily things that one would necessarily put together, and one feels that Mr Cuthbert pushes things a little when he says in his address that Robert Burns "had he been living in our times, would have identified himself with Temperance reformers".

History tends to give a rather different impression, although it must be admitted that the Tam O'Shanter, for example, does conclude with a salutary lesson of what happens to someone on an alcoholic bender.

Be that as it may, tonight saw an excellent programme of entertainment of ladies and gentlemen's choirs, and a few individual contributions from Miss Peters, and Messrs Forsyth and Donaldson, while recitations were provided by Mr Raffan and Mr Roy.

A good time was had by all, and of course the great advantage of a Burns Supper organised by the Forfar Temperance Club is that no-one woke up the following morning with a sore head. Nor was Church attendance adversely affected the following morning!

January 25 1932

Today was a rather sombre Burns Day in Forfar for it was also the funeral of Provost Andrew Peffers, who had taken ill after speaking at a Burns supper a few nights ago.

He had suffered a "seizure" and died at his house a few hours later in the early hours of the following morning. He had only been Provost a matter of months but he had been on the Town Council for 34 years. He was 62.

He was born in Forfar, attended the old North Burgh School and Forfar Academy and began to work in his father's dyeing works, but then opened his own accountancy business.

There was hardly any aspect of Forfar life that he did not take part in, and although he was occasionally gruff and found it difficult to suffer fools gladly, there could be little doubt that he had the interest of his fellow Forfarians at heart.

The turnout of what *The Courier* estimates to be 1,000 (one tenth of the town's population) at his funeral speaks for itself.

In 1914 he was 44 and could well have been excused military service on account of his age, but nevertheless insisted on serving with the Black Watch Territorials. He was invalided home and immediately became a member of the Food Control Committee.

He was survived by his widow and seven grown-up children, and there could have been no greater honour given to him than the decision to name the new row of houses being built between Bell Place and North Street as "Peffers Place".

He would have loved that.

January 26 1959

There was still a certain amount of work to be done yet, but it was now looking as if the new Station Park stand was going to be more or less ready for the big game on Saturday when Rangers came to town in the Scottish Cup.

Rangers had been here last year as well, but this time there was to be a new stand. The old wooden one had finally been demolished after a few storms and many years' yeoman service.

People joked that there was a film on The Regal about the old stand. It was called "Gone With The Wind"! The new one was thrown up in indecent haste with many supporters lending a hand with labouring work on Sundays.

Their efforts were praiseworthy and indeed allowed the game to be played at Station Park when it might have had to be played at Gayfield or Dens Park. Sadly not really enough attention was paid to the angle of the seats, and the result was that the near touchline could not be seen very well, and from the back of the stand you could not really see very much at all!

And no-one was more aware of that than the volunteers who had done the work on Sundays. They were given the back two rows of the stand, and soon found that if they wanted to watch the game, they had to stand up!

However, the rest of the structure was sound enough for the game on Saturday 31 and was duly passed by the inspectors. Forfar gave a reasonable account of themselves, but lost 1-3.

Station Park 1959, with the new stand being built

January 27 1899

Today's edition of *The Forfar Herald* contains a piece that simply would not be allowed in the 21st Century, but which in 1899 no-one would take offence at.

Indeed, it would be looked upon as a very laudatory and flattering piece of writing, and it was obvious that the performance of the Forfar Amateur Minstrels at the Reid Hall to which he refers was greatly enjoyed both by the writer himself and the audience.

The problem lies in the use of the word "darkies" to describe the Chorus in some of the numbers particularly a song called "The Coloured Four Hundred".

It was part of a collection of Dixie songs which were very popular in late Victorian Britain, particularly in the music hall, but which sadly are not allowed today. One can't help feeling that in some ways, this is society's loss, for these songs are cheerful and happy, even though they refer to the dark days of slavery.

The rest of the programme however was very well done with one unfortunate exception of a song for which the singer had only had very little notice and for that reason, his performance was to be excused.

The evening finished with a pot-pourri of Studentenlieder, songs culled from the International Students Song book, and that was particularly well done as the reception from the packed Reid Hall indicated.

The Forfar Herald congratulates the Conductor Mr D Wilkie Neill on the performance of himself and the rest of the troupe and understands that the group are going to perform similarly in Brechin and Arbroath in the near future.

January 28 1953

Today saw a traumatic incident at the Cross on which a woman was badly injured by what can only be described as a runaway lorry!

It was just after 3.00 pm on a cold, sour day. A lorry, belonging to Mr R Smith of Balmashanner Farm, had been parked in front of the Town House. Clearly the hand brake was faulty, or had not been secured properly, and it began to roll down the slight incline towards Castle Street.

In the meantime, Mrs Bella Rodger of Sparrowcroft, wife of George Rodger, master painter, was looking in the shop window of Graham Pool's shop in Castle Street along with her friend Mrs Forrester of Dundee, and of course as the engine was not engaged, she did not hear the lorry heading towards her.

Mrs Rodger was knocked straight into the glass window and suffered multiple lacerations to the face and leg. It was a fairly delicate procedure to extricate Mrs Rodger from the window with slithers of glass all over the place, but it was soon established that although she was injured, her injuries were not life threatening.

Fortunately Graham Pool's shop was one of the few in Forfar in 1953 that had a telephone and the ambulance was soon summoned. Mrs Forrester fainted and had to be revived with smelling salts.

Both ladies were taken to hospital. Mrs Forrester was released soon after, but Mrs Rodger, still suffering from shock, was detained overnight. It was certainly an unusual sort of accident, but traumatic nevertheless for all concerned, including the spectators.

January 29 1933

It doesn't happen every year, but a rumour spread round the town that "The Loch's bearin"!

This meant that people were able to skate on the Loch, and it also mean that this Sunday "the Loch was ferr black wi fowk" as hundreds of Forfar people took advantage of the frozen, hard, windless conditions to try their luck on the ice.

Skating had one great advantage as well in those days of the economic depression, namely that it was free! Some folk had skates, but solid tackety boots did just as well today!

Mothers naturally feared that the ice might not be as thick as it appeared, but in fact it was and a superb time was had by all, even some of the older ones who insisted that the Loch used to freeze for weeks on end "in my young day".

Thick ice meant of course thinner attendances at Kirks, and Jack Frost seemed to have put one over the Almighty for one day, but at least one local Minister was seen having a walk round the Loch on the Sunday afternoon smiling tolerantly at some of his parishioners and even sympathising with some who had a fall.

A feature today was that nightfall did not halt the proceedings. The strong moonlight meant that the skating could go on for some time after the sun had gone.

It was as well however that the ardent pupils did not heed too literally the advice of one "expert" who told them that the secret of skating was not to put one foot on the ice before lifting the other off it!

January 30 1927

The idea of learning how to render First Aid to the injured had become very popular in recent years.

There had clearly been a need for it during the Great War and industrial accidents were now becoming very common, as increasingly were motor car accidents.

It was one of the many hobbies that women, often war widows, took up in the 1920s and it was appropriate that two ladies tied for the award of the Cumming Cup at the Forfar St Andrews Ambulance Association at Forfar Station today.

Twelve entrants presented themselves for the award which was conducted by Dr J Ewen Cable, honorary "surgeon of the section" and it consisted of an examination in three parts — written, oral and practical.

After due consideration, the honour was awarded to Miss FSS Hamilton, of 1 Morley Place, and Miss Pat McLean, whose address is given as "Bookstall" who achieved 99 per cent, generally agreed to be a magnificent effort.

Miss Hamilton was awarded the Cup, while Miss McLean was given the financial award of a half sovereign.

The stress was always, of course on the word "First" for it was very important that some sort of action was taken immediately, before an ambulance, a nurse or a doctor could get there.

Lives could be saved if prompt action was taken, but it was also vital that First Aiders should not consider themselves to be doctors and able to make any diagnosis.

Increasingly, more and more First Aiders were seen at theatrical events and football matches, and it was another sign of the times that more and more women were doing such jobs.

January 31 1908

Today *The Forfar Herald* announced the decision of the Reverend George Johnstone Caie to retire from the pulpit at Forfar Parish Church, a position he had occupied since 1875, the first Minister to be elected by popular choice rather than royal patronage following the abolition of the Patronage Act in that year.

33 years was a long time to be a Minister and he was very much looked upon as the Minister of the town, rather than just the Parish Church. It was becoming obvious to some of his parishioners that his health was failing, and concern was expressed for him because he was much loved and respected.

He was a Canadian, born in New Brunswick in 1840, had qualified in Edinburgh but had returned to Canada to preach for some years before taking over in Forfar.

He had been responsible for considerable renovations of the inside of the Church, and devoted himself to the supervision of the work. He was a fine preacher and constantly attendant to the needs of his flock, being particularly strong in the local temperance movement, having seen for himself, no doubt, the evil effects of alcohol on so many families.

A man with a certain social conscience, Reverend Caie had also been a member of the School Board for many years and Chairman of the Forfar Infirmary. He was said to be of "kindly and genial disposition" and very easily approachable. His sermons were interesting to some, but over the heads of others.

He had a wife and six children, one of whom, Norman, became a Minister.

He said that he would live on in Forfar "the town that I love" after his retirement. He died three years later in 1911.

February

February 1 1862

This Saturday a meeting was held in the County Hall of the Subscribers to the new Forfar Infirmary for the purpose of approving the Constitution and electing Directors. On the motion of Provost Lowson, Sheriff Guthrie Smith was elected to the Chair.

The building had recently been completed, but there was now need for beds and furnishings before staff could be appointed. The concept of an Infirmary was a new one but had been given a boost by the Crimean War a few years previously, where many soldiers' lives had been saved after they had been tended and cared for.

Some people even believed that the life of Prince Albert (who had died in December 1861) of typhus might have been saved by more specialist care.

The Chairman remarked on how a handsome and spacious building it was and in a fine location on the outskirts of the town on the Arbroath Road, close enough for the transport of patients but also far enough away to safeguard the town from infections and foul smells.

It was intended that it would be opened officially in July and would have accommodation for 36 beds, 16 for typhus fever, 4 for scarlet fever and another 16 for surgical cases. It was pointed out that it was one of the best of its kind in the country.

The whole cost had come to £2,304 17 shillings and 5 pence, but the Treasurer had been able to pay off all the contractors. Subscriptions had come from Kirriemuir and Oathlaw as well as Forfar itself, but now more money was needed to furnish the Infirmary before it could be officially opened.

February 2 1979

Forfar's remarkable character Andrew Smyth died to-day in his home in West High Street.

He was almost universally known and universally loved, not least for his bad eye-sight which often led him to nod to lampposts on the street, and his glasses which looked "like the bottom of lemonade bottles" as some people put it.

He was 75, and had served on Forfar Town Council for 50 years without a break, having been a Bailie and then Provost between 1951 and 1956, during which time he met the Queen Mother. Legend had it that he said to her "Juist ca' me Andra" and she did, apparently!

He was one of the real characters of local government and served on many national committees, always being seen to go to them by public transport, and telling all his yarns to his fellow passengers.

Not for "Andra" was the idea the Councillors were "on the make". He never took a penny for all that he did. It was all done for sheer love of the town and its people. He may occasionally have played at being a fool, but he was anything but stupid!

He was at his best when chairing a meeting, when he had the ability to see the problem and make a quick and sensible decision. He also excelled at School Prize Givings when he introduced the speakers, looked proudly on as prizes were presented to his "bairns", and then led the children in three cheers for the Holidays while assuring the children that their "Uncle Andra" would look after them!

He worked on the railway before he retired, and he never forgot that he was a "Farfar loon", speaking to every person on the street that he met — and even, of course, the occasional lamppost!

February 3 1943

It was far from home, and the weather was nothing like a cold day in February in Forfar, but at least one Forfar man would, in later years, recall this day as the day that the Prime Minister Winston Churchill came in triumph to Tripoli.

Tripoli had fallen to the Desert Army on January 23, and the British were now in charge of this city enjoying a few days rest before re-commencing their relentless pursuit of the Afrika Korps into Tunisia.

Not only was this Forfar man in the guard of honour at Tripoli Aerodrome, but he was also given the job of guarding Churchill's caravan at night. At one point, a cigar butt was thrown out, and he would have loved to grab it as a souvenir, but of course he was standing to attention on guard duty!

In the afternoon he had heard the Prime Minister saying how the fame of the British Eighth Army had spread through the world, how they had pursued in three short months the Hun from Alexandria through the desert to the green and pleasant land of Tripolitania, and how if anyone ever asked what he did in the war, it would be sufficient to say "I marched and fought with the Desert Army".

There was still a long way to go, difficult days awaited in Tunisia, Sicily and Italy, but there was now no doubt that the tide was turning and that the British success in Africa, coupled with the Russian victory at Stalingrad, meant that the war was going to be won.

February 4 1924

A serious fire at the North School in Wellbraehead was today put out by the Fire Brigade.

The damage was estimated at £200, but fortunately the fire occurred at a time when the children were not there. It was after school when janitor Alexander Robertson discovered a problem with the heating in the basement at the back of the school and that the wooden surrounds of the boiler were burning furiously.

He attempted to put the fire out himself but did not succeed and telephoned the Fire Brigade. The horse drawn fire engine arrived promptly to loud cheers from the neighbours but by that time the fire had spread to the classroom immediately above the boiler room, which was not used at the moment as a classroom but rather as a storeroom for spare desks and equipment.

They were extensively damaged but Firemaster McLaren was soon able to put the fire out. The incident attracted a large audience from Bell Place, Wellbraehead and the surrounding area, but the children were disappointed to learn that there would be no "holiday" tomorrow!

The North School was looked upon as the showpiece of Forfar education — it had now been open for about 16 years — and the damage was a blow to the finances.

It was also a bit of a shock to the janitor, but at least no children were harmed.

February 5 1909

The Suffragette movement has as yet not been much in evidence in Forfar.

Today's *Forfar Herald* in the context of the imminent by-election for the County of Forfarshire has an announcement.

Mrs Drummond who calls herself "The General" of the National Women's Social and Political Union, is to set up her headquarters in Forfar to co-ordinate a campaign to influence all candidates in the coming by-election and to spread propaganda about their cause.

There are three Suffrage movements, the National Women's Social and Political Union, the National Union of Women's Suffrage and the Women's Freedom League, and that of Mrs Drummond is looked upon as the most extreme and the most disruptive, although the Women's Freedom League has a few strong characters as well.

Their argument is that women deserve the vote because more and more of them are now working, more and more of them are going to University and they now wish to play a greater part in political life. So far, they have not succeeded, but Miss Fraser recently addressed a meeting in Kirriemuir and was given a tolerant, if cool, reception.

They have been very disappointed in the attitude of the Liberal Government who were their main hope. On the other hand, some men support their cause, although the Church, with a few exceptions, tends to oppose them. It is to be hoped that, whatever happens, things remain peaceful.

Already there have been a few reports from London of post boxes being set on fire, paintings in art galleries damaged and things like that, while even in Dundee their MP Mr Churchill has had a little trouble from some ladies.

February 6 1952

"Awfa sed news the day! The Keeng's deed!"

King George VI had indeed been found dead in his bed this morning at Sandringham Palace. He was 56. Although it had been obvious for some time that the King had been in poor health and had recently undergone an operation, it was still a shock.

When the news reached Forfar, the flags on all the public buildings were lowered to half mast. TV had not yet in 1952 reached Forfar, so it was the radio that gave out the details.

Great sympathy was expressed for this man who had become King in the most bizarre of circumstances when his brother Edward VIII refused to give up his American mistress (or the "Yankee hoor", as some Forfar people put it rather more crudely.)

King George VI, on the other hand, had been a family man with two charming children. It was stretching a point somewhat to say that his widow Queen Elizabeth was from Forfar — she had spent a large part of her life at Glamis Castle and had been confirmed in the Episcopalian faith in St John's Church in East High Street, Forfar.

The King's daughter was now to become Queen Elizabeth II, although that caused a certain amount of stir in Scotland because there had never been a Queen Elizabeth I in Scotland!

The new Queen was currently in Kenya and was now flying back home. Arrangements would soon be in hand in Forfar for the Coronation next year, but in the meantime it was all grief for the loss of a much loved and much respected King.

Forfar, 1840

46

February 7 1940

Tonight's *Forfar Dispatch* contains what strikes us as a strange appeal.

It is from the Overseas League Tobacco Fund and is asking for donations of cigarettes and tobacco for troops serving abroad.

The *Dispatch* is prepared to be a collecting centre, and quotes many letters that it had already received from soldiers so grateful from those at home who had thought of them.

Some 80 years down the line, we are tempted to think that these poor lads were already in so much danger of early death that it was not really befitting for Forfar people to send them anything that might further endanger their health and welfare!

Although these were the days when tobacco was considered to be a little self-indulgent on occasion perhaps, on the other hand, it was looked upon as a valuable sedative in times of stress and was even occasionally prescribed by Doctors for that purpose!

Smoking was not necessarily universal, but certainly practised by well over 80% of the population, and no-one really noticed how foetid the atmosphere was simply because it was so prevalent.

And for young men abroad, far from home and in potential danger at any minute, smoking was a great stress reliever in the same way that people at home worrying about their menfolk would also smoke cigarettes without suffering any general opprobrium.

The problem at the moment however was one of boredom, for nothing was happening. Not without cause was it called "the phoney war". But everyone knew that it was soon likely to change, and change dramatically.

February 8 1958

Forfar awoke this Saturday morning to see the worst fall of snow for over 10 years, probably since the bad winter of 1947.

Communications were badly affected, trains were running but were badly disrupted, and road were blocked, although by mid-morning the road to Dundee was described as "passable with care".

The roads to Brechin and Kirriemuir, however, remained blocked for some time, although the problem was, as usual, not quite so bad near the coast and it was possible to get to Arbroath — if anyone would want to.

Football was of course off (it was as well that it was this week, and not next week when Rangers were due to come to Forfar in the Scottish Cup).

Shops made a brave effort to stay open, and both picture houses remained open, reaping a rich reward for their endeavour in the shape of large "houses" as Forfarians trudged their way through the snow to The Regal and The "Gaffie".

Power supply of electricity and gas was by and large unaffected, and the remarkable thing was just how quickly the snow disappeared. By the Sunday, there were signs of a thaw and by Monday and Tuesday, life had returned to normal, albeit with a mess of slush and a few burst pipes as the temperature rose.

The main topic of conversation in the town was the Manchester United air crash on Thursday which had claimed the lives of so many of the "Busby Babes" while Matt Busby himself was fighting for his life.

Even in this tragic situation, Forfar sense of what was important prevailed, for we were assured by the local gossips that "it was jist as weel there were nae Farfar leds there"

February 9 1924

The popular and hard-working Headmaster of the West School, Mr D Herald, retired today after 15 years at the West School; his departure was marked by the presentation of a tea and coffee service set from his pupils and staff, as well as a newspaper rack specially designed by David Napier, a former pupil of the school.

Mr Herald was a native of Kirriemuir and he had trained in the Church of Scotland Training College in Dundas Vale, Glasgow before then entering St Andrews University in 1888. (The other way round from what we would have expected, perhaps!).

He had taught in Broxburn, Perth, St Andrews, Cullen, Cowdenbeath and Forfar North before becoming the Headmaster at Forfar West in 1909. He had led the school in difficult times of war and economic problems, and had been looked upon generally as a very fair, if somewhat strict Headmaster.

In his retiral speech, Mr Herald told his audience that he had not had the best of starts in life, being ninth in a very large family, but this had equipped him well to understand the challenges that some children faced.

It was not always the brilliant pupil that did best in life, and most children should "plod" along and they would eventually achieve some success by this "plodding".

He had always tried to make the school a pleasant place for his pupils and staff, and to create a good family atmosphere in the school. He would always have a special place in his heart for the West School and its pupils.

February 10 1945

Forfar's "Dad's Army" (although they were not to be called that for another 20 years!) had their Social Evening tonight in the Legion Hall in Academy Street.

The members of No 10 Platoon "C" Company of the Home Guard with their wives and lady friends enjoyed a dinner and entertainment.

A total of 70 people were there and the meeting was presided over by Platoon Commander Lieutenant A Nicoll and second in command Lieutenant A Boath. Guests were Major and Mrs Smith and Captain and Mrs Wilson.

Songs were provided throughout the evening by various singers including some of the soldiers, and there was dancing with music from Balfour's Band.

The highlight of the evening was the resume of the Platoon's Activities since its inception by Sergeant J Watson. "Interesting in the extreme, intermingled with gems of humour and here and there touches of pathos" was the way that it was described in *The Forfar Dispatch*.

The Home Guard were generally highly regarded in town, although there were a few jokes about even if the RAF and the Black Watch are wiped out, there is still the Home Guard.

But they did do a few useful jobs like Air Reconnaissance and other things, and they did seem to have a good time together in their camps and weekends away, and the occasional "march" through the town (cruel people called it a "limp") to Church parades.

In any case the war seemed to be drawing to an end, so the boys of the old brigade might not be needed to invade Europe after all!

February 11 1911

It was not often that Forfar Athletic enjoyed the attention of all Scotland.

This was the result that rocked Scotland, as Forfar beat Falkirk 2-0 in the Scottish Cup. Falkirk were looked upon as one of the better First Division teams in that era, finishing second in the League in 1909 and 1910, and in 1913 they would win the Scottish Cup.

They were not quite as good as Celtic, but managed by a man called Willie Nichol who rejoiced in the unlikely nickname of "Daddy" and with players like Willie Agnew, Tommy Logan and Jimmy Croall, the Bairns were more than a match for Rangers, Dundee and Hearts.

A huge crowd of 3,000 assembled at Station Park to see this game, and a small temporary stand was erected in the north east corner of the ground to allow more people a seat.

The weather was cold but dry and the pitch was good. Forfar surprised their visitors by going ahead through "Jummer" Petrie and then before half time Dave Easson scored another with his knee.

It was scarcely credible stuff from a team who were not yet even in the Scottish League, and Falkirk launched a barrage on Forfar's goal in the second half.

But Bill Paterson in Forfar's goal was in inspired form, and towards the end, Forfar launched a counter-attack and gained a penalty kick, unfortunately missed by Geordie Low.

Not that it mattered, for Forfar had already "staggered humanity", as Paul Kruger might have put it.

Forfar's team that day was Paterson, Gibb and Hannan; Lawrence, Chapman and Bruce; Lavery, Low, Bowman, Easson and Petrie.

Forfar Athletic 1910/11

February 12 1919

The war has been over for three months now, but *The Forfar Herald* still has the melancholy task of reporting casualties of soldiers who have died of their wounds or of the flu which is still ravaging both soldiers and civilians.

There are other after effects of the war as well. Tonight the Parish Council had an interesting case to deal with. It concerned a war widow who was asking to be relieved of her "poor and school" assessments in the rates.

She had been left with three children and currently received a war pension of 29 shillings, which was clearly not enough. So she had taken a job which brought in another 17 shillings and sixpence per week. Even this she did not feel was enough and was asking for a rates rebate.

Ex-Bailie Peffers supported her application on the grounds that a women who was doing so much to help herself deserved some encouragement. Councillor Ritchie said "She is paid for her work", a remark which did not seem to advance the argument in any direction, but then said "But if fowk winna work, they canna live, let alane pey their rates" from which it seemed that he was supporting the case of the war widow.

Councillor Whitson, however, was afraid that this might set a precedent, but such were the persuasive arguments of the energetic Bailie Peffers that it was agreed that the war widow should be relieved of her assessment. Sadly, Forfar had loads of war widows in such circumstances.

February 13 1818

All of Forfarshire was plunged into sadness to-day at the news of the death of George Dempster of Dunnichen.

He was 86 and was buried at Restenneth Priory a few days later with many people from Forfar, the town that he loved and which loved him, making their way out to Restenneth to pay their respects.

He had been born in Dundee in 1732 and was just too young to have taken any part in the Jacobite Rebellion of 1745, although he would undeniably have known all about that event and its far-reaching consequences.

Dempster can be fairly described as a member of the Scottish Enlightenment in that very exciting time when ideas like liberty and advancement were bandied about by politicians. George was the MP for Perth Burghs which included Forfar between 1761 and 1790.

Being a politician in the 18th century was a dirty business and one did not normally get oneself elected without spending a great deal of money on bribery, but George rose above that and became known as "Honest George" and was much thought of by people like Robert Burns.

"A title, Dempster merits it

A garter gie to Billy Pitt"

Dempster realised that although one had to help the poor, it was far better to eliminate poverty by improving methods of agriculture and he used his Estate at Dunnichen and the village which he created, Letham, to put his ideals into practice.

In Parliament he was much opposed to the war with America and sided with the Whigs. He worried a little about the French Revolution of 1789 but argued that the way to stop a similar thing happening here was to treat his labourers well.

Very few people seem to have ever had a bad word to say about this man who was a benevolent landowner in an age when such people were very few.

February 14 1892

A particularly awful crime was discovered this Sunday afternoon in the premises of Charles Greenhill, butcher of 129 East High Street.

One of the shop assistants had gone to the premises for the purpose of feeding the guard dog. When he arrived there he found that the animal was dead and that the safe weighing two hundredweight had been removed.

The killing of the dog aroused particular horror and it seems to have been done by someone who knew how to slaughter animals, possibly even a former employee of Mr Greenhill who would also know the premises.

A lady who lived near the shop claimed to have heard a noise of a "spring cart" at about 3.00 am, and also a "spring cart" was heard to pass through the gates of Clocksbriggs Station about an hour later, so police investigations were centred on this lead.

The safe was believed to contain between £20 and £30 (an awful lot of money for 1892) and the thieves also helped themselves to some meat. It was clear that they were "professional" or "career" criminals, for it was a brilliantly executed job.

There must have been several of them to remove the safe. They seem to have gained entrance through a window at the back, which was not secure. Naturally a crime of this sort, although by no means uncommon in late Victorian times was much discussed in the town and rumours spread about a horse and "spring cart" being found near Cunninghill Golf Course.

Station Park, 1958, for the visit of Glasgow Rangers in the Scottish Cup

February 15 1916

While there had been a general decrease in crime in Forfar in recent years (possibly because of the recent severe restrictions on the sale of alcohol, but also because so many young men were away at the war) there was today a case of seven young boys appearing before Bailie Michie charged with damaging property in the Reid and Steele Parks with knives.

Initials like GB and WH had appeared carved on various benches along with references to the love life (real and imagined) of various Forfar characters. However *The Forfar Herald* is impressed by some of the mothers who "took up the role of Portia" in the role of defending their boys.

The charges were basically admitted but one of the mothers said that "they a' goat a guid lickin'" while another said she would rather see them "getting a guid thrashin' rather than see them policed (sic)".

So the quality of mercy was tempered somewhat by the mothers whose apparently unanimous view was in favour of a good hammering "which never did onybody ony hairm" rather than the more conventional view that one would expect in the 21st century of "counselling" or "understanding"!

Bailie Michie agreed that it was better not to take the matter any further, although he and Chief Constable Thomson both thought that carving initials on seats and on the walls of shelters was a serious problem — there were apparently 119 sets of initials carved! — and both of them were concerned about where the boys got their knives from.

Now, there was an area in which mothers could play a constructive part!

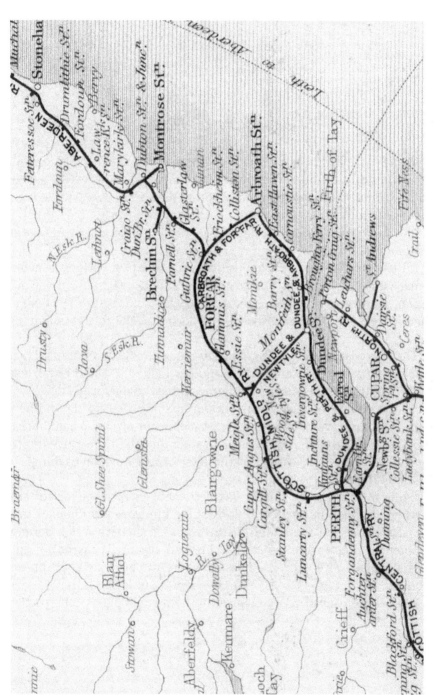

The railways round Forfar in 1851 (Map by Talis)

February 16 1848

A "tragic and melancholy" accident took place on the new railway line being built at Padanaram this afternoon.

A new stretch of line was being laid west of Forfar and heading eventually to Coupar Angus and Perth, and *The Courier* tells us that it involved John Baird, the contractor, who was near to the top end of the line.

He took charge of one of the empty waggons to roll it back to pick up more material for the new line that was being built. He ran alongside it, but at one point his foot slipped and he fell in front of the rolling waggon. Before he could recover, the wheels passed over him, smashing his head and killing him instantly.

Help was summoned immediately from Forfar, but it was obvious from an early stage that there was no hope. Mr Baird was not, apparently, a local man but came from the Glasgow direction. The town was nevertheless plunged into mourning.

Mr Baird was one of the many casualties of the railway development which went on throughout the United Kingdom in the 1840s with everyone rushing to get lines built in a hurry as "railway mania" took over.

The stretch of railway being built by the Scottish Midland Junction Railway would eventually lead to Glasgow, and Forfar would consider itself to be well placed to take advantage of the obvious benefits that were to accrue.

This afternoon's sad occurrence, however, was a reminder that there was often a price to be paid for progress, and it was paid in human lives.

February 17 1909

Bailie Killacky had two cases of people sleeping in the wrong places this Wednesday morning at the Police Court!

The less serious "offence" (if it could be called that) was that of George William, labourer, who was found asleep in the pavilion of Strathmore Cricket Club. He was admonished and allowed to depart.

The more serious offence of illegal sleeping was James Smith, mason, who took up his lodgings in a first class (first class, mark you!) railway carriage belonging to the Caledonian Railway Company at Forfar Station. He admitted the offence but said that he had nowhere else to go.

The Chief Constable said that there had been numerous complaints about people sleeping in railway carriages, and at 1.30 am this morning, Sergeant Doig, on examining the carriages in a railway siding found Smith sound asleep on the floor of a first class compartment.

Smith was apparently a serial offender and the last time he had slept in a railway carriage, he had left the carriage in a "verminous condition". And this was a first class carriage!

Possibly, Bailie Killacky might, to advantage, have dismissed the harmless vagrant or made arrangements for him to be accommodated in the Poorhouse, but instead he fined him 5 shillings or 3 days in prison.

It is hard to see how Smith could have acquired 5 shillings, so one feels that a prison cell might have been the next place for the wretched Mr Smith. Had it been a third class carriage, it might not have been so bad, but... a first class carriage! "We canna hae that!"

DOUGLAS YOUNG

to the

Electors

of the

Kirkcaldy

Burghs,

1945

FREEDOM FOR THE SCOTTISH PEOPLE

to enjoy the life and wealth of Scotland—
That is the purpose of my campaign.

We are facing a crisis in our nation's affairs. The basic existence of our whole people is endangered. We have been warned.

From many varied examples—the Forth road bridge, Prestwick airport, Rosyth dockyard, the mid-Scotland ship-canal, the housing scandal, *Bevinism*, the coal-muddle, the fish-muddle, the oatmeal-muddle, the Education Bill, the Board of Trade's discrimination against the Fife linen-manufacturers, the anti-Scottish conduct of the B.B.C.— we can judge by results how the British Parliament and the London State-Departments sabotage practical schemes of Scottish betterment.

Our Local Authorities' plans for housing and public services, the projects of Scottish private enterprise, the reasoned demands of cultural associations such as the E.I.S. and the Saltire Society, even of the Churches—all alike are carelessly neglected or arrogantly prohibited by a government outside our borders over which we have no control.

Scotland must have a new system—or our people will perish.

Douglas Young in 1945

February 18 1947

The worst weather on record did not prevent a large crowd of Forfarians trudging through the snow to the Meffan Hall to hear a lecture delivered on behalf of the Scottish National Party by the famous Scottish poet, politician and academic called Douglas Young.

The first thing that struck the Forfar audience was his size. He was about 6 foot 7 inches tall. Young, like his Chairman, Arthur Donaldson had enjoyed a chequered career so far and was no stranger to prison for his "unwarlike activities". Tonight he spoke cogently and eloquently for over an hour in his rich, throaty voice.

He had already had two unsuccessful attempts to win the seat of Kirkcaldy at Westminster elections, and although he found himself to a certain extent in favour of the current Labour Government, he remained convinced that independence was the answer to Scotland's problems.

A heckler asked him if Scotland leaving the United Kingdom was not dissimilar to rats leaving a sinking ship. He replied that it was more like kidnapped passengers escaping to freedom, and reminded everyone that the Act of Union had only been forced through in 1707 by wholesale bribery and intimidation.

He insisted that "Dominion status" (like Canada and Australia, for example) would be wholly appropriate for Scotland. He then attacked the Government for the fuel crisis, while Arthur Donaldson insisted that there was no fuel crisis in Scotland, which had enough natural resources to cope with its problems.

But then it was back out into the snow for people to trudge home. Young never did become an MP but he did become an excellent Lecturer in Greek at St Andrews University.

Arthur Donaldson, Scottish Nationalist and journalist
with *The Forfar Dispatch*

February 19 1662

There was a clear sign today that the zeal for witchcraft in Forfar was abating, and that there seems to have been a general revulsion and indeed sympathy for the way in which some so called witches had been convicted on the flimsiest of evidence and burned to death.

Today Christen Pearson was released from the Tolbooth (believed to be where the Cross is now) after no individual had laid evidence against her, something that immediately raises the question of why she was arrested in the first place?

There was a bizarre condition to her release and that was that she had to agree (not, however, in a formal confession) that she had practised witchcraft and that if anyone were to denounce her, she would face the penalty for it.

Those of us who cannot understand the complexities of the 21st century legal system will certainly have a few problems with understanding this one!

Not that it bothered Christen Pearson for she disappeared out of town immediately and was never seen or heard of again! Maybe she went to Dundee to see the devil!

It is certainly a very dark part of Forfar history but it must be seen in the context of what was going on in the rest of the world at the time. It was a nervous, worried, distressed people, following civil wars in both Scotland and England, and it was only natural that a scapegoat needed to be found.

Christen Pearson was only one of a series of women accused of consorting with Satan, a creature who was taken very seriously indeed in the 17th century.

February 20 1928

A rare treat for Forfar football fans tonight as Celtic's Manager Willie Maley came to town to deliver a lecture on the development of Scottish football in the Masonic Rooms.

The event had been organised by ex-Bailie Tom Hanick, a personal friend of Willie Maley, and attracted a huge crowd to listen to Maley as he showed his lantern slides of early and current players.

Maley was as usual charming and genial, going out of his way to say that Forfar was his favourite little town and that "my friend Jim", pointing to James Black, was doing a great job with Forfar Athletic.

He talked at length about his own great players like Jimmy Quinn and Patsy Gallacher, and great players of other teams, including Forfar's own David McLean and Alec Troup.

The evening was concluded with songs from Miss Maxwell of Forfar and Messrs Stoddart and Anderson of Glasgow while Mr Moir of Forfar was the accompanist.

Guests included Provost Lowson and Jimmy Brownlie of Dundee United, but everyone was impressed by what an ordinary man Maley was as he chatted amiably to everyone about football in general.

A few tried to embarrass him by talking about religion and Ireland, but Maley was able to deflect any awkward questions, preferring to talk about his new prodigy called James McGrory whom he rated "in the same bracket as Quinn".

He also showed a remarkable knowledge of local Forfar football. He stayed the night with his friend Tom Hanick, but had to leave on the early morning train the following day for his team were playing at St Mirren that afternoon. He left a lasting impression.

February 21 1914

There was great excitement in the town today!

Trains arrived at the Station throughout the morning from Glasgow bringing hundreds of the "Keelies", the "Glasgow Irish" — those who loved the Glasgow Celtic who were playing Forfar Athletic at Station Park today in the Scottish Cup.

They were ragamuffins, ill clad, some of them without proper footwear with only stockings on their feet, but they were cheerful, happy and sociable, singing their Irish songs and some of them with penny whistles and bugles, the better to support their team, the one that had revolutionised football the past 25 years or so.

They talked to the locals and chatted up the girls; although some Forfar matrons uttered dire warnings to their children to watch for pickpockets, others even offered them bread or biscuits.

And then the train came in with the team on it! There was Manager Maley and even Scotland's greatest living legend, the Bhoy from Croy, the redoubtable Jimmy Quinn, now at the end of his playing career, not playing today.

Humble enough to be there with them, he helped carry the hamper off the train to the charabanc which would take them to the Queen's Hotel for lunch. Jimmy was smoking a clay pipe and in the immortal words of one Forfar lady "He looked just like an ordinary man!"

They had lunch at the Queen's Hotel and then changed in the Baths in Chapel Street before being taken in the charabanc back up to the ground for the game. They won 5-0 — no real surprise there — but the people of Forfar would never forget the day that the mighty Celtic came to town.

Forfar Athletic v Celtic, 1914

East High Street from the Cross, 1900s

February 22 1890

The weather was fine this Saturday for a race between the Forfar Harriers and the Kirriemuir Harriers with some of the Dundee Harriers joining in on an individual basis.

Athletics and running had grown in popularity in Forfar over the last twenty years, and a great crowd assembled all the way along the route to watch.

For the purpose of the race, both clubs divided their runners into the "fasts" and the "slows" with the "slows" being given a start in a primitive form of handicapping.

The "hares" were let off at 4.15 pm, the "slows" at 4.20 pm and the "fasts" at 4.25 pm.

The race started from Bankhead then they went along Craigie Loch, Balmashanner and back by the Lour Road and Castle Street which was particularly well-populated with well-wishers and supporters.

The "hares" arrived back some 25 minutes after the "fasts" departed, then came a posse of the "slows" with Forfar first and third in that category through Sim and McPherson, with Steven of Kirriemuir in second place.

Almost immediately afterwards came that great Forfar Sportsman John Killacky (who would soon become famous as a cyclist as well) clearly winning the race for the "fasts".

He was cheered and clapped all the way along Castle Street, but the real excitement came in the race for second place between Sherridan of Forfar and Captain Hendry of Dundee with the Forfar man just edging home.

The time taken by Killacky was 29 minutes, which was considered to be a good time for a distance of about five miles.

February 23 1917

Today's *Forfar Herald* appeared as usual, and it is difficult to find anything in the four pages that does not have some reference to the war.

This being winter, the casualty lists are comparatively low, although there is an account of Private Alexander Meffan who has been reported killed. He was actually 46 but had been a soldier in the past and had volunteered at the start of the War.

But the main issue seems to concern the Burgh Tribunal on conscription. Conscription had been introduced last year, and the Tribunal had the job of deciding to whom certificates of exemption were to be issued. The issue this week was factory workers. Previously, tenters (engineers who maintained looms) were considered to be exempt as being necessary to the war effort at home, but a tenter had this week received instruction to proceed to Perth and had been given a single railway ticket.

He was in fact being called up. What seemed to be happening was that there was a slight change in emphasis in that the military would call a man up, then it would be up to him to lodge an appeal to the Tribunal for exemption. Previously, tenters had been automatically exempt.

It was a clear case of the net tightening, although there was also the clear argument that it was better to keep a man in a job as a good tenter than to take him away and make him a bad and unwilling soldier.

1917 was not a time of logical thought, however. Hysteria was in the air!

February 24 1892

James Christie, a labourer who lived in South Street, did not have a very good day today at the Forfar Police Court before Provost Doig.

He was on a charge of using abusive and scurrilous language to Mrs Nicol, the wife of John Nicol, lamplighter, a crime that he had been convicted of six times previously!

Why he did not like Mrs Nicol is not obvious, but it would probably not be a huge leap of faith to suggest that there might have been, in the past, a liaison of sorts which had possibly ended acrimoniously.

But suddenly Mr Stirling, the Superintendent, suggested that the Crown should desert the diet *pro loco et tempore,* i.e. abandon the case in the meantime.

Christie was now on a far more serious charge, namely with two others, William Mudie of Reedmakers Close and John Steele of Nursery Feus, breaking into the butcher's shop of Charles Greenhill in East High Street and stealing a safe, £28, a cheque of £3 6s and 10 pence and 10 lbs of steak.

The case was remitted to the Sheriff Court and that very afternoon they were examined by Sheriff Substitute Taylor and committed to prison pending further enquiry with no bail allowed.

Mudie was subsequently released but the other two were likely to face the charge. One can imagine the feelings of Mrs Nicol and indeed Mr Nicol at this point, for Mrs Nicol would certainly not have to face any abusive behaviour from Christie for a while because Mr Christie was likely to be behind bars!

February 25 1947

It was the middle of what was regarded as the worst snow on record, certainly in the Twentieth Century.

Forfar Town Council tonight faithfully reflected the two predominant and perennial strands of Forfar thinking, namely "We'r a Farfar fowk thegither in wir bra wee toonie" and the less respectable and somewhat contradictory one of "Ah dunnae see hoo he gets it an' ah dunnae".

In the first place, Streets Convenor Whyte paid tribute to all those council workers and even a few volunteers who had done such a great job of clearing the streets.

In particular tribute was paid to the firm of AT Mungall's who had provided their lorries and their men free of charge, and many householders had done their bit by clearing the front of their houses.

As a result of all this, civilisation had more or less continued in Forfar. But wait a minute! There was a letter from some of the greetin' faces of Lilybank, Easterbank and Graham Crescent.

Their areas of town had to a large extent been neglected. Councillor Smyth replied that it was only right that the main roads where all the traffic was should be done first, but it also appeared that if a Councillor lived in your street, you tended to get slightly more favourable treatment.

Taylor Street and Lour Road, for example, were "spotless" whereas Robertson Terrace and Hanick Terrace were not. Now that it was late February, it was beginning to be hoped that the worst had passed, and that everything was going to thaw anyway.

Sadly there was still a while to go yet in this horrible winter of 1947.

February 26 1929

Reverend WG Donaldson of the Old Kirk made his first appearance on the bench as a Justice of the Peace today.

A considerable figure in the community, he was clearly a great believer that members of the Christian Church should involve themselves in as many aspects of local life as possible.

His decision to become a JP had been met with a little criticism from a few members of his congregation who felt that he had enough to be going on with in his Church.

A few had even turned a little theological on him and pointed to a text which said "Judge not, lest you yourself be judged". Most of this was light hearted stuff, but Mr Donaldson felt compelled to make an oblique reference to it in his sermon when he said that "The trouble is that so many people think they are always right" as he thumped the front of his pulpit in his traditional manner which earned him his nickname "knockie"!

However that may be, he took his place on the bench and his very first case was a pathetic young labourer from Arbroath who had been found at the back of Colliston village hall "in a state of intoxication and incapable of taking care of himself".

In an exemplary piece of Christian forgiveness, Reverend Donaldson looked at the young man who indeed looked as if a plate of soup might be a better idea than alcoholic refreshment, and said that as this was the first ever case to come before him, the young men was to be admonished and dismissed.

"God bless you, sir" was the reply from the repentant young drunkard.

February 27 1910

This Sunday morning saw the sudden death of Mr James Baxter, the Manager of The Gas Works who passed away at 5.00 am in the Forfar Infirmary.

He was only 52, and although he had been in indifferent health for some time, his death came as a shock. It was generally agreed that he had never been the same since his wife died a few years ago, and he was survived by a son and two daughters.

He was a very significant man in Forfar history for his decade as Manager of The Gas Board since 1900 was the era in which the gas lighting of the town had improved beyond all measure from being in a rather primitive state to being one of the best in Scotland, and much remarked upon by visitors.

Mr Baxter had not only been a scientific and skilful gas engineer but had also been a capable and economic Gas Manager, introducing various labour-saving and other economical improvements at the works.

He had started off as a plumber but had now been in the gas industry for 23 years, watching the industry grow as people began to understand more and more about gas, and beginning to become less and less afraid of it.

Mr Baxter was a native of Paisley and that was where his funeral was going to be held, but his cortège went along North Street towards the station passing the Gas Works where the flag was at half-mast.

Shops in North Street lowered their blinds as a sign of respect, as people came out to the pavement and bowed their heads. The coffin was escorted to the station by the Provost, Town Councillors and his workers at the Gas Board.

February 28 1911

A major panic today in the agricultural community with the fear of anthrax.

Anthrax was not so well understood or as easily controllable in 1911 as it is now, and of course, apart from anything else, it could be spread to humans.

Today a bullock died suddenly at Nether Bow Farm, about a couple of miles to the north of Forfar, without any previous sign of being ill; at the post mortem Dr Inglis the Veterinary Inspector for the area found anthrax to be the cause of death.

This obviously had serious implications for the agriculture of Angus. Everything possible was being done to prevent contagion and the police were called to enforce preventative measures. All the workers on the farm were quarantined for a spell, and no cattle were allowed to be bought or sold from the farm.

In the town, posters were put up at the Cross, near the "mert" and in public houses known to be frequented by farmers and farm labourers warning them about what had happened at Nether Bow.

The measures certainly seem to have been effective, because there are no reports of the "mert" having to be cancelled.

Anthrax was (and still is) a rare but serious disease believed to have been caused by something that the animal ate from the ground.

Cases of anthrax occurred from time to time, but were usually fairly easily containable, and nowadays, it can be treated by antibiotics or, for preference, by a prophylactic vaccination. But in 1911, it was "an awfa waydaein at the Boo".

What Well Dressed Forfar People Looked Like in 1935. They are watching the Opening Ceremony of the Strathmore Cricket Club Tea Pavilion

February 29 1972

Leap Year's Day and at last the Miners' Strike of 1972 is over!

Well, it is not really over, for there were a part two and a part three to come yet in future years, before coal mining was finally destroyed in the mid-1980s.

The miners had been on strike since soon after the New Year, and from an early stage it was obvious that they were winning it.

Coal mining, on the face of it, did not seem to have much to do with Forfar, but of course in the highly industrialised society that Great Britain still was in 1972, the Miners' Strike did have a great effect including putting the factories on a three day week because of lack of electricity, and football matches played on a Sunday because people were working on a Saturday!

"It's nothing tae dae wi us" did not really apply! And yet there was a genuine feeling of shock in this peaceful town — with no great recent tradition of labour problems — to see so many men on strike with the scenes of violence on the picket lines, shown gleefully on TV, a particular cause of horror.

It was the first Miners' Strike since 1926 and it would be fair to say that opinions in the town varied. The thuggery of the miners on picket lines certainly did nothing to excite sympathy, but there was also a feeling that the Government of Edward Heath had done a great deal to provoke the conflict while doing nothing to solve the underlying problem of inflation which was affecting everyone.

But today the North of Scotland Hydro Board announced that there would be no more power cuts to the electricity supply, and the situation returned to normality — for a spell!

78   Advertisements from 1938

March

March 1 2018

The 1st of March is normally reckoned to be the first day of spring, but this is no ordinary March, because Forfar, like the rest of the country is in the grip of the meteorological phenomenon commonly known as "the beast from the East".

What actually caused it no-one really knew other than it was a combination of circumstances but crucially, it was an east wind. Normally winds come from the west and are generally milder.

It would be a very ambitious claim for anyone to say that it was Forfar's worst ever snow — there were after all a few candidates in the 1970s and 1980s, not to mention the big freeze up of 1963, and the one that was generally agreed to be the worst of the 20th century, 1947.

It was certainly quite severe with schools closed, roads blocked and the other disruptions to life, including snow piled up high at the side of the road. All the Forfar old ladies said that it was "yokie" or "an afa weydaein" and tending to begin sentences like "Ah mind fan..."

But the emergency services kept going, and the saving grace was that, it being the end of February when it started, daylight was that little bit longer and whenever the wind changed, the thaw came fairly rapidly.

A week later the snow had virtually gone, and everyone wondered what all the fuss had been about. It did shut the "climate changers" up for a while, though! We had no need to feel guilty about mild winters for a while!

March 2 1900

The news today from South Africa is good, in that Ladysmith had been relieved.

This happened a couple of days ago, but the good news was confirmed today and reported in *The Forfar Herald*.

This war has been going on for a few months now, and it is good to hear of some success, for there are one or two politicians and even members of the public beginning to wonder what this is all about, and why it is that the British Empire has not already crushed a few uppity Dutch farmers.

Naturally there is a great deal of concern about how "wir leddies is daein" in that faraway country in a war that is not readily understood.

The Forfar Herald is able to give a list of 51 men from Forfar — militiamen, reservists, regular soldiers and volunteers — currently serving in South Africa. One man, Private A Bett of the Zoar has been killed while serving with the Royal Highlanders, Private J Laird of Roberts Street, also with the Royal Highlanders, is missing and at least three others are wounded, one of them, Private E Ramsay of North Street, being captured in Bloemfontein.

It is an extremely worrying time for quite a few families, but there is a funny side to it as well. We are told, for example, of an old Forfar lady when she was told that Ladysmith had been relieved, who said "Relieved? Relieved? Efter Ah the bither she has caused wir leddies, I wad wring her bloody neck for her!"

March 3 1971

Forfar today lost one of its foremost brains in the death of Dr Jack McKenzie at his home in St John's Cottages, Service Road.

He was Principal Teacher of Classics at Forfar Academy, and died "in harness". He had performed this job with distinction from 1956 and was much loved and respected by his pupils.

Born in 1913, his father having been a Master Painter and Decorator in the town and a veteran of the First World War, Jack had studied at Forfar Academy before going on to St Andrews University where he graduated MA Hons in Classics.

He then went on to London to do a degree in English and finished off his education with a Ph D on the role of actors in medieval Scotland. He also served in Naval Intelligence in the Second World War.

He taught at a Primary School for a spell, and then Lawside Academy in Dundee teaching Classics, but Forfar Academy was the job that he always wanted.

He had a genuine love for his subject and the ability to infect others with his enthusiasm always saying that there was nothing he enjoyed more than Latin or Greek Prose Composition.

He was a well-known local character as well with his bicycle and battered suitcase, a lover of golf and a performer in the Forfar Amateur Dramatic Society, and yet essentially a very quiet man with his own ideas on what was right in education and everything else.

His funeral at St James's Kirk and at Forfar Cemetery on the Saturday after he died was very well attended.

As Burns once said of another Classics teacher, "the fawts he had in Latin lay, for nane in English kent them".

March 4 1946

There was an elephant in the room at tonight's AGM of the Forfar Infirmary, but it was never mentioned.

It was of course the imminence of the National Health Service, already being worked on and scheduled to begin in summer 1948.

This would change things totally and in ways that no-one could in 1946 predict, apart from the fact that all health care would now be free.

Tonight with Provost Lowson in the Chair, tribute was paid to Mrs Fyfe-Jamieson of Ruthven who had passed away.

The Convenor of the Management Committee reported that new X-Ray equipment would be delivered soon and that Forfar Infirmary might well be used as a training hospital for Nurses, if Forfar and Arbroath Infirmaries were to amalgamate.

Treasurer AC Smyth reported that last year there was an average of 43 patients per day, there had been 325 operations (almost one per day!), 1665 outpatients had attended and there had been 1876 X Rays. It was clearly a well-used hospital, and its use was increasing over the years.

Mr Dalgety had reported that Balgavies Convalescent Home had also been well used by Forfar people but also had patients from Dundee and Glasgow. The Home had been adversely commented upon in a Government report, but Mr Dalgety questioned the right of Government Inspectors to inspect a private Home.

Various bequests were reported upon, and a new Committee was elected for next year. Although the future was obscure, there was no reason to believe that the Infirmary would not continue to serve the community of Forfar.

March 5 1938

The Forfar Dramatic Society tonight finished their performance of JB Priestley's "Spring Tide" before an appreciative audience.

The Society of course enjoyed a very high reputation in Scotland in those days with their successes at festivals, and this performance was also much enjoyed by the locals, even though it was generally agreed that it was not one of JB Priestley's better plays.

The play was produced by Miss Cita Angus who generally demonstrated fine knowledge of stage technique, although now and again she made the mistake of having the actors sitting with their backs to the audience, something that did not lend itself to the Reid Hall's occasionally unreliable acoustics.

The play concerned a London boarding house with a few dysfunctional characters, and how life changed for them when they all migrated to a houseboat. This of course necessitated a change in setting, but the Society handled that very well.

The old favourites, Aggie Smith, Fred Milne, Connie Tait and Harold Adamson were all very much involved, with Harold in particular being very impressive with his Irish brogue, and the Society also took the opportunity to blood a few youngsters, some of them proving an instant success with the audience — James Bruce, James Crofts and Agnes Milne.

The rest of the cast included James Findlay, Louise Steele and David Jolly, and the evening also contained music at the interval provided by Fred Mann on the violin and Mr HC Carver on the piano. The Forfar Dramatic Society maintained its high reputation with this performance and they were rewarded by large audiences.

Forfar Jute Mill

March 6 1885

The Forfar Herald, while in the past pretending to be neutral and impartial in the issue of compulsory vaccination, now attacks two recently published books — *The Great Delusion* by William White of London and *Forty Five Years of Registration Statistics proving Vaccination to be both useless and dangerous* by Alfred L Wallace LL.D.

Neither of these two books impress *The Forfar Herald* which states that before compulsory vaccination, "almost every tenth man or woman that one met was deeply marked with smallpox and the disease was undoubtedly more fatal and hideous"

Furthermore in the last epidemic in Forfar, by far the greater proportion of the deaths caused by smallpox were of those who had never been vaccinated or who had been improperly or imperfectly vaccinated.

There was even a case in Forfar of a woman who was vaccinated two days after she had caught smallpox. The vaccination mitigated the effects of the disease and the lady duly recovered.

So *The Forfar Herald* thinks that the Government was right to introduce compulsory vaccination and is not impressed by the book of Dr Wallace. It also reminds its readers that Dr Wallace is also associated with Spiritualism.

The whole issue of vaccination was very much a live one in Victorian Britain with many people of the opinion that it didn't do any good, that it interfered with nature and that it was not God's will.

Most local doctors however and apparently here the local press were of the view that although smallpox was undeniably a dangerous disease, it could nevertheless be dealt with by insisting on immunisation.

March 7 1924

Today saw a terrible happening when 22-month old Agnes Ferguson of 20 North Street died in Forfar Infirmary of severe burns.

This had followed an incident in North Street a few days before when her mother Mrs Ferguson had ill-advisedly left her with her four-year-old brother while she nipped along the short distance to Hebenton's North Street Dairy to buy some milk.

It appears that a gas ring had been left on, and somehow, the little girl's dress had caught fire. When the mother came back, she met the little girl and her brother in the close with the girl's clothes on fire.

She ran back and Mr Hebenton the milkman was able to wrap a blanket round the little girl, and to summon help from Dr Cable who happened to be in the district.

Dr Cable arranged for her to be taken to the Infirmary but it was immediately apparent that the burns were serious. For a while it was hoped that her life could be saved, albeit at the cost of some horrendous burns to her body, but she died a few days later to the tremendous anguish of the family and neighbourhood.

It was of course very easy to be judgemental and to criticise the mother for her fatal mistake, but she was hardly alone in leaving children unattended and most people would admit that they had done the same in the past and got off with it.

No charge seems to have been brought against Mrs Ferguson which was only right because she had surely suffered enough.

March 8 1918

The longer the war goes on, the more "tight" becomes the food supplies with the Atlantic Ocean now looked upon as one of the major theatres of war with German U Boats wreaking all sorts of havoc.

The food shortage is having its effect on Forfar, although it has not reached crisis point, but Finavon at least is fighting back!

A new ploughing record is being claimed by The County Food Production Committee. This was achieved by Mr McBeth of Messrs Simpson, Motor Engineers, who ploughed 34 and a half acres in 67 and a half hours in his paraffin driven tractor.

This means that seeds for the crops can be planted at an early stage and the harvest can consequently be ready all the earlier! It is an excellent example of how the war is being fought on the home front as well as abroad, and how people like farmers, bakers, butchers and food shop staff are doing as much for the war effort as the soldiers and sailors.

In the meantime the coming of spring brings a certain apprehension about the resumption of hostilities on the Western Front, now that the Germans have won in the East. Some Forfar soldiers were lucky enough to get some leave at the New Year, but they have now returned to face the onslaught.

Of course, we now have the Americans, but the Germans are tougher foes than the Red Indians, and no-one is really expecting a great deal from those "transatlantic blow bags" who have taken their time about arriving!

March 9 1855

The town has been in a fervour for the last few weeks because of the by-election.

The previous MP, the Radical Joseph Hume had died a few weeks ago, and the by-election to replace him had caused no little argument, discussion and even a threat, now and again, of public disorder.

The candidates were William Baxter, the Radical, and Sir John Ogilvy, the Whig.

Forfar was part of the constituency called Montrose Burghs which also contained Montrose, Arbroath, Brechin and Bervie. Although this constituency had only 1,585 electors, this did not mean that the rest of the population was not very actively involved in the election.

There are reports of meetings and demonstrations at the Market Muir and elsewhere, mainly in favour of the Radical Baxter who was a Dissenter and belonged to the United Free Church and not above implying that Sir John Ogilvy had sympathies with the Church of Rome.

Surprisingly, little seems to have been said about the Crimean War, which was the big issue of the day. The polling booth was at the Cross and each elector declared publicly who he was voting for, usually to loud cheers or boos.

Forfar voted 123 to 105 in favour of Baxter, and although Arbroath and Brechin voted for Ogilvy, Montrose, a very Radical town, voted overwhelmingly in favour of Baxter.

The telegraph wires in 1855 were somewhat primitive, and unreliable, but "horse flesh" propelled the couriers with the news from the other burghs. As everyone declared their vote, it was registered there and then, there was no complicated "count", and by 5 o'clock it was clear that William Baxter the Radical was elected to Westminster.

March 10 2019

Forfar today has an Earl and a Countess!

On his 55th birthday, Prince Edward, the third son of the Queen, was given the "Earl of Forfar" to use in Scotland as distinct from the "Earl of Wessex" which he uses in England.

As to how he came to be given this title which had been long extinct no-one really knew, but it was believed to be given as a reward to the town for its exceptional loyalty to the Crown over the centuries, and because the Queen Mother often claimed to have come from Forfar (a slight exaggeration, perhaps, although she did live her early life in Glamis Castle).

Prince Edward, born in 1964, was a late baby, but it was generally reckoned that he was one of the more sensible of the royals, tending to avoid the limelight and having married a sensible woman called Sophie Rhys-Jones, now the Countess of Forfar!

Certainly their life has been more or less totally free from scandal, however hard the gutter press has tried to stir things up, and Edward had the courage to give up his career in the Royal Marines (for which he was clearly not suited) and take up a career in the theatre instead.

Sophie also had a career in public relations.

They visited Forfar for the first time later in the summer of 2019 and were presented with the Forfar Tartan from the Strathmore Woollen Mill.

They came across as a nice couple, possibly embarrassed at the antics of some of their relatives but themselves free from foolishness, and it was good for the town of Forfar to be associated with them.

Forfar Masonic Hall

March 11 1906

Sunday in 1906 was usually a quiet, sombre, guilt ridden experience where everyone, after going to Church was expected to go for walks, possibly read a book and talk very little.

This Sunday was a glorious exception for last night there had been dancing in the streets of Forfar! For the first time in their history, Forfar Athletic had won the Forfarshire Cup, and the town was nursing a huge collective hangover and thinking of nothing other than football!

We are told that the team arrived at Forfar Station last night from Montrose after beating Arbroath in the Forfarshire Cup final. They were ushered into a series of brakes and driven through the streets of the town. Crowds lined North Street, East High Street and Castle Street to see the procession, led by the Forfar Instrumental Band playing "See! The Conquering Hero Comes!", before the team was taken to a hostelry for a celebration with Chairman Mr Cruickshanks and Vice Chairman Mr Grant!

Particular glory was bestowed on Geordie "Purkie" Langlands who had scored the first goal and had a hand in the second in the 2-1 victory. It was said to be the "biggest crowd ever seen at Links Park" with train loads of supporters from both Forfar and Arbroath, and the Montrose "neutrals" siding with the "black and navy" of Forfar.

The receipts were £54, exclusive of the stand. Forfar's team on that historic day was Roger, R Murray and Shand; Melvin, A Murray and A Fairweather; Blyth, Langlands, W Fairweather, Petrie and Ritchie. After the game, and before Forfar's triumphant return to the town, both teams had been well wined and dined at the Commercial Hotel in Montrose.

Celebrations went on in Forfar until the early hours of the morning!

March 12 1945

The end of the war is expected any day now (in fact it would have another two months to run) as the Allies are closing in on the west and the Russians on the east.

It was probably round about now that the joke about the Russians "driving them back" became current. ("Driving them back? I'd make the buggers walk" said the old Kingsmuir lady to the Minister!), but there was increasing concern about the Polish soldiers who had made such a favourable impression on Forfar people.

They had arrived early on in the war (Great Britain sadly not having been in a position to save them, other than to offer them a temporary home) and they had been billeted in the Reid Hall (until it went on fire in 1941) and a few private houses and on local farms.

Most of them were now in France fighting in the British Army, but what would they do after the Germans surrendered? Their land would now be in the hands of the Soviet Union, who were hardly a great deal better than the Germans.

Would they be welcomed back to Poland? Would they want to go back? There was, of course, an alternative urged on them by many young Forfar girls in their letters to them. They could always "bide here".

Thankfully, so many of them did. This also of course gave rise to another Forfar joke about the Forfar lady who gave birth to a wooden baby, but that was because she was married to a Pole!

March 13 1931

If there were any doubt about the economic recession hitting Forfar, it would have been dispelled by the announcement today of some huge losses in Manor Works, commonly known as Craik's.

The loss for the year comes to a massive £2897 16 shillings and 3 pence. Fortunately, there is still sufficient capital in the Reserve Fund, but it is still a massive loss.

The £490 for Directors' Fees probably raised a few eyebrows in the town, when the accounts were published. The background to this had been that Craik's had done well out of the Great War (with the "war profiteer" sneer often being hurled at them) but then of course once all the military contracts dried up, recession hit them in the early 1920s, their cause not being helped by a bad fire in autumn 1920.

But then things picked up considerably in the mid 1920s until the Wall Street Crash of autumn 1929 triggered off a worldwide depression which showed every indication of getting totally out of control.

"When America sneezes, the whole world catches a cold" and as a great deal of jute went to America, the trade was badly affected with the other factories in town also struggling and having to lay off workers or put them on "short time" of working half the week.

Sadly, Ramsay MacDonald's Labour Government seemed to have no solution to this problem of international capitalism, and the outlook was grim. It was not as if poverty were anything new to Forfar people, but the prospects for jute in particular were far from bright.

George Dempster of Dunnichen

March 14 1921

Reverend WG Donaldson of the Old Kirk is not happy these days about the employment of young boys to deliver Sunday newspapers.

He has delivered one or two sermons to this effect recently and now in the Parish Newsletter "old Knockie" (so called because of his habit of thumping the pulpit when upbraiding Forfarians for their sin and sexual desires) warns clearly about the evil that this practice can do to a youngster (and he may never be able to rise above it!).

The problem seems to be that not only does a boy deliver newspapers, he sometimes sells them and takes money for them. Presumably the danger lies in the temptation to cheat customers or the real possibility that he might be attacked by "vagabonds" for his money.

Not only that, but newspapers are brought round in a "hurdy-gurdy" in wheels which makes a noise to disturb the peace of a Sunday morning along with the strident cry of "Post!"

And worst of all, the boy is sometimes not finished in time to go to Church! The problem of course is a comparatively new one. Although Sunday newspapers did exist before the war, what had made the difference is the Dundee based *Sunday Post.* This began in 1914 to give soldiers local news, continued after the war and is more or less universally read in Forfar because, for example, it always gives a report on Forfar Athletic's games.

Sunday newspapers seem to be one of the many examples of how the Church is now beginning to lose control over life and society.

March 15 1895

A very full meeting of ratepayers was held tonight in the Drill Hall, New Road with Provost Anderson in the Chair to consider the proposal of Councillor Ritchie to turn the Gushet Nursery into a Public Bowling Green.

The Gushet was near Wellbraehead, and the lease of the Nursery on the land there was about to expire. It was most unusual for the Town Council in 1895 to consult the "vox populi" on any issue but this was one which clearly aroused a great deal of interest.

Councillor Ritchie's argument was that Forfar had very few areas for recreation in comparison with towns of comparable size like Montrose, for example.

There was a certain amount of the class war involved in this issue, for although bowls was a very long established sport (since the days of Sir Francis Drake!) and was played widely in Forfar, it was a very expensive sport and tended only to be played in private clubs.

This idea of Councillor Ritchie would ensure that "the working place would benefit". The counter argument was put by Treasurer Fenton who outlined the expenses and the disadvantages of the site at The Gushet which might not really be big enough.

Councillor Craik then said that what was needed was more fields for football and cricket, pointing out that there were pieces of land available for bowls at Lilybank, the Myre and North Mains.

An amendment was introduced that the idea of a bowling green at the Gushet should not be persevered with, and the amendment was carried amidst a certain amount of "hissing" from those who disagreed.

March 16 1916

Forfar may be in the middle of a dreadful war, but a glance at today's *Forfar Dispatch* shows that there is no lack of social activity going on in the town.

There is no football, sadly, for the simple reason that there are not enough men around the sustain all of Forfar's teams, but the women of the town are rising to the challenge.

For example, the ladies of the Parish Church Choir have organised a concert "to entertain wounded soldiers tonight in a genuinely homely evening where they can spend a few hours in the sunshine of ladies' smiles".

There are of course quite a few wounded Forfar soldiers, some of them quite seriously wounded, after last year's battles at the Dardanelles or Loos.

And last week, the Meffan Hall was crowded to hear the Annual Reciting and Singing Competition organised by the West End Debating Society in which 24 young reciters and 7 singers took part.

The high standard of "histrionic talent" was an eloquent testimony to the efforts of the Debating Society in keeping going during difficult times.

And of course, there are Forfar's two Cinemas — the Gaffie or Pavilion which has been open since 1910 and Shand's Palace in Roberts Street. The Pavilion is showing "The Broken Coin" while Shand's Palace is showing "Charlie At The Bank", "the best film ever seen in Forfar" involving Charlie Chaplin, although such is the innate Forfar desire to pronounce things differently from the rest of the world that he is commonly referred to as "Chairlie Chippleton"!

March 17 1785

Today Andrew Low was hanged on the gallows tree on Balmashanner Hill, apparently the last man to be hanged in public in Scotland.

There was a certain revulsion of feeling about this public administration of justice, but the main reason for the stopping of public hangings was the fear of disturbances and even political demonstrations. The Jacobites had now long gone, but there were other subversive movements around, and the American Revolution and the loss of the colonies had caused a great deal of alarm.

Today in Forfar, crowds had gathered from all around the county to see the hanging of Andrew Low. Records of the court cases make it clear that Andrew was indeed a habitual criminal, but he had not murdered anyone, and the sentence of execution did seem hard to the enlightened people of the 18th century.

Transportation to a distant part of the world, or prison with hard labour seemed to be more appropriate. Nevertheless, the town was all agog to see what was going to happen. It probably wasn't Andrew, but a previous criminal who had uttered the immortal remarks from the cart that was taking him up the road "Fut are ye a' hurryin' for? There'll be nae show tull I get there!"

Nevertheless, we can imagine all the excitement as the red-coated soldiers escorted the hapless Andrew on his last journey. There was even, apparently, some sympathy shown for him by a few, and many cheers for him as he passed through Castle Street, the Pend and up the Lour Road for his appointment with the executioner.

March 18 1892

The Forfar Herald today publishes a laudatory report on Forfar man Dr James A Lowson, who is currently doing very well for himself in Hong Kong.

Dr. James A Lowson,
one time Provost of the town

He was well known as a golfer and a cricketer before he left Forfar, but it is now hard to decide at which of the two he really excels. He had frequently been praised as a golfer but it is as a cricketer that he is glorified today.

The Hong Kong Telegraph contains a report of a cricket match in Hong Kong where the home team beat Shanghai by an innings and 122 runs. Dr Lowson took 6 for 56 in the first innings and scored 49 when Hong Kong batted. His innings included "a brace of fours", to the delight of the watching Governor and a host of interested guests and spectators.

In the evening after the dinner, there was a "smoke" (sic) put on by the Governor and Dr Lowson there proved his versatility and all round ability by singing a couple of songs.

This is only another episode in the fascinating and unusual life of Dr Lowson who, among other things survived a shipwreck. After supervising and dealing with an outbreak of bubonic plague, he fell ill himself with tuberculosis in 1901. He decided to come back to Forfar, where he served on the council from 1905 onwards, eventually became Provost before his death in 1935.

He did a great deal to improve the general health of the town, having the reputation of practising medicine with poor families and not asking for payment.

One of Forfar's greatest sons, one feels.

March 19 1932

The Drummer in *The Forfar Dispatch* is beside himself with joy today. As unemployment rises inexorably, it is good that there is something to be happy about. It is all to do with local lads who have worked hard at their hobby and earned a reward.

Forfar Instrumental Band tonight "swept the boards" by winning everything at the Forfarshire Amateur Bands Association competition at Kirriemuir. The general standard was very high but Forfar won every single competition.

There were 12 teams entered for "the quartette" from seven clubs — Forfar, Brechin, Kirriemuir, Montrose, Arbroath, Dundee RNVR and Dundee Trades (some clubs entered more than one quartette) — and Forfar no 1 won the handsome John Killacky Challenge Cup, with Brechin City no 1 being the runners up.

In the individual sections Dave Rattray won the cornet section, Willie Cook the horn, Jimmy Towns the euphonium and Bill Harvey the bass.

Cook, by the narrowest possible margin over Rattray, was adjudged the best of all the soloists taking part with his rendition of "Cherry Ripe" which the adjudicator Herbert Bennett from Glasgow described as "absolutely delightful".

The prizes were presented by Provost Peacock of Kirriemuir and the Vote of Thanks was given by Mr Ritchie of Arbroath, the President of the Association, both of whom commented on the "Forfar monopoly".

It was the first time that a "clean sweep" had ever happened in the history of the competition. The event was well attended by an appreciative audience, and it was a great reward for all their hard work during the winter months.

March 20 1947

Tomorrow will be the spring equinox but there is still no visible let up in the hard winter.

For a few days, it looked as if it was beginning to thaw out, but the snow returned with a vengeance at the start of the week, disrupting transport and blocking roads again.

One train to Brechin could get no further than Justinhaugh, but fortunately the passengers were able to get out and make their way to the Justinhaugh Hotel, unlike those who had been stuck at Kirkbuddo a few weeks ago and had to spend the night in their train!

There was now official confirmation that this had been the worst February for 133 years since 1816, which was the first winter after the Battle of Waterloo!

Yet, there were worse places to be snowed in than Forfar. Food supply disruption was minimal and hardly anyone noticed, because rationing did that job anyway!

Football was, of course, out of the question but the cinemas remained open, Churches remained open and the social life of the town remained, to a large extent, unimpaired. In any case, Forfar people, some of whom had now lived through two dreadful world wars, were used to hardship and, as always, looked out for each other.

Of course *The Forfar Dispatch* had the Chronicles of Mary-Ann, who said "The lest onding made me that thrawn I wiz company for naither man nor baist" which could be translated as "The last heavy fall of snow caused me to be so angry that neither humans nor animals found my company congenial."

March 21 1934

In recent weeks a new book has appeared on bookshelves in London, Edinburgh and elsewhere called "The Birth Of The Future" written by a Forfar man called Peter Ritchie Calder.

Peter Ritchie Calder, famous scientist and peace campaigner

It is his first book and is described as a "pilgrimage" taken by the young author through various places of work, laboratories and educational establishments to chart what life is going to be like in future years.

The Forfar Dispatch is extremely impressed by the work of this loon, particularly in his "buoyancy of language" which allows mortals and laymen to understand the mysteries of science.

Even HG Wells was impressed by this work. Later in 1934 he will produce another book called "The Conquest of Suffering". Peter Ritchie Calder is the son of Mr DL Calder, former Manager of Station Works, and he is a journalist with *The Daily Herald,* having taken up that career as a journalist on the suggestion of his English teacher at Forfar Academy, David Mackie.

His first essay apparently appeared in *The Forfar Dispatch* when he was eleven years old! His interest in science dates from only two years ago, possibly as a result of the economic depression in which he began to look to science and the future for answers to the world's problems.

It was as a scientist that he became famous, but he was also an ardent peace campaigner in the 1950s, eventually earning a peerage and becoming Baron Ritchie-Calder of Balmashanner in 1966. His family are well known, and the BBC Travel Correspondent Simon Calder is his grandson. He died in 1982.

March 22 1920

Today saw the funeral of James Neill who had died at his home at Ythanbank, Forfar on March 18.

He was 86 and a retired Dancing Teacher. He was commonly known as "Dancie Neill" and held his classes at his premises of 46a Castle Street for many years.

Anyone who had ever been at his classes held him in the highest esteem and regard, and he taught both juveniles and adults. His classes were a prominent feature of Forfar's social and educational life for well over half a century; it was only a couple of years ago that he had retired, even late in his life offering, in dancing, some solace for those suffering the privations of war.

"Dancie" was an untiring and enthusiastic teacher and at four score years, he still had the sureness of touch, the lightness and suppleness of step, and the precision and artistic poise which mark the born exponent of his art.

He had a distinctive walk, almost as if he were walking on tiptoes all the time. *The Forfar Dispatch* is convinced that in his case his dancing was the passport to longevity.

Certainly, he took great pride in the fact that in his 64 years of teaching, there were some Forfar families of whom he had taught four generations.

He was equally proud that he had taught the Strathmores, the Airlies and the Atholls to dance. His wife had died in 1918 and he was survived by three sons and four daughters. His funeral was well attended by grateful ex-pupils.

March 23 1904

Tonight at the Town Council a letter was read out from Mr David Steele, banker, offering the Town Council a ten and a half acre field to the west of the Reid Park and to the south of Viewmount for the purpose of recreation for the town.

This gift would have immediate effect and the field could be used by the public in the meantime while the field was being made into a "park".

It was not often that anything received universal approval in the Town Council, and even less often that anything received a round of applause, but tonight was an exception. It was envisaged that this new recreational resource would be a perfect adjunct to the Reid Park which was possibly not suitable for team games like football and cricket.

Provost Adamson was naturally very happy with the gift, and the offer could not have come at a better time because the Council had been looking for areas suitable for leisure activities, for at the moment there was only really the Market Muir.

The Lochside had been considered but there could be problems with the Earl of Strathmore who owned the land, and in any case there could be drainage issues.

Mr Steele was, of course, "merriet oan a Lowson" (as they said in Forfar) and this is another example of how the town was indebted to the Lowson family. By next July, the Steele Park (as it was now called) would be used for the Forfar Games, and its value has been proved countless times in the next 100 years and more.

March 24 1919

The town was still struggling to come to terms with the new situation of the post-war world.

Every day saw more and more ex-Serviceman returning, some of them claiming to have served with the Royal Air Force which was an amalgamation in April 1918 of the Royal Flying Corps and the Royal Naval Air Service.

There can be little doubt that the recent war had provided a great boost for flying and some young men had arrived back in town claiming to have had a trip in these flying machines, which were used for reconnaissance and even the dropping of bombs on the enemy.

It would appear however that it might be some time before Forfar could become an air base in the way that Montrose, for example, was used, apparently during the war. Now it appeared that the possibilities of aerial travel were being considered for commercial purposes!

A letter arrived to the Town Clerk and it was duly read out at tonight's council meeting. It was from a Company offering to consider any proposals for the aerial transport of either passengers or mail that the town of Forfar might care to make.

The idea was met with stony silence while the Councillors racked their brains to consider any way that this idea might become a possibility. Bailie Lamb at last came up with the idea that as some Councillors were due to attend a meeting soon in Edinburgh on town planning, possibly a flight by air might be a possibility! Everyone then had a good laugh at that idea and moved on to the next item of business.

March 25 1943

Today's *Forfar Dispatch* contains a heart-warming story about Forfar folk far from home.

Mrs Scott, manageress of The Pavilion (The Gaffie) cinema received a letter from her son Robert "somewhere in India" (censorship didn't allow him to say more than that) who was sitting in a café one night when someone tapped him on the shoulder and asked him if he was Bob Scott.

It turned out it was a chap called McKay who was "marriet oan a Low" (as the Forfar idiom put it) and whose sister in law was currently working in the pay-box along with Mrs Scott at The Gaffie.

Not only that, but there was someone else with him who was a nephew of Davie Guild who had worked there for so long. This was the legendary "Granny" Guild whose aphorisms included "Come oan noo, you leds, behave! It's no outside ye're in!"

He told everyone that he worked here "One nicht every nicht and twa nichts on Seturday!"

So, much was the reminiscing about Forfar and "The Gaffie" including the old one "Fut's oan the Gaffie the nicht?" "The Roof".

They might have been interested in the far fields of India to know that what was really on at The Gaffie tonight was a film called "Man Power" starring Edward G Robinson, George Raft and Marlene Dietrich.

Mrs Scott had also received another letter from her son Jimmy who was in a POW camp in Germany, but was healthy and well along with some Australians! And they were able to play cricket!

March 26 1927

Tonight finished "The Yeomen Of The Guard", the annual performance of the Forfar Amateur Operatic Club in the Reid Hall.

It was well performed by the group and well received by the local audiences on all four nights that it was performed. The group had enough talent and strength to "double cast" several characters, something that has the great advantage that it covers for illness and other problems.

It also guarantees large audiences, for some people are happy enough to come twice to see and compare parts. The drama critic of *The Forfar Dispatch* is very impressed by the individual singers with Ernest McLaren singled out for his brilliant performance of Jack Point "a wise man playing a fool" which is not easy.

But the other Principal singers were also good in both sets of performances. The critic is less impressed by the Chorus of the Yeomen. They were like the Curate's egg — good in patches.

Some of the men sang well and paid due attention to the business in hand. Others spent rather too much time staring at the audience, presumably looking for their friends!

The Orchestra were sometimes a bit too strident and gave the impression of being more interested in their own performances rather than being part of the show, although he exempts the pianist Miss Amy Smith and ex-Bailie Lamb from such criticism.

The Stage Manager permitted rather too long intervals, and the continuity was not always as slick as it might have been, and the result was that the opera went on for far too long, not finishing before eleven o'clock; the benches at the Reid Hall are somewhat uncomfortable!

March 27 1918

Today at Albert in France, the Reverend Gilbert Elliott, Minister of the West United Free Church in Forfar met his death through enemy fire.

It was several months before his fate could be ascertained but in August *The Forfar Herald* reported that he was now considered dead. It merely confirmed what had been suspected since the spring when he failed to return to his unit.

Rev Gilbert Elliott,
West Free Church,
killed in World War 1

Three of his companions reported that they had seen Lance Corporal Elliott fall when surrounded by Germans and when he refused to surrender. He left behind a grieving wife and a small daughter and his congregation were devastated by the news.

He had been the Minister of the West Free Kirk since 1915, and had decided to join up last year, although Ministers could gave applied for exemption. He could also have applied to be an Army Chaplain which could have kept him out of the line of fire, or he could have applied for Officer Training, but he preferred to be a Private in the Royal Scots because he "loved the common man".

Very soon, he became a Lance Corporal, but was one of the many casualties of the German Spring Offensive launched a week ago, and which was so successful that it looked for a spell as if the Germans were going to win the war.

Reverend Elliott was one of the "higher profile" Forfar casualties of the war, and he was much mourned by his fellow Ministers, for it was felt that this personable, intelligent and kindly young man had so much to offer to Forfar and the world. It was probably the West Kirk's saddest day.

March 28 1948

This Easter Sunday evening, after all the eggs had been duly rolled in the Reid Park and elsewhere on what was a fine spring day, (very few chocolate eggs, for chocolate was very much on the ration in 1948!) saw Forfar musical people enjoy a rare treat.

This was a very fine Cantata performed in the Old Parish Church to the delight of *The Forfar Dispatch's* critic who thought that in the past Cantatas were often "gey thin stuff". Cantatas had been very popular in the late Victorian age, but their popularity had waned in recent decades.

Tonight, the Old Parish Church Choir, under the very able Direction of William D Bernard, Music Teacher at Forfar Academy as well as Organist of the Old Kirk, performed Gaul's Holy City which seemed to "accord well with the sunny radiance of a fine Easter Sunday. The music was never banal and always mellifluous."

The individual parts were taken by Mrs McQuarrie, Evelyn Petrie, Robert Petrie junior, William Dundas, Ruth Linton, Mrs McKenzie and William Millar.

What was particularly pleasing was the performance of the young singers with young Bob Petrie in particular being highlighted for his versatility. Mr Bernard himself conducted, accompanied and played some pieces on his own.

The performance was very well received by a large audience, and there is no doubt that the Old Kirk particularly lent itself to this sort of performance. It is large, capacious and apart from a few odd places with pillars etc. had very good acoustics.

March 29 1898

The Montrose Review has clearly no sense of humour. It has no idea of what Forfar is all about, and basically it does not seem to like Forfar. No doubt some recent event on a football or a cricket field caused all this, but its report of the Forfar Police Commissioners Meeting is well worth a read.

It seems that Councillor Esplin takes the brunt of the Montrosian attacks. Now, Forfar people knew what Councillor Esplin was like, and it would have to be admitted that he occasionally was known to "open his mooth and let his belly rummle", as they say in Forfar.

Tonight, according to the shocked Montrose journalist, Esplin had a go at Provost McDougall saying "It's a lie. I dinnae care a farden aboot fut you say", "Hold your tongue, sir", "A nonentity, a mere nothing" and then a bizarre threat to "throw somebody's hat at you".

Bailie Milne was told that "You are a nothing, sir. Your principles are not worth candy!" — and all this at a rather boring meeting about police pay and how far out the road the power of the Forfar police extended!

The Montrose Review extends sympathy to Provost McDougall and wonders why the other members of the meeting did not intervene.

One feels that the earnest journalist from Montrose is here ignoring one of the basic principles of Forfar life, no doubt as true in 1898 as they are now — namely that in Forfar to survive and prosper, you really have to be two-faced, and able to dish out and take abuse! And as far as can be ascertained, Provost McDougall did not challenge Councillor Esplin to a duel because of this!

March 30 1885

Bailie Moncur was a busy man at the Police Court this Monday morning.

He first had to deal with a bunch of unruly young men, William Lowson of North Street, Robert Milne of Carseburn Road, Henry Smith of Market Place and George Purvis of Montrose Road, (the last three being described as factory workers whereas Lowson is just a "boy"). Their whose behaviour was described by Bailie Moncur as "disgusting and disgraceful". At the corner of North Street and Don Street, they had thrown eggs at three women, Mary Hill and Jessie Miller of North Whitehills, and Jane Cuthbert of Victoria Street, described as factory workers or dressmakers.

The eggs had struck them on their heads and damaged their dress. It is not clear whether this was just a piece of silliness which went too far or whether the women were innocent adults and it was done maliciously. The boys were all fined 2 shillings or two days imprisonment, the comparative leniency of the punishment making one think that the women were girls who were not totally innocent either.

Rather more serious was the case of Isabella Morrison or Milne, factory worker of Dundee Loan who broke two panes of glass at the house of her estranged husband William Milne of Dundee Road.

She denied the charge, but was found guilty on the evidence of neighbours and as she had been guilty of this sort of thing on nine previous occasions, she was given a straight sentence of twenty days.

March 30 1851

The 1851 Census for Scotland was taken on the night of 30/31 March 1851. The following information was requested:

Place (name of street, place, or road, and name or number of house); Name of each person that had spent the night in that household; Relation to head of family; Marital Status; Age; Sex; Profession or occupation; Birthplace; Whether blind, or deaf and dumb.

James Lowson, Linen Manufacturer, born in January 1815, who had married Agnes Barry, born in September 1813, in 1833, was living in Kirkton, Forfar,.

Their children were Andrew, 15, James, 14, John, 12, Agnes, 10, Mary Anne, 8, Eliza, 6, Euphemia, 4, William, 3, and Margaret,1.

Their two live-in servants were 19-year-old Margaret Esplin and 17-year-old Ann Lowson.

Ann Lowson was the daughter of John (61) and Margaret (59) Lowson, both Hand Loom Weavers (flax), and living in the North Lone with their youngest daughter Margaret, like her sister a Domestic Servant..

March 31 1915

The war had been going strong for well over six months now, but after initial fighting which had involved the loss of Belgium but the saving of Paris, the war had now settled down.

An offensive or "push" was expected soon, but meantime life in Forfar continued almost as if nothing was happening with the Town Council tonight getting upset about the report from Mr Caw of the Scottish National Gallery.

Provost James Moffat

He had taken some of Forfar's pictures and portraits away last Thursday from the Town Hall to Edinburgh for examination and reported back that it would cost the Council about £80 to restore.

It was agreed that this should be done and in the meantime, Provost Moffat had bought at an auction a portrait of the famous Forfar fiddler of last century James Allan and was proposing to donate it to the Town Hall, if not to the Library or the Museum.

Bailie Hanick, in acknowledging this gift on behalf of the town, said that some of the "gentlemen" previously here, pointing to the empty places where the portraits had been, had now taken their departure.

"They have gone to the front, I believe" he said making a joke about the non-return of the portraits from Edinburgh.

Bailie Ritchie even questioned whether Mr Moffat's gift was the real James Allan, the famous Forfar fiddler, but Councillor Lamb pointed out that he had a fiddle in his hand, so it must be him! The war seemed a long way away from such mighty deliberations.

March 31 1901

The 1901 Census for Scotland was taken on the night of 31 March/1 April 1901. The following information was requested:

Place (parish and name of street, place, or road, and name or number of house); Name of each person that had spent the night in that household; Relation to head of family; Marital Status; Age; Sex; Profession or occupation; Whether an employer, worker, or on own account; Birthplace; Whether Gaelic or G & E; Whether blind, or deaf and dumb; Number of rooms in house with one or more windows.

John Fyfe Craik, Jute and Linen Manufacturer, was born in November 1848. He married Mary Jane Coupar, born in Sacramento, California, in 1875; she died in 1894.

He lived in Briar Cottage, Glamis Road, Forfar. His family - John, 31, was a Commercial clerk. Elizabeth, 20, and Catherine, 18, were not working, Stella (16), Claude (14) Beatrice (12) and Cecil (6) were all still at school. A step-son, George Craik (8) was also present. Their cook was Janet Cant, aged 23; Barbara Walker, 20, from Aberdeenshire, was their other servant.

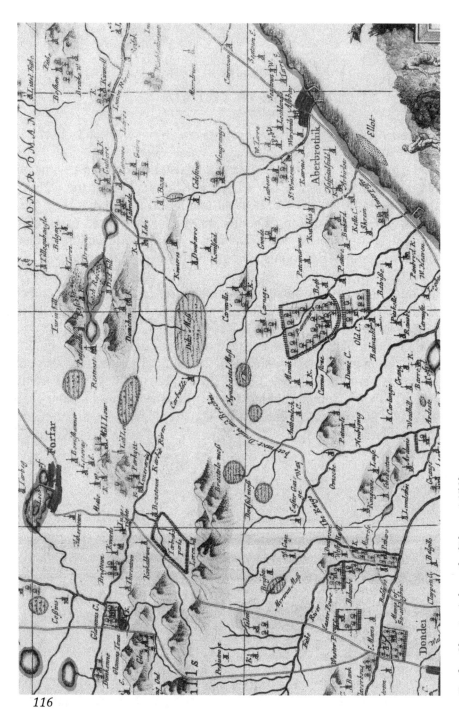

Forfar, Glamis, Arbroath, (Blaeu, 1653)

1890

In This Year
Traders in Forfar

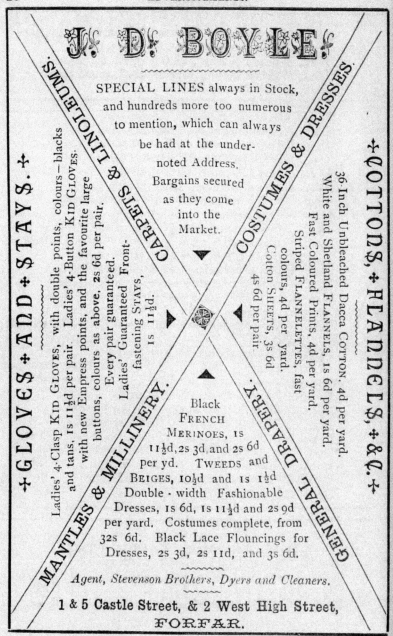
xviii

GEORGE DONALD,
SLATER,
18 NORTH STREET,
FORFAR.
All work done under personal supervision.

MILLINERY.

FLOOR CLOTHS.

THE
RECOGNISED HOUSE
FOR
ALL KINDS OF DRAPERY GOODS
IS
STEWART'S,
140 EAST HIGH STREET,
FORFAR.
Agent for the PERTH DYE WORKS.

WALL PAPER.

DRESSMAKING.

JAS. GLENDAY,
BOOT AND SHOEMAKER,

Begs to intimate that he has always in Stock a Large and Choice Selection of BOOTS, SHOES and SLIPPERS of the Best Manufacturers, and which he will sell at the LOWEST POSSIBLE PRICES.

MEN'S BOOTS from 7s 6d.

Try our MEN'S LORNE BOOTS, Clamps and Tackets, at 9s.

WOMEN'S from 4s to 10s 6d.

All sorts Boots and Shoes Made to Measure, at shortest notice.

Repairs carefully attended to.

77 EAST HIGH STREET, FORFAR. 77

M. M. DONALD,

TOBACCONIST,

8 CASTLE STREET,

Has always on hand a LARGE SELECTION of FANCY GOODS,

Habana, Indian, and Mexican

CIGARS AND CHOICE TOBACCOS.

ALSO,

EGYPTIAN ✳ AND ✳ AMERICAN ✳ CIGARETTES

OF THE BEST BRANDS.

D. P. THORNTON,

BOOT AND SHOEMAKER,

✦ 84 WEST HIGH STREET, ✦

HAS always on hand a First-Class Assortment of BOOTS and SHOES, from the Best Manufacturers in the Trade, at VERY MODERATE PRICES.

I would call special attention to my Stock of BOYS' and GIRLS' BOOTS which for Durability and Price cannot be surpassed.

BOOTS and **SHOES** of all kinds Made to Measure. REPAIRS of all kinds executed on the shortest notice.

NOTE THE ADDRESS

84 WEST HIGH STREET, FORFAR.

CYCLE STORE.

GEORGE H. DOUGLAS,

CYCLE AGENT,

53 WEST HIGH STREET, FORFAR.

Machines on Hire. Requisites kept. Inspection invited.

GENT.'S GARMENTS MADE TO MEASURE IN FIRST-CLASS STYLE AND FINISH.

WILLIAM DICK,

CLOTHIER AND HATTER,

INVITES Inspection of his Stock, purchased from the best Manufacturers, including all the Newest Styles; Fabrics and Colourings—Quality and Price unsurpassed.

Ulsterings, Overcoatings, and Worsted Coatings.
Scotch Saxony, Cheviot and Homespun Suitings.
West of England Cloths and Suitings.
Trouserings and Vestings.
Satin and Felt Hats.

Dress, Oxford, and Wool Shirts—all sizes.
Fronts, Collars, and Cuffs.
Lambswool and Merino Underclothing.
Scarfs, Gloves, Braces. and every Requisite for Gentlemen's Outfit.

20 WEST HIGH STREET, FORFAR.

WILLIAM SCOTT,

Joiner, Cabinetmaker, and Glazier,

109 CASTLE STREET, FORFAR.

FURNITURE made of Well-Seasoned Wood.
Modern in Design and Moderate in Price.

JOBBING CAREFULLY ATTENDED TO.

"HERALD"
GAS
ENGINE.

LARGEST
IN
DISTRICT.

FORFAR HERALD

PRINTING WORKS,

OSNABURG STREET, CROSS.

In these Premises, which were Built Specially for the purpose,

LETTERPRESS PRINTING

in all its Branches is carried on. A large and efficient Staff of Workmen is employed, and some of the most modern Machinery is used.

Orders receive every attention; and the work is turned out Neatly, Quickly, and at Moderate Charges.

GEORGE S. NICOLSON, PROPRIETOR.

READY-MADE CLOTHING,

Men's, Youths', and Boys',

IN GREAT VARIETY, GOOD QUALITY and CHEAP

ALSO,

SHIRTS, DRAWERS, TIES, SCARFS,
FRONTS and BRACES.

INSPECTION CORDIALLY INVITED.

WILLIAM A. GIBSON,

25 DUNDEE LOAN,

FORFAR.

JAS. W. ROBERTSON,

Painter, Paperhanger and Decorator.

52 CASTLE STREET, FORFAR.

Always on hand a Large Variety of Cheap Paperhangings
Best Quality.

ESTIMATES FURNISHED.

PICTURES FRAMED

GLASS CUT TO SIZE.

HOOD'S
BOOTS & SHOES.

ALL who really want Good Value should Try HOOD'S BOOTS, SHOES, and SLIPPERS. They are of First-Class Workmanship, and manufactured from the best materials. Universal Satisfaction Guaranteed to all.

REPAIRS.—Special attention is given to this Department — the best materials used, and the Lowest Prices Charged. BOOTS RE-GUSSETED.

CUSTOMER WORK.—As HOOD is a practical Tradesman in all the Branches of the Boot and Shoe Trade, and employs none but the best Workmen, he can with confidence recommend his own make—Pegged, Rivetted, and Sewed.

ADDRESS—
HOOD'S, 96 CASTLE ST., FORFAR.

xxxviii

xxxix

xl

xli

OSNABURGH BAR.

ALEX. ROBERTSON,
WINE AND SPIRIT MERCHANT,
OSNABURGH STREET, FORFAR.

Luncheons, Teas, &c., on the Shortest Notice, and at Moderate Charges.

A. R. having possession of OSNABURGH STREET HALL will be prepared to take engagements for Marriage Parties, Balls, Suppers, &c. ESTIMATES GIVEN.

—— :o: ——

PRICE LIST.

	Per Bot.
PORT WINE, ...	2s 6d to 3s 6d
SHERRY, ...	2s 6d to 3s 6d
Fine Matured BRANDY,	4s 6d to 5s
Fine Old Highland WHISKY, ...	2s 6d to 3s
ROBERTSON'S BLEND,	2s 6d to 3s

ROBERTSON'S do.,17s 6d to 18s 6d per Gal.
"The Bailie Nicol Jarvie" Blend of Old Scotch WHISKY, ...3s per Bot.
Do., do., 18s per Gal.
Old Jamaica RUM,3s to 3s 6d per Bot

BASS'S BITTER BEER,	...	...	2s 6d per Dozen.
EDINBURGH ALES,	...	...	2s 3d ,,
LONDON PORTER,	...	...	2s 6d ,,
TABLE BEER, ...	...	...	2s ,,

DUNCAN FLOCKHART AND CO'S ÆRATED WATERS.

Any Quantity Supplied to the Trade at Wholesale Prices. All in Splendid Condition.

Agent for D. NICOLL'S SUPERIOR LEMONADE—Manufactory, Fleuchar Craig, DUNDEE.

LARGE QUANTITIES AT WHOLESALE PRICES.

ALL ORDERS PUNCTUALLY ATTENDED TO.

OSNABURGH BAR.

TRY

☞ **PETRIE'S** ☜

FOR THE BEST AND CHEAPEST

HAND OR MACHINE-MADE BOOTS AND SHOES,

Our Whole Stock of BOOTS, SHOES, and SLIPPERS are only of the very best Material and Workmanship, at Prices (for same quality), that cannot be beat. Every pair guaranteed.

BRING YOUR REPAIRS.

PETRIE'S SHOE SHOP,

113 EAST HIGH STREET, FORFAR.

EVERY SUCCEEDING SEASON

✚ JARVIS BROTHERS ✚

SHOW a largely increased Selection of High-Class Drapery Goods—comprising the Latest Novelties in MILLINERY, DRESS, and MANTLE MATERIALS, Ladies' JACKETS and MANTLES, FANCY TRIMMINGS and FURS.

TAILORING, MILLINERY, DRESS, and MANTLEMAKING, under Efficient Superintendence at very Moderate Charges. Fit, Style, and Workmanship guaranteed.

Every requisite for Family Purposes at

JARVIS BROTHERS'

68, 70, & 72 CASTLE STREET,

FORFAR.

THE ROYAL HOTEL.

Hugh Greenhill, Proprietor.

The ROYAL HOTEL, Forfar, is furnished in the most approved style of modern Decoration and Appointments; and the accommodation provided is in every way in keeping with the requirements of a first-class modern Hotel.

☞ 'Bus Waits all Trains.

Dinners, Suppers, Pic-Nic Parties, etc., are carefully attended to.

POSTING IN ALL ITS BRANCHES.

Telegrams promptly attended to.

The Royal is well ventilated and fitted up on the most approved sanitary principles—Families and Gentlemen will find the Establishment replete with every Comfort.

Commercial, Coffee, Billiard and Stock Rooms, Baths, Lavatories, etc.

All the Finest ALES and STOUT kept on Draught and in Bottle.

The Finest Brands of CHAMPAGNE, SHERRY, PORT, WHISKY CLARET and all other Liquors always in Stock.

HORSE-HIRING AND LIVERY STABLES.

Good Service at Reasonable Rates.

The Largest Stud of Horses for Jobbing in Town.

Broughams, Landaus, 'Busses, Brakes, Waggonettes, Chapel Carts, Gigs and Phætons.

HEARSE AND MOURNING COACHES.

(Black Belgian Horses.)

ROYAL HOTEL, FORFAR.

SALUTATION HOTEL.

HOTEL.

Airy and Comfortable Beds.   Liquors of the Best.
Charges Moderate.

HIRING.

Horse-hiring carried on in all its Branches.   Orders
taken at County Stables or at Salutation Stables
will have prompt attention.   Good serviceable
Horses and Modern Machines.

COACHBUILDING.

The Proprietor of the Salutation would direct attention
to this New Department of his Business which he
has lately added, and where, under efficient charge,
every effort is made to furnish Coachwork at the
lowest Prices possible for Good Work.   Jobbing
Carefully attended to.

WORKS: ACADEMY STREET.

NOTE.—Parties at the West End of the Town can
leave their Orders at the County Stables where prompt
attention will be given.

WILLIAM PETRIE,

PROPRIETOR.

l

DAVID STURROCK,

TAILOR AND CLOTHIER,

✢ 63 CASTLE STREET, FORFAR. ✢

———o———

REASONABLE CHARGES.   GOOD WORK.   LATEST PATTERNS.

M'BETH & MILNE,

Plumbers, Gasfitters, Zinc-Workers, Coppersmiths, and

Bellhangers.

◆

ESTABLISHED 1868.

◆

All Orders carefully executed by experienced Workmen, and only material of the best description used.

◆

GREEN STREET, FORFAR.

PARTIES FURNISHING

SHOULD VISIT

HEBENTON'S

IRONMONGERY WAREHOUSE,

57 CASTLE STREET,

GREAT VARIETY AT LOW PRICES.

lv

April

April 1 1856

The Crimean War is over!

The Treaty of Paris was actually signed on March 30, but no-one actually thought to tell Forfar until today when a newspaper to this effect was placed in the news-room or the reading room, as it was sometimes called.

The news spread like wildfire, for there were quite a few Forfar families with soldiers still in the army. Several had gone and not been heard of since.

There was the vivid example of "Eck" who had gone to the Crimea and come back with only one leg with a rumour going around the town that a local joiner was going to make a wooden one for him!

The gentlemen of the town met at Morrison's Hotel to celebrate the event with Mr Lowson of Kirkton acting as toastmaster and Mr Roberts in the Chair.

For some reason the Provost was not there, but he was not as indispensable as he thought and the meeting proceeded with great merriment.

After a massive meal, toasts were drunk to the Queen, Prince Albert, the Emperor Napoleon of France and local heroes Lord Panmure and the Earl of Clarendon.

Songs were then sung, while all the time in the town, bonfires were being lit, squibs were crackling, crackers were flying about, houses were decorated with lanterns and a few fiddlers and pipers appeared to supply music for "the loons" to dance with "the lassies" on the streets.

It was a great night, but it was an anxious one as well, for there were quite a lot of families (about 20, perhaps) who had someone who had gone to the war, but had not been heard of for some time.

Ednie & Kininmonth

GENERAL FURNISHING, and BUILDERS' IRONMONGERS,

14 CASTLE STREET, FORFAR

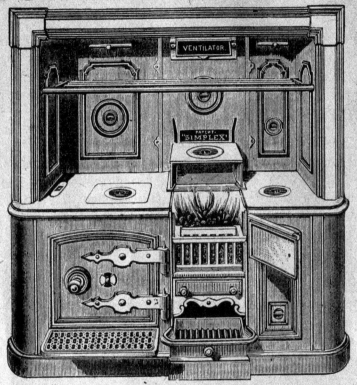

SPECIAL LINES.

DINING ROOM, DRAWING ROOM, AND BEDROOM GRATES, TILE HEARTHS, and FENDERS.

Large and Varied Stock of LAMPS,

Including Table, Floor, Suspension, Wall, Hand, and Reading Lamps.

Some specially pretty Designs in Floor Lamps.

Oil Heating and Cooking Stoves and Gas Heating and Cooking Stoves.

Extensive Range to select from.

Silver-Plated Goods.—A Unique and carefully selected Stock suitable for Marriage Gifts, &c.

Ednie and Kininmonth Advertisement, 1900

April 2 1911

The 1911 Census for Scotland was taken on the night of 2 April 1911

There were new questions relating to fertility of marriage: on duration of marriage; the number of living children born to each marriage; and the number alive at the time of the census.

There were changes to several others:

(1) categories for people with disabilities were revised and the introductory section to the third report on the 1911 census refers to the intended use of the terms as: (a) lunatic - in cases where the infirmity had been acquired during life, (b) imbecile - in extreme cases where the infirmity had existed from birth or an early age, and (c) feeble-minded - in milder cases where the infirmity had existed from birth or an early age.

(2) the question on occupation was extended to find out which industries or services a worker was connected to in addition to their personal profession or occupation

(3) the question on place of birth was extended to include nationality for those born in a foreign country, that is, outwith British territory, colonies and dependencies.

April 2 1871

The 1871 Census for Scotland was taken on the night of 2/3 April 1871. The following information was requested: Place (name of street, place, or road, and name or number of house); Name of each person that had spent the night in that household; Relation to head of family; Marital Status; Age; Sex; Profession or occupation; Birthplace; Whether blind, or deaf and dumb.

Reverend Alexander Cumming, Minister of the First Free Church, was born in October 1829 in Edinburgh, and lived at 23 St James Road, Forfar.

Sharing his house were Mary, his wife, born in Ceylon in 1838, his widowed mother-in-law Mary Boyd, now aged 74, born in the West Indies, three children (James, 7, George Hay, 3, and Alexander, 2)

Their servants were Isobella Paterson, 25, and Margaret Porter, 19, both from Aberdeenshire, where all the children had been born.

William Dowell, the choirmaster, had come to Forfar from Stirling. He married Isabella Tawse Mitchell in 1866, and lived at 17, East High Street, Forfar.

Their young family consisted of three children — Isabella, 3, William and Alexander. Isabella's mother-in-law was living with them.

They had one servant, Julia Fyfe, from Dunnichen.

As a Master Painter, William employed two men and two boys.

April 2 1982

Excitement was in the air today.

It was the end of the school term and the much longed for Easter Holidays were now here!

Not only that, but Forfar Athletic were (incredibly) playing in the Scottish Cup semi-final tomorrow against Rangers at Hampden Park, yet even that was not the main topic of conversation in comparison with the news that kept breaking throughout the day.

At first it was not believed in East High Street and Castle Street, but the BBC kept saying it. It appeared that Argentina had invaded the Falkland Islands in the South Atlantic, and that Britain would apparently be sending troops to get them back.

Even though many Forfar people could not have told you accurately where the Falkland Islands were, this sounded like war, and concern was immediately expressed for all the Forfar boys currently serving in the Army, Navy and Air Force.

The last time there had been any event like this had been Suez in 1956. Fortunately, that fizzled out pitifully, but there was now the possibility of Forfar blood being spilt in conflict for the first time since 1945!

Parliament was meeting at Westminster tomorrow afternoon at the same time as the football was on! That showed how serious it was! In the meantime this Friday night, we had the main BBC news interviewing the Prime Minister, the Cabinet and military experts.

The Scottish news featured interviews with Forfar's Chairman, Directors, Manager and even the groundsman Wull Watson. Tomorrow promised to be a very exciting day!

April 3 1911

All Forfar was amazed at the conjuror CH Charlton who appeared at the Pavilion this week.

The Pavilion had now been open for a year and had attracted quite large audiences of many occasions. It was central and comfortable and was sufficiently adaptable to show films as well as variety performances.

The Forfar Herald says that they had seen many fine magicians in their time but that CH Charlton "takes premier position with an extraordinary conjuring and mystifying performance".

He had performed four times before the late King Edward. His cards tricks were clever, and his flags and handkerchiefs were bewildering but what really intrigued the Forfar audience was with a kettle with which he supplied any kind of drink.

"Call your favourite beverage and the kettle does the rest". Mr Charlton invited the audience to name any drink, and for ten minutes he filled up glass after glass. Beer, whisky, stout, gin, port, milk etc. were supplied from the kettle without the slightest hesitation.

"The whole performance, as we have said, is mystifying and bewildering and really has to be seen to be believed".

One does indeed wonder how this was done, for clearly no-one in Forfar in 1911 had the slightest idea. There was also James Brady, the comedian, who did four successive numbers and was unfailingly humorous.

There was something "new" about him and that was very refreshing, and there was female representation in the comedienne Grace Dalton who also sang very sweetly.

April 3 1881

The 1881 Census for Scotland was taken on the night of 3/4 April 1881. The following information was requested: place, name, relationship to head of family, marital status, age, gender, profession, birthplace, and whether blind, deaf, and dumb.

Over 480 people with the surname Lowson were living in Forfar. Some of the households were:
  Alexander Lowson, Hotel Keeper, 95 North Street
  Andrew Lowson, Dresser in linen factory, at 3 Academy Street
  Ann Lowson, Hotel Keeper, 97 and 99 North Street
  George Lowson, Manufacturer, at Painters Croft
  James Lowson, Agricultural Labourer, at 18 Dundee Road
  James Lowson, Linen Manufacturer, Ferryton House, Hillside Road
  James Lowson, Railway Labourer, at 24 Market Place
  John Lowson, Linen Yarn Warper, at 47 North Street
  Peter Lowson, Factory Worker, at 15 Newmonthill Street
  William Lowson, Factory Worker Linen, at 27 Market place
  William Lowson, Manager of a Linen Factory, at 16 North Street
  William Lowson, Writer and Bank Agent, at 27 West High Street
  William Lowson, General labourer, at 87 North Street

April 4 1898

Enforcing school attendance on reluctant pupils has never been an easy job even up to the present day.

However since the Education Act (Scotland) of 1872 and its subsequent amendments and additions provided for compulsory education for all, attempts had to be made to enforce the law even though, in some cases, it was obvious that nobody was going to win.

In the case of single-parent families where the parent was out working, it was a particular problem. This morning at Forfar Sheriff Court, Sheriff Lee had two cases to deal with.

The first was James Low, a labourer, of Couttie's Wynd, charged with "failing to provide efficient education" for his 12-year-old son James who had registered only 100 attendances out of 190.

Sheriff Lee granted an "attendance order" which was seen (in 21st century football language) as the "yellow card", as it were, before the "red card" of prosecution.

More complicated was the case of John Lamb, engine driver, of 22 Market Place who had also failed to enforce his son's attendance at school.

There were special circumstances involved here — it was not specified what they were but one can hazard a guess that Mr Lamb was recently widowed — and on this occasion an attendance order was issued, and also that Mr Lamb should be immediately informed by the Headmaster whenever his son was absent.

It would be interesting to know what happened next, but it is difficult to believe that there was any great success. Truancy, hookey, plunking, jouping, ticking — all these many words for not going to school tend to indicate that it is a perennial problem.

April 5 1886

Mr WH Thomson. Registrar for the Parish of Forfar tonight presented his quarterly report.

Since the turn of the year, there had been 91 births (13 of which were illegitimate), 23 marriages and 45 deaths. These figures would tend to indicate that the population of Forfar was effectively doubling as twice as many babies were bring born as there were people dying off!

This was in fact true because the jute industry (in spite of its reputation of being an unhealthy, boring job) was indeed attracting more people in from the land simply because jobs were available.

The death rate was quite low, simply because there was no major outbreak of an epidemic nature in the town at the moment, although there was still a distressing amount of childhood mortality. It was the lowest death rate since the introduction of compulsory registration in 1855.

It is interesting that in spite of all the efforts of the Churches, there was a distinct failure to prevent the ongoing occurrence of illegitimate births. (The Churches were similarly unsuccessful in their attempts to curb alcoholic drink!)

Although illegitimacy was a stigma, it was by no means an uncommon phenomenon. What was a lot more of a "disgrace" in Victorian society was for a woman to remain unmarried, and oddly enough, the "condition of spinsterhood" was easier for the working classes than for the middle classes.

A working class woman could easily get a job in the factory; a middle class woman often had no obvious way of earning a living and had to stay with a brother or some other relative.

April 5 1891

The 1891 Census for Scotland was taken on the night of 5/6 April 1891. The following information was requested:

Place (parish and name of street, place, or road, and name or number of house); Name of each person that had spent the night in that household; Relation to head of family; Marital Status; Age; Sex; Profession or occupation; Whether an employer, employed, or working on own account; Birthplace; Whether speaks Gaelic or Gaelic and English; Whether deaf and dumb, blind, or lunatic, imbecile, or idiot; Number of rooms in house with one or more windows.

Peter Reid, the confectioner, was living with his wife Agnes at 54 East High Street. Their servant was Catherine Forsyth.

Lodge Kilwinning in the 1890s with Peter Reid sitting second from the left

April 6 1927

Normally such proceedings are conducted in circumstances of the strictest secrecy, but tonight a deputation from the Provincial Grand Lodge of Forfarshire under the leadership of Brother AC Anderson solicitor and one time Provost of Arbroath visited Forfar Lodge Lour at their place of meeting in the Osnaburgh Hall, thereafter visiting Lodge Forfar Kilwinning.

There was a large attendance of members, greetings were exchanged, and of course, there were many handshakes!

Brother Anderson then took the chair, expressed his pleasure at the way things were going in Forfar and in particular their wonderful temple in which they now met, and wished them all the best for the future and hoped that they would show themselves worthy of their craft and the noble cause of Freemasonry.

For Lodge Lour, Brother James Graham replied, and the rest of the evening was spent with a few drinks, song, entertainment and reminiscences. It is probably true to say that at that time there were nothing sinister in freemasonry in Forfar.

Other parts of the world, not least the west of Scotland, could look upon the freemasons as a secret society who went around with their trouser legs rolled up, did some bizarre things at initiation ceremonies and arranged "jobs for the boys" in order to kept Roman Catholics out, but in Forfar they were looked upon with benign tolerance.

It was all about friendship, and of course as everyone knows that there can never be a "secret" in Forfar for very long, there was no point is trying to maintain a façade of mysterious exclusivity!

Ian McPhee receiving Scottish League Second Division trophy in 1984

April 7 1984

George Orwell wrote a book called 1984, threatening everyone with dictatorships and a generally depressing existence.

He was clearly not thinking about Forfar who today won the Scottish League Second Division. This was pay-back day!

All the years of hurt and pain which we had spent standing on cold and wet terracings watching dreadful Forfar teams were suddenly wiped out!

They did this by beating Stranraer 5-3, even though Stranraer scored first with a fine strike described by the man standing beside me as "a some rekker, that een" — a phrase incomprehensible to someone who doesn't come from Forfar.

But this Forfar team were not winners of the Scottish League for nothing, and Jim Liddle scored twice and John Clark, Billy Gallacher and Ronnie Scott once each to release delirium for Doug Houston's men and their supporters.

Chairman Sam Smith, the man who had done so much to bring all this about, was in his element on the loud speaker, telling everyone in the 2,142 crowd to go to Jarman's and buy themselves a drink which he would pay for. (One assumes he was only kidding!)

It was also a time for sadness and reminiscing about the supporters no longer with us, but with us in spirit. One thought for example, of the famous Willie Wilson, inhabitant of the "Poors House" with his club foot, speech impediment and, frankly, not very much going for him.

He was the pioneer of the "That's hut!" phrase when something pleased him. I'm sure I heard a ghostly voice saying it that day as Ian McPhee lifted the trophy.

April 7 1861

The 1861 Census for Scotland was taken on the night of 7/8 April 1861. The following information was requested: Place (name of street, place, or road, and name or number of house); Name of each person that had spent the night in that household; Relation to head of family; Marital Status; Age; Sex; Profession or occupation; Birthplace; Whether blind, or deaf and dumb.

Over in Fife, Police Constable Ebenezer Donaldson was living with his wife Mary Galloway, from Auchermuchty but now living in Cove Wynd, Pittenweem.

Together with their children Mary Stark, born in 1857, and Jane, born in 1859, they were anticipating the birth of their third child, a boy called William Galloway, on 17 June.

The Donaldsons went on to add six more children — four sons and two daughters — to their family.

William Galloway Donaldson, by now Reverend, arrived in Forfar in 1908.

Ebenezer died in 1916 in Kirkcaldy. His career had taken him to be Governor of Cupar Prison and latterly Keeper of the Sheriff Court Buildings, Kirkcaldy. His estate of £1939.3.2 was divided among sons George, William, Ebenezer, and David.

April 8 1938

Forfar Station was a busy and animated place this Friday night with a party of Forfar people, mainly men but with a few women as well, awaiting the arrival of the train to the south.

It was not like departures to wars or emigrating overseas where the atmosphere was one of sadness mingled perhaps with pride.

No, this one was total happiness with references to "the kerry-oot" — a brown bag which made a clinking sound as one moved with it and frequent cries of "be careful" and "dinnae drap it".

There was even a piper — not a very good one, it would have to be said, but if you listened hard enough you could hear something like the "bonnie, bonnie banks of Loch Lomond".

"Ah hope we get a sit on the tren."

"Oh, we'll hae tae get a sit. We canna stand a' that wey"

"Twa nichts oot o wir beds! Ah'll sleep on Sunday nicht"

"Och aye, we'll speak aboot this a' the rest o wir days"

"This is my third time".

All these statements had made for weeks previously and the occasion had been much talked about in the factories, the pubs, the streets and even the school playgrounds.

It had been much looked forward to, and much saved up for, because although short time working and unemployment were now things of the past, it was still a very expensive trip.

"Here comes the tren! Ah hope thae Aiberdeen leds are weel behaved. Oh good, there are loads o' sits. We'll a' get thegither". On they climbed, excitement clearly in the air. It's arrived at last...

They were a happy bunch, and even happier when they returned on Sunday, for Scotland beat England 1-0 at Wembley.

April 9 1910

This was Geordie Langlands' day!

It was the Scottish Cup final at Ibrox Park between Dundee and Clyde. Geordie a Forfar man had indeed played for Forfar Athletic until 1908 when he joined Dundee.

In 1909 he would have won a Scottish League medal if Davie McLean had not inspired Celtic to win their famous 8 games in 12 days to pip them at the post, but today he was playing for Dundee in the Scottish Cup final.

Many of his friends decided to go that day to watch him in Glasgow, a Glasgow that was still buzzing with excitement after Scotland's great win over England last week at Hampden.

60,000 were there, including a large contingent from Dundee and not a few from the neighbouring towns of Angus, keen to see the Scottish Cup go north of the Tay for the first time ever.

It was not looking very good at all for Langlands or Dundee when Clyde were 2-0 up with less than ten minutes to go and quite a few Dundee fans had left to head home for an early train.

Some of the newspaper reporters had already filed their report saying Clyde 2 Dundee 0. When John "Sailor" Hunter scored a scrappy goal to pull one back, it did not seem to matter until the very last minute.

A corner kick came to the feet of Geordie Langlands who hammered the ball home to give Dundee a draw which they did not really deserve. Eventually, at the third attempt, they won the Scottish Cup, and Langlands became the first Forfarian to win a Scottish Cup medal.

He served in World War One, returned to Forfar Athletic to finish off his career and to set up his plumbing business in Queen Street. He died in 1951. Some man was "Purkie" Langlands!

Geordie Langlands, Forfar Athletic and
Dundee

April 10 1921

It had been a matter of some regret that Strathmore Cricket had been unable to fulfil any fixtures in 1920, but it had been felt that there were simply not enough cricketers in the town of sufficient quality to do the club justice.

In addition, there had been problems with the ground which had not been used for a long time. But today, a Sunday, a group of young men were seen at the Lochside having a look at the ground and what equipment they had, and they were generally of the opinion that there was no reason why cricket could not start in 1921 once the weather got better.

There had been a meeting on Friday night in the Royal Hotel when a Committee had been formed and Mr DH Gourlay of Glamis Road had been appointed Captain and Secretary.

His first task was obviously to arrange fixtures and he had already sent letters to Arbroath, Brechin and some of the Dundee teams. Forfarshire had managed to play at Forthill in 1920, and the First Class game in England had proceeded.

Indeed England had already lost the Ashes in Australia and both teams were sailing back on the same ship for another series in England. Some of the Strathmore players had been able to have the occasional game during the war for regimental teams, and there was no lack of enthusiasm.

Everyone was on a high in any case for in the football International yesterday, Scotland had beaten England 3-0. But of course, what was always needed for a game of cricket was good weather!

April 11 1892

Effectively, a union of the Forfar Libraries was brought about tonight.

The Forfar Free Library which was based in the Meffan Institute agreed to accept a "loan" or a "gift" of the Old Forfar Library which had been struggling for some time, but which still contained some old and valuable books.

At the moment, these books were sitting in a house in East High Street that used to belong to Peter Reid, but they were going to have to be removed from there.

The Forfar Free Library agreed to take these books for the price of £25 which would be enough to clear the debts of the Old Forfar Library and to liquidise the company.

They would also pay for the removal expenses for the considerable number of books. There was an element of politics in all this, because The Forfar Free Library did not really have enough room for all these 1,500 books, but this would be a lever on the Trustees of the Meffan Institute to give them extra premises.

Otherwise the Trustees would be responsible for the Free Library having to throw out such a large collection of old, antiquarian books and a collection of folios!

Forfar Free Library was very proud of the use of the word "free" in its title, and the reading habits of Forfar people were well known throughout Scotland. Now that the Education Act of 20 years ago guaranteed a high and increasing standard of adult literacy, the popularity of the Free Library would continue.

April 12 1864

A great attraction in the Town Hall today brought a large crowd to see a Fancy Bazaar in aid of Kinnettles United Free Church.

The doors were "thrown open" at 11.00 am today. Within a few minutes the Town Hall was crowded with everyone gasping in amazement at stalls and flags with pot plants of an exotic and unusual nature on sale, and they sold well. Various other items of food, flowers and artefacts were also available to be bought.

Upstairs, the Band of the Glamis Company of Rifles, under the leadership of Mr James Anderson, played at intervals throughout the day. At four o'clock the place was closed for a tea interval, by which time the astonishing amount of £100 had been drawn.

The Town Hall opened again at six, and this time there were even more people who appeared, including this time a great many from the outlying districts of Kirriemuir, Montrose and Coupar Angus, the railway now facilitating travel in a way that it had not done before.

Almost everything was sold, and it was a great day for Kinnettles. Much was the talk about a possible railway link to Kinnettles, but that did not seem to be likely to happen for some time.

People also discussed the war in America which now seemed to be veering in the direction of the Northern or the Union States, and quite a few questions were beginning to be asked about the British Prime Minister, Henry Temple or Lord Palmerston who was now not far short of his 80th birthday.

Three Factory Lums – the Tails, the Hauchie and the Mull

April 13 1931

As if there weren't enough industrial problems going in the world with the recession and the rise in global unemployment a dispute seems to have developed at St James's Works.

It seems that the employers, under the guise of efficiency and with the alleged intention of keeping the factory going as long as possible, have instituted a system of "monitoring" as they called it, (or "close espionage" as *The Forfar Dispatch* puts it) to make sure that none of the workers is cheating in the work that they claim to have done and the bonuses claimed.

While *The Forfar Dispatch* agrees that "slackers" do exist and need to be pulled up, in the context of the sometimes bitter days of the 1930s, this invasive supervision of the workers does remind people of the "means test", not to mention the sort of thing that goes on in Russia and will soon be apparent in Germany as well.

Not only that, but it is contrary to the Forfar tradition where weavers are an independent-minded bunch and resent any unwarranted interference. One women was apparently so upset at being spied upon that her productivity suffered and she was eight shillings down on her normal wage — something that clearly indicates that spying is counter-productive!

Whatever happened to resolve this particular dispute, no-one actually knows but it soon disappeared under the more general problem of the mass unemployment which was hitting the country. It was possibly to do with the over-zealous manner in which one particular overseer carried out his duties.

April 14 1896

The great days of the militancy of the Forfar Factory Workers' Union would appear to be over.

It was only a few years since the resistance to the great lock out of 1889 as spearheaded by Tommy Roy and Adam Farquharson, but now the Union seem to have lapsed back into apathy.

Tonight at their half-yearly meeting in Robertson's Hall, Osnaburgh Street, only a small number turned up. The meeting however was quorate and went ahead under the Chairmanship of Councillor Ritchie. The financial situation was very satisfactory with the grand total of £2,333.

A great deal of that had been paid out as funeral expenses for members and ex-members, and it was usually appreciated very much by recipients in very trying times and circumstances.

What was disturbing however was the threat by "the masters" to make some workers redundant with threats having been posted that workers were liable to be "turned off " at any minute, depending on economic circumstances.

Councillor Ritchie deplored these events and said, to loud applause, that one would get further through courtesy than through fighting and he therefore deplored the tactics of the factory owners. It was important however to stay together.

The meeting was very harmonious tonight with various other things discussed like future social events of dances and trips to Glen Clova.

Someone mentioned that the famous radical politician Sir Charles Dilke, along with Lady Dilke, was likely to visit Forfar in September during the Trades' Union Congress, and that it might be an idea to invite him to address the Union. This was duly agreed to.

April 15 1940

The Fyfe Jamieson Maternity Hospital has now been in existence for little over a year, and came in for a great deal of praise at the County Public Health Committee with Provost Mitchell clearly very proud of his new local asset.

It had good modern equipment and a high level of quality staff which supplied a long felt need in the County. It was also quite amusing to think that people who lived in Brechin and Arbroath, for example, and expressed uncomplimentary feelings about Forfar at football and cricket matches, nevertheless, had their sons and daughters born in Forfar!

But the downside in these pre-NHS days was the cost. It was reluctantly decided to increase the cost from 6 guineas per week to 8 guineas for private wards, and to £3 per week for women of limited means on "insurance" in general wards.

The Committee had to allow for the fact that some families would not be able to pay anything, and these had to be budgeted for as well.

Dr Sinclair, the County Medical Officer of Health, reported that in the past year, 271 babies had been born, 201 of them in the general wards. Eleven had to be brought back for treatment for "failure to thrive".

The average number of patients at any given time was 12, and the average length of stay was 16 days. To modern women who often leave the maternity hospital a couple of hours after giving birth, this must come as something of a surprise. Equally surprising is the cost. £3 per week was a lot of money in 1940!

April 16 1746

Today of course was the Battle of Culloden and the final defeat of Bonnie Prince Charlie.

It marked the beginning of troubled times for Forfar, particularly those Forfarians who had sided with the Chevalier. Lord Ogilvy's Regiment called the Forfarshires had fought in the Jacobite Army and were 800 strong. The battle was of course a total rout, but it was what happened afterwards in the pogrom of The Duke of Cumberland that was even worse and Forfar was not spared.

The Episcopalians were the main object of the persecution. Forfar did not at that time have an Episcopalian Church or place of worship, but they had a secret Meeting House (in East High Street) and a Clergyman called William Seaton.

Had Forfar had a formal Church of Episcopalian worship, it would have been burned down, as happened in many other towns at the hands of the victorious and unforgiving Hanoverians. They were backed up by the Presbyterians, who were similarly not renowned for their magnanimity or religious tolerance.

All Episcopalian clergy were asked to sign a statement renouncing the Stuarts and swearing an oath of allegiance to King George II. They refused of course, and until more tolerant times returned, the Episcopalians were always on the run, having to worship in the open sometimes.

The lack of any definite evidence of what went on in the Church in those days is perhaps an indication that these were indeed bloody times, but not only did the Episcopalian Church survive, so too, in a funny sort of way, did the Jacobite Rebellion flourish in the romantic fiction of it all, and it did bequeath us a whole collection of lovely Jacobite songs and music. Fifty years later Robert Burns, himself the grandson of a Jacobite, collected all these songs and of course wrote some himself.

East High Street in 1932

April 17 1929

Dr J Ewen Cable, Medical Officer of Health for the Burgh, today pulls no punches in his Annual Report on the town's health in which he states that so many houses in the town are sub-standard.

He states that there is urgent need for at least one hundred "working class houses of the two-room type" to replace houses which should be closed and demolished. Sadly, of course, they cannot be "closed and demolished" until such time as new houses can be built.

In the meantime pressure must be put on landlords to make sure that the houses were wind and water tight, no easy task given the general age and state of repair of these houses. One hesitated to use pejorative words like "slums" and there was little real overcrowding. Nevertheless, urgent action was required.

There were of course some better houses being built by the Town Council and they would be very welcome, with inside toilets and running water. The problem was private landlords who were not, frankly, always as interested in the welfare of their tenants as they ought to be or as they claimed to be when standing for the Town Council!

On the other hand, there were two respects in which Forfar did rather well — one was the water supply which was sufficient in quality and quantity for the town's needs, and the other was the collection and disposal of rubbish which was done in a way that was entirely satisfactory.

The only problem was the housing, and a walk round the town would immediately indicate that Dr Cable had a point.

April 18 1936

This was the greatest night in the history of the Forfar Dramatic Society when it won first place in the Scottish Community Drama Association's One Act Festival at the Lyric Theatre, Glasgow.

The play that they performed was "The Dreamer" by the author from Cardenden, Joe Corrie who was at the performance on Saturday night and was one of the first to congratulate the Forfar team on their magnificent rendition of his work.

The play centres on a young girl who is so depressed about unemployment that she starts to read "socialist books" and eventually gives up her relationship with her intended. It is hard, raw, 1930s stuff but the lead was played by Agnes Smith, a lady who was still going strong on the Forfar stage 40 years later. It was her acting that won the day, but she was well supported by Harold Adamson, Mary Patullo, Ina McDonald, Bella Wilson and David Milne.

The play was produced by Catherin Hollingworth and she was given the greatest compliment of them all when the adjudicator, Mr Richard Southern of London, said that it did not even look as though there had been a Producer, because the play came together as if of its own accord.

There had been a total entry of 400 teams when the competition started in February, and this was the first time that a team from Angus or Dundee had ever won the Festival. There were eleven teams in the finals on the Thursday, Friday and Saturday; Forfar had been the very last of the eleven to perform on the Saturday night.

April 19 1910

Tonight the "Electric Pavilion" was opened to the public on the site of the old Canmore Bowling Green.

There had been a special performance for the Town Council and a few invited guests the night before, but tonight it was opened to the public with the prices 9d, 6d and 3d and children 2d.

Last night had included a few variety acts of live performances, but tonight was the first night where the entertainment was entirely "bioscope films".

The Pavilion was built by Messrs Fyfe and Fyfe who were already well known for providing high class entertainment in the West of Scotland. They announced that there would be a complete change of programme every Monday and Thursday. Although the main entertainment would be films, there would nevertheless sometimes be other forms of entertainment, such as the Forfar Instrumental Band under John Lamb, or the bagpipes of John Smith, or local artistes like Billy Oswald and Madge Locke.

There was accommodation for over 700 people and next week's films already looked promising with "Nero", the Roman Emperor who burned his city down, and "Laddie", a story of a mother's love for her son.

It was not the only Forfar picture house for there was "Shandies" (Shand's Picture Palace) in Roberts Street, and the Reid Hall could also show films, but this new picture house promised to be the best of them all.

Indeed, it would still be showing films all of 60 years later, and it became to be known as "The Gaffie" the centre of local entertainment and much visited by people from all over the county.

April 20 1836

Today saw the induction of Rev James Y Strachan and the opening of the new Church which came to be known at St James's Church.

It is fair to date the Church from this date, but it had followed a prolonged period of negotiations well and laboriously detailed for us in *St James's Forfar, the Story of a Congregation* by Rev John F Kirk, one of the later incumbents.

The origins lay in "the Chapel" (hence Chapel Street) built originally by Episcopalians for a place to worship following their persecutions after the Jacobite Rebellions. It had been taken over by the Established Church and used as an "overflow" from the "Big Kirk" when that Church, although itself only recently built in 1790 for 2,000 people, was struggling to contain that amount of people, and had to find some place for their surplus.

A new Church would eventually emerge for this purpose — St James's Church. Ecclesiastical History is traditionally a very complicated subject and this is true in Forfar as much as anywhere else, but St James's Church remained a strong bulwark of Christianity for the next 150 years.

In 1836, slavery had only recently been abolished by the Whigs (the slave *trade* had been abolished some 30 years previously); the Government had only recently decided that education was something spending money upon.

Parliament had only recently been reformed, King William IV was quite rightly referred to as "silly Billy" and the monarchy was not held in high esteem — but what was this that dominated so much of Forfar conversation? A railway! A steam engine without horses! Running on metal rails? All the way to Arbroath? No, it could never happen!

April 21 1955

There was a large turnout today at Newmonthill Cemetery for the funeral of John Killacky, one time Councillor and Bailie of this town and also Scottish Champion Cyclist on many occasions in various events, particularly in 1894 and 1897.

In 1894 he had been the Champion at both the Five Mile race and the 50 Miles event and in 1897 he had won the sprint at Celtic Park on a bicycle that he had made for himself.

He had been born in Dundee but had moved to Forfar at an early stage of his life. He was 84 and had been in poor health for some time and had died in King's Cross Hospital a few days ago. His wife had predeceased him.

He had two sons, one a well-known golfer. He had been "mine host" at the Queen's Hotel for many years, and was a popular and well-loved Forfar character, being known as "Kalac" and "Killacky o' the trackie".

Not only had he been a cyclist himself, he also built and designed bicycles, and was accredited with having been the first person to own a motorised cycle in Forfar — a tricycle.

He had played at other sports as well, notably golf and athletics, and had been President of the Forfar Instrumental Band and the Forfar Factory Workers' Union.

He was also a well-known lover of Forfar Athletic. Among his other hobbies were the collecting of clocks and coins. A kindly man with the ability to be sociable to everyone, he was the perfect man to run a hotel, and he did the job with conspicuous success.

Harry Lauder and Jean Hanick

April 22 1936

The Reid Hall tonight had one of its biggest ever occasions when Sir Harry Lauder appeared before a full house.

This was to fulfil his promise to his friend, the late Provost Tom Hanick. Sir Harry had promised to come and sing for him in aid of funds for the Old Folks Jaunt which the late Provost had organised but was now in the hands of his sister.

Sir Harry brought with him some supporting artistes from Dundee, but it was Lauder himself that the Forfar crowd had come to see for his fine singing and couthy Scottish humour.

He had last been in the Reid Hall well over thirty years ago, and quite a few remembered him. He sang all his old favourites like "She Is My Daisy", "The Saftest O The Familie", "Roamin In the Gloamin" and "When I was Twenty One", and before finishing up with "Keep Right On To The End Of The Road", he paid tribute to the late Tom Hanick: "I never met a more hospitable and willing fellow in my life".

The other artistes also performed well with Mr AH Petrie singing the John McCormack favourite "I Hear You Calling Me". Every single ticket was sold, the receipts were £147 10 shillings, and another £6 was raised through the auctioning of a water colour gifted by a Dundee art dealer.

The evening finished with "Auld Lang Syne" and "God Save the King" and it was an evening that would be remembered for a very long time by those who were there.

April 23 1991

Today saw Forfar host an International Cricket Match for the first time when Scotland played Lancashire in the 55 Over competition.

The decision to award this game to the Lochside Park ground was a tremendous compliment paid to the Strathmore Club for all their hard work to bring the ground up to International standard, and the decision was rewarded with good weather and a reasonably sized crowd, considering that it was a Tuesday at the start of the season.

It was certainly the opinion of some of the Lancashire players and the Umpires that they had seldom seen such a beautiful ground, and it was a shame that they did not come in mid-season when the trees would have been in bloom.

It was clear that the Scotland team lacked match practice whereas the Lancashire squad had been training together for weeks. Lancashire won the toss and put Scotland in to bat.

With the very first ball Philip de Freitas, a Test match player, had Ian Philip of Stenhousemuir lbw, and when Arbroath's George Salmond was dismissed for 6, Scotland were 9 for 3. Reifer and Russell then put up some resistance, but Scotland struggled to 163 for 8 on their 55 Overs.

That was never likely to be enough, and although Dave Cowan of Freuchie took two wickets and Jim Govan of Dunfermline one, good knocks by Gehan Mendis and Graeme Fowler saw Lancashire home with a degree of ease.

It was however a great opportunity for Forfar people to see Test Match players, and the day was voted a success. There would be more Scotland Internationals in Forfar in the next few years.

April 24 1933

Forfar today lost one of its best people today in David Mackie, teacher of English at Forfar Academy at the age of 65.

He had been in indifferent health since he had been compelled to retire through illness in 1927. A native of Cupar, his lasting contribution to Forfar was his book *Forfar and District In The War*, but he had enjoyed a great teaching career at the West School, Headmaster at the Lower Academy, and then at Wellbraehead School before becoming head of English at Forfar Academy.

It was a job in which he revelled, as he was one of the lucky people in the world whose job was also his hobby. Another of his hobbies was writing for *The Forfar Dispatch,* for which he was from time to time "The Drummer", combining interest in the people of Forfar and penetrative analysis of social problems with a fine sense of humour.

Particularly in the War when *The Forfar Dispatch* was short staffed, David Mackie would offer his services for free, writing odd paragraphs and taking copy and advertisements.

He had also been Chairman of the Library Committee and Curator of the Museum — and all that after a hard day's teaching.

He had a sound knowledge of Classics, the Bible and of course his own subject of English literature. It had been his intention in his retirement to write a comprehensive history of the Burgh, but he was thwarted in his ambition by poor health. His book on the war is a masterpiece and much consulted to this day. His funeral was attended by a large crowd of former colleagues and former pupils.

April 25 1885

Forfar Athletic fans have occasionally been criticised for bad behaviour.

Moronic criticism of the players, referees and opposition would seem to have a long pedigree. Here as early as 1885, the very first season of the team's existence at the then somewhat primitive Station Park, we have a man called "A Spectator" writing in *The Forfar Herald* to complain that three pence is far too much to pay to watch football when his enjoyment is spoiled by his fellow fans.

He starts off by saying that football has developed into the most popular sport in the town, and it is a great game when properly conducted. But today we had Dundee Harp, one of the many Irish teams in Scotland at the moment.

They wore green jerseys, something that led a few of Forfar's more intellectually challenged individuals to shout a few inanities about "Boilin Water" (believed to have something to do with the Battle of the Boyne two centuries ago!).

Both "young Forfar" and "old Forfar" indulged in the pastime of ridiculing the Dundonians' appearance and even the colour of their hair.

"Offensive epithets" were hurled, and the abuse was not confined only to a "few ignorant persons" but "the general round of the large concourse of spectators".

"A Spectator" concludes that what made it worse was that "the fair sex were invited" (and even admitted free of charge) and he hopes that in future "they may not have their ears contaminated and their finer feelings shocked by improper language".

(In the 21st century, we don't get such behaviour at Station Park, do we? Certainly not! Good heavens, no!)

April 26 1956

The Queen Mother today received the Freedom of The Burgh of Forfar.

It was a day much looked forward to, but there was a touch of anti-climax about it as well. She arrived at the Cross and was introduced to the Provost Andrew Smyth (whom the Pathe News called "Smith"!) before the actual Ceremony in the recently refurbished Reid Hall.

She then crossed the road to the Strathmore Woollen Mill (commonly known as "the Tweed") to see tartan being woven. She was then taken to see Forfar's 1,000th council house in Gallowshade before being taken for a drive round the Reid Park to see all the school children.

It was April, but we are all aware that April can be a cold month, and today was a collector's item. To keep children (2,500 of us) awaiting for over an hour to see a car driving past with a woman inside it waving (one of those rolling waves for which she was famous) was not the greatest idea in the world and it was no great surprise that behaviour became a little fractious.

It was when they started to say that she was a "Forfar lass" and "one of us" that even eight-year-olds began to wonder!

Nevertheless she was a woman held in high esteem locally, and because in 1956, expressing disloyalty to the Royal Family was more or less treason, I held my tongue. I did wonder however why some people lived in palaces and castles, while there were still houses in Forfar which did not have an indoor toilet! But then again, I was always considered to be a dangerous socialist and radical!

JD Henderson, Strathmore and Forfarshire

April 27 1946

More and more signs are apparent that Forfar is returning to normal after the Second World War. Most of the soldiers, seamen and airmen are now home, although some who have been in the Far East theatre of war are taking longer to get home.

This is particularly true of those who have been prisoners of war because their rehabilitation is taking a long time. But jobs are now plentiful and today Strathmore Cricket Club played their first game of the post war era.

There had been some cricket at Lochside during the war particularly towards the end of the hostilities, but today Strathie travelled to Duffus Park, Cupar to play their first game. Rationing was still in force which caused problems with cricket clothes and equipment, and the tea at Cupar was not as rich as it was pre-war, although the Cupar ladies had done their best.

A bus was hired (although petrol was scarce) leaving Littlecauseway at 12.45 pm and the team was JF Farquharson, DH Chapman, JD Henderson, J Samson, J Forbes, E Balfour, D Donald, JD Howie, G Martin, R Towns and D Balfour.

Cupar batted first on a very chilly day (That hadn't changed since before the war! The weather is always cold at the start of the season!) and toiled for over two hours to reach 91 for 9, being well pegged down by the bowling of Henderson and Towns.

Strathie reached the total for the loss of 5 wickets with Davie Chapman and Ernie Balfour hitting 30s. It was a "meritorious" start to the season, according to The Forfar Dispatch, and one of the advantages of taking a bus is that the players can have a drink and a chat with their Cupar counterparts afterwards!

Forfar and District in the War, compiled by David
Mackie and published in 1921

April 28 1921

The new book *Forfar And District In The War* is now in the hands of the printer, and today *The Forfar Dispatch* carries an advertisement asking people to book their advance copy of the book.

> "The book will be of limited circulation and is a very large book, so it would be appreciated if people could give an indication of whether or not they would like a copy of the book".

It will cost five shillings, and was written and compiled by David M Mackie, Teacher of English at Forfar Academy. He has been working on this book for more than two years and feels that it is an important contribution to the recent cataclysmic events which have affected the town so much.

Great pains have been taken not to omit anyone who served, but nevertheless, inevitably some names may have slipped through the net. There is a Roll of Honour of those who failed to return. The Roll of Service of those who took part from the Burgh of Forfar and the Parishes of Kinnettles, Oathlaw, Rescobie, Tannadice and Inverarity is complete with rank, regiment, theatre of service and other things.

The book is covered in Forfar linen boards. The front picture is that of a Black Watch man gazing wistfully at his local town.

In addition, there were a few very interesting articles by Forfar man Professor George Duncan, for example, who was chaplain to Field Marshall Sir Douglas Haig, and a few accounts written by Forfar people of life in Mesopotamia, Salonica, Palestine and an account of the surrender of the German fleet.

There are also a few indications of what the home front was like during the conflict, as well as a tribute to the fallen.

April 29 1901

The South United Free Church decided tonight at their Congregational meeting to extend their premises by building a new hall.

For a long time, their Session House at the back of their Church in Little Causeway had been inadequate for their purposes and was clearly impeding the work of the Congregation, since it limited their ability to hold meetings for their various organisations and fund raising activities.

Sometimes they had had to move elsewhere at somewhat ruinous cost. Now under their young, enthusiastic and active Minister, Reverend Dr Grieve, plans were afoot to consolidate and to increase their premises.

There was a considerable amount of ground behind and at the side of their existing Session House for their premises to be extended. Plans had already been drawn up by Mr Bain the joiner, and it was estimated that the cost would be £300.

This was, of course a lot of money in 1901, but the Church had a very active Ladies Missionary Work Society and a considerable amount of the money had already been raised.

There was still a little more to be raised, however, but Reverend Dr Grieve and the president of the Congregation, Mr Andrew Whitson, were confident that the Congregation would find "other ways to make voluntary contributions".

It was intended that the money could be paid before the work started — something that sat well with the Christian ethics of 1901, and *The Forfar Herald* is suitably impressed by their enterprise and commitment.

There were two other United Free Churches in town — the East and the West, and one suspects there was an element of competition and one-upmanship here!

April 30 1818

In the aftermath of the wars against Bonaparte, the country is seized with a fever of canal building, the idea being to find a way of transporting goods quickly.

The North of England in particular is seeing a great deal of canals being built. There had been some discussion of the possibility of building a canal between Forfar and Arbroath for some time, as Forfar manufacturers felt that it would supply a method of transporting raw materials from Arbroath to Forfar, and linen and other goods from Forfar to the port of Arbroath.

It had been an idea of George Dempster of Dunnichen for some time. The idea would be that the canal would start at the sea at Arbroath Harbour, and end up at the Forfar Loch. There were a couple of possible plans and they were submitted today to a Joint Committee of Arbroath and Forfar Town Councils.

There were various technical problems concerning the depth of the water at various points, but the major problem seemed to be that a canal would not really be viable in that it would not attract enough "trade" to justify the enormous expense that the sinking of a canal would take.

A possibility might be to extend the canal westwards to go as far as Coupar Angus, but that would cause further problems.

Today's meeting resolved nothing, and the issue would continue for a few years yet before finally being shelved when news reached Forfar and Arbroath in the 1820s about a horseless locomotive powered by steam which could travel speedily along a couple of rails. This would be known as a railway.

James Mackintosh,

General Blacksmith & Engineer,

CANMORE IRON WORKS, QUEEN ST., FORFAR.

Lawn Mowers Repaired and Sharpened.

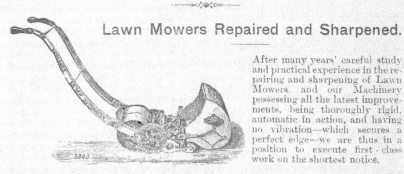

After many years' careful study and practical experience in the repairing and sharpening of Lawn Mowers. and our Machinery possessing all the latest improvements, being thoroughly rigid, automatic in action, and having no vibration—which secures a perfect edge—we are thus in a position to execute first - class work on the shortest notice.

HORSESHOEING.

This Branch of the Business is conducted on scientific principles. Every description of shoeing done with the greatest care by first-class workmen.

MATCH PLOUGH. This Plough has proved that it stands second to none. It has all the latest improvements, and is constructed so that the packing is complete, light of draught, and very easily manipulated by the operator in every way. Farm Implements of every description made or Repairs done.

KILN BEDDING supplied and fitted on. Reapers and Binders repaired and sharpened. Skates repaired and hollow-ground. Mangles, Wringers, Grates, and Ranges repaired. Gates and Railings. Engine and Mechanical Jobbing of every kind.

J. M. conducts his business by close personal attention, and at prices strictly moderate for first-class work. ESTIMATES GIVEN.

May

May 1 1887

There is a rather bizarre mention in *The Forfar Herald* at the end of this week of a few noisy women appearing with some sort of a flag in Horsewater Wynd.

Today is a Sunday and this is significant for *The Forfar Herald's* somewhat opinionated leader writer who uses the *nom-de-plume* of Luke Lively had been having quite a campaign about noisy behaviour on the Sabbath.

Running, shouting, foul language, drinking and other things are going on from those who apparently objected to the tyranny of the Churches and their excessively vehement stance on what a Sunday should be like.

But today is also May Day, and even as early as 1887, May Day was looked upon as some sort of special day for the Victorian equivalents of socialism and feminism.

So was it a political point, or was it simply something rather rude along the lines of "Be quiet, Luke Lively!"?

We are not likely to find out, but we can read what *The Herald* says.

"The most violent noise in the West on Sunday proceeded from a number of young women with a flag at the foot of Horsewater Wynd. I hope these same young women and the male hybrids [sic] who accompanied them did not go there in consequence of anything I have said."

"Curiouser and curiouser" as the current best seller Alice in Wonderland might have said, although it is hard to believe that using words like "hybrids" were ever likely to endear Luke Lively to anyone's cause.

It is one of these things that we wish we knew more about.

May 2 1916

For the second time in a month, the Forfar population was terrified by the appearance of Zeppelins.

Exactly a month ago, there had been a few of these "Hunnish airships" spotted, but nothing had happened, even though the Church bells, normally silenced during war time, had rung out to warn the population.

Tonight again had been heard the monotonous droning noise of those airships which had already caused some destruction in England. Fortunately perhaps tonight was a dull, cloudy and misty night which meant that in the same way as Forfar could not see the Zeppelins, the Zeppelins could not see Forfar.

Yet panic was in evidence, and children, who all thought this was great fun, were hidden in cupboards by edgy mothers who had been influenced by all sorts of rubbish that the Germans were in league with men from Mars!

Very few people in Forfar would ever have seen an aeroplane before and attack from above was a terrifying thought. But the sound of the Zepps lessened and disappeared to the north, to the relief of the town.

No-one ever found out what this was all about — possibly just a reconnaissance mission, it was believed — but it was enough for The Drummer in *The Forfar Dispatch* to deliver a stern warning to all its readers about being careful to make sure that lights were not visible from above and to follow all the blackout instructions.

A platform had now been erected on top of the Peel Monument in the cemetery to allow soldiers to keep an eye open for Zeppelins.

May 3 1928

The town of Forfar was somewhat distressed this morning to realise that the county in which they lived was no longer to be called Forfarshire, but Angus.

The name "Angus" was of course a very ancient one which can be traced back to Aonghais and other medieval worthies, and there was even a connection with the Trojan Aeneas who played such a distinguished part in the founding of Rome, according to Vergil's Aeneid.

But it was a decision taken by the County Council, ironically enough at yesterday's meeting in the County Buildings, Forfar and it was seen as a victory for Arbroath who had long since resented the name "Forfarshire" when Arbroath was now a lot bigger than Forfar.

They had clearly "chappit on a few doors" in Brechin, Montrose and Kirriemuir, and they had now won their point, with Colonel Fotheringham in the Chair absolutely triumphant.

Forfar Parish Council had objected on the grounds that it was "unnecessary, wasteful and contrary to the wishes of the public" and in any case, the Council was acting "ultra vires".

Bailie Peffers and Bailie Malcolm had spearheaded the objection, but the objection had been over-ruled, and the change would go ahead.

It would be a long time however before people stopped talking about "Forfarshire" — certainly in sporting circles — for there were the Forfarshire Cups in both Senior and Junior football. Of course there was Forfarshire Cricket Club, based at Forthill, Broughty Ferry and extremely unlikely to want to change their traditional and honourable name to "Angus CC" or even "Dundee CC".

May 4 1933

Tonight at the Reid Hall took place the Finals of the Burns Competition organised by the Forfar Burns Club under the Chairmanship of Mr JN Strachan, and Mrs Strachan presented the prizes.

The local Press are impressed by two things — one was the very high standard in both speaking and singing from the youngsters, and the other was the complete lack of jealousy among the competitors who cheered and clapped the efforts of each other and seemed genuinely delighted with each other's success.

There was also a little regret that some of these songs and poems weren't heard as often as they should be because the Burns culture had waned a little in recent years. Such commemoration of Burns as there was tended to happen entirely at Burns Suppers at institutions like Golf Clubs where there was rather too much emphasis on alcohol!

There were nine sections — Boys aged 10-12, Boys aged 12–15, Girls aged 10–12, Girls aged 12–15 in both Speaking and Singing, and a section for Violin Playing.

The Violin Playing was won by Sidney Chalmers; the other winners were Jean McDougall, Gordon Simpson, Sheena Allardice, William Thom, Marjory Stewart, George Birse, Davina Galloway and Frank Massie.

There were a large number of proud parents in Forfar tonight, and a great deal more happy people who had enjoyed a real night of Burns Entertainment.

The judges were from Dundee and Coupar Angus, while Jean Hill of Forfar acted as the accompanist for the Singers.

Cattle Market

May 5 1903

The profession of "cattle droving" does not come out very well in the proceedings of the Forfar Sheriff Court today.

On trial was Isaac Brown of Pyot's Close, East High Street charged with assault of William Liddle, Auction Mart keeper, North Street by hitting him on the left eyebrow with a stick.

The accused denied the charge. The incident occurred when Liddle and James Mollison were sitting in the drovers' bothy at Forfar Station awaiting the arrival of a cattle train from Aberdeen. Brown and another drover called Malcolm entered the bothy and were immediately ordered to leave by the yardsman.

Why they were" invited to depart" is not immediately apparent but they refused to go; a dispute arose about a key to the bothy which had, apparently, been lost presumably while in the possession of Brown.

Foul language "unbecoming to cattle drovers" (laughter in court) was then used by Brown. In the dispute Liddle claimed to have been hit by Brown's stick, but this was denied.

James Mollison then appeared as a witness but his face was "woefully covered with blood" and he was unable to testify because he was clearly intoxicated, having presumably fallen on his way to court!

He was then ordered to stand down, but to remain in court. The trial then proceeded and Brown was found guilty, fined £2 or an alternative of 21 days in prison.

Mollison was then brought back, told that he was being held in contempt of court for appearing "in a state of drunkenness and incapacity" and ordered to reappear on Thursday for sentencing.

May 6 1926

The General Strike seems to be passing Forfar by!

The factories are still working, schools are still functioning, shops are still open and both local newspapers *The Forfar Dispatch* and *The Forfar Herald* managed to produce a paper in spite of some men being on strike.

Some other Forfar men on the railway and road transport are on strike, often against their better judgement, but some trains are still managing to run and some lorries are seen on the streets as well. The Bus Services to Dundee have stopped however.

It is probably true that opinion is split 50/50 about the cause of the miners. There is sympathy for them in that they have a difficult, dangerous job hewing the coal that we all need and their employers are far from sympathetic to them, but is this the best way of addressing the problem?

A tough looking bunch of miners from Fife had been seen at Forfar Station on picket duty, but one of the local factories was able to pick up its raw materials by the device of sending a man with a speech impediment (a result of a war wound) with a horse and cart. He was also the most foul tempered, foul mouthed man you could imagine.

When asked by the pickets where he was going, the man said something that they did not understand, but they took it to mean food for the rather emaciated looking horse, and allowed him free passage!

On the way out, to forestall any search of what was under the tarpaulin, the foul mouthed man suddenly turned sociable and started talking about football. They still couldn't understand a word of what he said, and were quite happy to wave him through!

May 7 1921

This was a football match at Station Park with a difference.

The football season was now over, as far as the seniors were concerned, but this was a Cup Final, the first ever Ballingall Cup for Primary Schools.

It was a 2-1 victory for the West (the Van Goolers, as they were called for reasons that are lost in the mists of Forfar antiquity) over the North. The game was well attended by doting parents and friends with more ladies than normal at a football match.

It was a fine spring day with a touch of a breeze now and again. As well as the football there was also a supporting programme of dancing from the pupils of David "Dancie" Kydd who did the Highland Fling and the Cake Walk, and a Gymnastic and Club Swinging Display by girls from Forfar Academy under the guidance of Captain Avery followed by a cycle race.

The Forfar Instrumental Band under Conductor ex-Bailie Lamb was also in attendance. But the main event was the Cup final and what a day it was for the red haired Harry Robb who scored the only goal of the game!

The Cup was presented by Dr Lowson who said that this was a great triumph for Captain Avery who had organised the whole event. He also thanked Mr Ballingall who had donated the trophy.

But the real heroes of the day were Samson, Massie and Bell; Strachan, Machan and Laird; W Christie, Cook, Lamond, Robb and A Christie who won the first ever Ballingall Cup for the West School.

Order of Divine Service

for the

Kirking of the Council

the

Commemoration of the Traditional Foundation by King Malcolm III (Canmore)

and the

300th Anniversary of the Confirming Charter by King Charles II

in the

PARISH CHURCH OF FORFAR, OLD

SUNDAY, May 9, 1965, at 11 a.m.

The Right Rev. DUNCAN FRASER, D.D.,
Moderator of the General Assembly of the Church of Scotland,
will preach the Sermon.

Officiating Ministers :
Rev. DAVID M. BELL, B.D., Forfar, Old.
Rev. D. DEWAR DUNCAN, M.A., Forfar West.
Rev. JOHN F. KIRK, B.D., Forfar St James's.
Rev. J. F. W. SYMON, M.A., St John's Scottish Episcopal Church.

Organist — W. D. BERNARD, L.R.A.M., A.R.C.M.

The Kirking of the Council

May 8 1945

Today was VE Day!

At long last "unconditional surrender" and the War in Europe was over. A certain confusion prevailed about whether factories and schools were to be open or not. This was because the announcement that today (Tuesday) was to be a holiday was not made until the Monday. And that, was of course the Spring Holiday.

Today however, in spite of the heavy rain, a large crowd gathered at the Cross at 3.30 pm to hear Provost Lowson announce the cessation of hostilities, half an hour after the Prime Minister had done likewise in London.

The Polish Allies were well in evidence, and although the weather put a damper on things, many people celebrated with their patriotic flags and rosettes.

Those of a classical bent recalled the destruction of the Long Walls of Athens in 404 BC "to the music of the flute girls, thinking that day was the beginning of freedom for Greece", while others recalled the words of Vera Lynn that "there would be fun and laughter and peace ever after".

Wives and mothers offered prayers and thanks that their "sodgers" would soon be home. That night there would be a Dance in the Reid Hall.

It was a great day ... and yet it was not great for everyone. Mr and Mrs Whyte of 61 Graham Crescent were informed that their 19-year-old son George of the Argyll and Sutherland Highlanders had been killed in Italy by one of the few remaining partisans. It was a timely and savage reminder that victory does not come without a price.

May 9 1965

This morning at the Old Parish Church there was held what can only be described as a huge Service for (wait for it!) The Kirking of the Council, the Commemoration of the Traditional Founding by King Malcolm III (Canmore) and the 300th Anniversary of the Confirming Charter by King Charles II.

That was quite enough to be going on with and there were to be five Ministers present — The Right Reverend Duncan Fraser DD, the Moderator of the General Assembly of the Church of Scotland; The Reverend David M Bell BD of Forfar Old; The Reverend D Dewar Duncan MA of Forfar West; The Reverend John F Kirk BD of Forfar St James's, and the Reverend JFW Symon MA of St John's Scottish Episcopal Church.

It is sad to note that a representative of the Roman Catholic Church was not invited in what were supposed to be the more enlightened times of the 1960s.

The Organist would be the much loved WD Bernard LRAM ARCM. But the most important "guest" today would be the BBC cameras, for the Service was to be recorded and broadcast the following week on BBC TV.

As could be imagined the Church was full. Indeed if it had been a football match, it would have been described as "all ticket" with all the local organisations given their place.

This service was of course only part of the ongoing celebrations of 1965 to celebrate mainly the Charter given by Charles II in 1665. The non-presence of the Roman Catholic Church was therefore even more mysterious, for, as the more perceptive asked, was Charles II not a Stuart who were all Roman Catholics?

Would it not have, in any case, made more sense to have them with us to show that we had moved on from the horrors of religious bigotry?

May 10 1940

The war came to life to Forfar with a bump this Friday.

Previously, things had been very quiet with jokes going around the town that BEF did not mean British Expeditionary Force but Back Every Friday!

The main topic of conversation was the annoying and seemingly unnecessary restrictions imposed on normal life by rationing and the blackout.

Casualties had so far been minimal and the army had looked safe behind the Maginot line, which George Formby kept singing about.

This was all very much in contrast with the intense action and permanent casualties of the Great War, but today came the news that Hitler had invaded the Low Countries, and apparently the British Expeditionary Force would not be back for quite a few Fridays.

Indeed they would come spectacularly to grief at Dunkirk in less than a month with a fair number of Forfar casualties. Those who listened to the late night news on the radio also heard that Mr Chamberlain had been replaced as Prime Minister by Winston Churchill, whom not everyone liked, but his wife's family came from Airlie, so there was some sort of tenuous local connection there!

In the meantime life continued. Strathmore had been defeated by Aberdeenshire XI last week at cricket, there were several Junior football matches scheduled for tomorrow, and there were, of course, the two cinemas.

The Regal had Claudette Colbert and James Stewart in "It's A Wonderful World" and *The Pavilion* was showing "Way Down South" with Bobby Breen. There was however a certain anxiety in the air now, for the war was coming closer.

Brechin Road with Reid Hall

May 11 1871

Tonight the Reid Hall was declared open by Provost Whyte at a ceremony in which there was also unveiled a bust of the benefactor himself, Peter Reid.

The Hall had cost £6,000 of which Peter himself had footed the bill to the tune of £5,000 while the Town Council paid the other £1,000.

The foundation stone have been laid on August 5 1869 and apart from anything else the construction of the Hall, an architectural beauty, had provided employment for many masons, bricklayers and general labourers.

The writer of *The Dundee Courier* is highly impressed. He tells us that the Hall is situated in the North of the town, next to the turnpike road to Brechin and Kirriemuir. It is only a short walking distance away from the Sheriff Court with the Railway Station beyond that.

The hall can seat 1,250 people, and there is a platform at the west end (not, in 1871, the east end) which is raised. There are adequate lavatories for both sexes, and it is a facility of which all Forfar could justifiably be proud, for it put the town well ahead of most other towns.

The ever-popular Peter Reid himself, not now far short of his 70th birthday, was cheered to the echo as he addressed the audience.

Indeed it is hard to think of any activity that has *not* taken place in the Reid Hall over the past 150 years since that day in 1871 — music hall, concert, drama, opera, flower shows, indoor sports, dances, billeting accommodation for Polish soldiers, receptions of Royalty and even the cinema (although the audience of 1871 would not have known what that meant!)

Coronation time in the factory

May 12 1937

Forfar was blessed with beautiful weather for their celebration of Coronation Day.

It was a particularly important day for Forfar because the new Queen was the daughter of the Earl of Strathmore of Glamis Castle, and of course her younger daughter, Princess Margaret had been born there.

Provost Graham was not in Forfar because he had been invited to London, but that did not stop the town celebrating. In the morning, there was a procession of lorry floats with many works, shops and organisations putting in a float.

The winner was the Forfar Amateur Dramatic Society with a beautiful tableau of "Mary of Scotland", even though a pedant asked the question of whether this was not a little treasonous today as Mary Queen of Scots was of a different lineage and religion from the Windsors!

There were many fine lorries, each of which was cheered by the crowd, but the man who stole the show was the well-known character "Joey" McDermid of Green Street who won the "pedestrian" section dressed as Gandhi of India.

There was a Church Service, then in the early evening there was a five-a-side football tournament at Station Park won by Forfar Celtic.

Later at night a magnificent bonfire at "Bummie", visible apparently from miles away, lit up the War Memorial, something which seemed in some ways to symbolise and glorify the sacrifice of those who fell.

It was a great day in every respect, but it could not disguise the problems that the new King and Queen would probably have to face every soon.

The news from Spain was not good, and everyone was worried about Hitler.

The first congregation leaving the Lowson Memorial Church in 1914

May 13 1919

In a time of such misery caused by the flu epidemic and the return of soldiers from the war often in a considerably less happy state than they left in 1914, it is gratifying for *The Forfar Herald* to report good news of the appointment of a Forfar man as Minister to the charge of Sorn Parish Church in Ayrshire.

This young man is David McMath who is not only a fine Minister, (currently an Assistant in Galston) but also a war hero as well.

He was the third son of Robert McMath of Canmore Street, he studied at Forfar Academy, then went to St Andrews University, taking an MA Degree in 1911 in "Mental Philosophy" and a BD three years later in 1914 after winning the Bruce Scholarship.

He was licensed by Forfar Presbytery in 1914 but war disrupted his plans. He was commissioned in the Gordon Highlanders then transferred to the Royal Field Artillery where he saw considerable active service and was awarded the Military Cross for gallantry and devotion to duty.

He was Captain when he was demobbed and took up his post in Galston. He had not been there long when he was called to Sorn, but then again, the Ministry like every other job was short of manpower in those desperate days of 1918 and 1919.

He had married a Forfar girl called Christina Cargill in 1915. Sorn was a small village in East Ayrshire in the very heart of the Burns country and it is to be hoped that Mr McMath had been well versed in the Bard in his Forfar upbringing!

May 14 1914

This Thursday afternoon saw the Dedication of a new Church in Forfar to be called the Lowson Memorial Church.

It had been erected by Mrs Steele of Beechhill in memory of her late father, jute manufacturer of the town. It certainly was required; both the other two Churches of Scotland in the town, the Old Parish Church and St James's Church were clearly oversubscribed and it was obvious that something was needed for the east of the town.

This beautiful piece of architecture, erected on an eminence at Lilybank which would also enhance the beauty of the town, would clearly fill that need.

It had become the habit over the previous twelve months for people to take their Sunday afternoon walk out to the east of the town to observe how the new Church was taking shape.

There was a huge congregation including Provost Moffat and members of the Town Council, and the sermon was preached by Rev A Wallace Williamson, Moderator of the General Assembly of the Church of Scotland. Various local ministers, notably Rev WG Donaldson of the Old Parish Church took part in the Service.

The main thrust of the Service was an exhortation to look beyond the narrow and limited constraints of the day and towards the eternal truth of God.

The Forfar Herald is clearly very impressed by the size of the Church, and photographer Mr DM Laing had photographs of the Church to sell. The next step would now be to "call" its first Minister.

Forfar Sunrise

May 15 1941

The war had been going badly this year, but this did not stop an undignified squabble in Forfarshire Junior Cup circles. Senior football had been suspended in Forfar, and for this reason junior football assumed greater importance, not least because it helped to take their minds off the horrors of what was going on in the world at this time.

On May 3 at Beechwood Park, Dundee, Forfar Celtic had beaten a Dundee team called United Juniors 3-1 in the final of the Forfarshire Junior Cup and had brought home the much coveted trophy.

Or so they thought! United Juniors brought a somewhat desperate protest on the grounds that three Celtic players Newton, Lamb and Moore had played in an unauthorised game, a Celtic-East End Select v The Army at Station Park on April 23.

This did not seem, at first glance, to be the most heinous of offences nor did it seem to have much impact of the Forfarshire Cup. It also was a game arranged for good causes and had attracted a reasonable crowd. "Clutching at straws" did not really seem to come into it.

Mercifully, the Forfarshire Junior FA threw the protest out, and Celtic were re-instated as winners of the Forfarshire Junior Cup — so congratulations were due to Celtic's team of I Ogilvie; Sturrock and Smart; Liddle, Smith and D Ogilvie; Dalgety, Nicholl, Lamb, Moore and Newton, who had lifted the Forfarshire Cup for the second time.

It was something that brought a little cheer to at least some people in the town.

May 16 1885

This is the day attributed by the excellent Centenary History of Forfar Athletic as the first ever game of the new club.

The origins of the club are complicated but they broke away from Angus Athletic to form a new club and their first game was against a Dundee team called Our Boys Rangers.

It was a good game, and Forfar Athletic won 1-0 in their black and white strips. It was played at Station Park which was described as "rather primitive" — basically a piece of flat grass with only temporary equipment.

But it was called Station Park because it was near the station and very handy for away teams. Today's opponents from Juteopolis were described as "plucky and clever", but they failed to "pass the leather between the posts".

Thus began Forfar Athletic Football Club, and their Secretary was James Black, a man who would be connected with the club for the next 66 years until his death in 1951.

It is believed that they acquired the nickname "the loons" because at one point before the breakaway from Angus Athletic they were the second XI, the youngsters and they all looked young.

Very soon Forfar Athletic would outstrip Angus Athletic, and become the main team in the town. Football was of course the big thing in the 1880s in Scotland, because Scotland had beaten England five times in a row, something that gave the game a great boost.

What also helped the development of the game was the fact that more and more employers were beginning to give their workers a half day on a Saturday.

May 17 1937

The Easterbank Housing scheme (first and second developments) is now complete and ready for occupation. Eight three-apartment houses, eight four-apartment houses and six five-apartment houses are now ready for allocation, and tonight a provisional list of tenants to whom a house would be offered was announced.

The people to whom they were offered were all living in houses that were too small for their growing families, and it was generally considered to be a great advance to get a house at Easterbank.

The disadvantages were that it was up a steep hill and a fair distance from the Cross and the Town centre, but the advantages were that the houses were modern, spacious by 1930s standards with a kitchen, an indoor toilet and most of all, running water!

Boundary fencing and gates for gardens had not yet been built, but a firm from Brechin had now won that contract and work was due to begin soon. In addition there were plans to build a gate into the cemetery from the new estate. This would allow entrance for people to walk to and visit graves, but it would also allow a thoroughfare through the cemetery and exit from the Newmonthill gate, something that would make it slightly easier for the inhabitants of the new estate to get to the centre of the town.

Those who had been allocated a house were the envy of those who hadn't, but in the meantime Easterbank was still a favourite walk for Forfarians of a Sunday afternoon to "hae a gawp at the new hooses".

Forfarian Frank Hill on debut for Scotland on May 18 1930. The game was against France in Paris and caused a little controversy because it was on a Sunday!

May 18 1843

This was the fateful day in Scottish Ecclesiastical History when The Free Church left the Established Church of Scotland.

In the case of Forfar, it was the Reverend William Clugston who had been in the new, large Old Parish Church with a comfortable manse and glebe who walked out of his house and job with about 80 followers to found (eventually) Forfar's first Free Kirk in what is now known as St Margaret's Church or the West Kirk.

For a long time it was called the West Free. It was a brave action of Rev Clugston to give up such an affluent lifestyle to preach in the open air sometime until suitable premises could be hired, bought or built.

The dispute between the Free Kirkers and the Establishment Church had been brewing for some time on several issues but what brought matters to a head was the business of who gets to appoint Ministers.

As it stood, a Minister was appointed by the King or Queen. Now clearly, Queen Victoria herself did not actually do it, but the Committee, who did the appointing, used parchment with the Queen's imprimatur on it.

Reverend Clugston decided to align himself with the rebels and walked out to a life of poverty and dependence on a few rich people. He was heard to preach (for he was a mighty orator) to a congregation of several hundreds in the open air in the Gushet (otherwise known as the Staikit Racie).

Eventually premises were found in the New Road in what became the Drill Hall. Sadly Mr Clugston did not live to see the West Kirk. He died in March 1857.

May 19 1900

Mafeking has been relieved.

The town exploded with joy. News reached the town late last night, but there were very few people about, and no-one really took the news seriously.

Today this Saturday morning, the news spread like wildfire, and by lunch time the town was all agog with excitement, as bunting and flags were on display from houses with even a string of them across East High Street.

Provost McDougall gave orders that the Union Jack was to be flown from the Town Hall and that the bells should be rung from the Old Kirk. The Post Office and the Railway Station were much decorated, and in Jarman's Hotel, a drawing of Baden Powell drawn by Forfar artist Mr A Barclay was on display.

In warm sunny weather appropriate to the occasion, The Forfar Instrumental Band, under Bandmaster Lamb, played "God Save The Queen" and Provost McDougall called for three cheers for the gallant garrison of Baden Powell.

In the evening, the band gave a concert at the Cross playing all the appropriate music of the day, and (shocking to some people) the Forfar Ladies Golf Club appeared in red, white and blue favours cycling (yes, ladies on bicycles!) through the streets and ringing their bells.

Such indecorous behaviour might have shocked the population at other times, but this was a great night for the Empire in its struggle against the Boers of South Africa.

Even the American flag, the Stars and Stripes, was seen waving from Newtonbank in Rosebank Road.

The only sour note for Forfar was the performance of Strathmore Cricket Club who travelled to play Dundee Victoria that day and lost.

May 20 1907

A farmer from the parish of Fearn was today charged with reckless driving, but this was driving a horse attached to a dog cart.

He was driving it in a "furious and reckless manner". It had followed a rather alarming occurrence in Castle Street.

Sergeant Doig was on duty and saw the horse being driven with no care or attention being paid to other drivers on the road or even pedestrians on the pavement.

The town was busy because it was a Monday — market day. The Sergeant called on him to stop, but he paid no attention and headed up the Brechin Road.

The man appeared to be under the influence of liquor, but as a dog cart yoked to a horse is fairly unusual, there was no problem tracking the man down. He was found in the Zoar public house and duly charged with the offence.

When he appeared before Bailie Lamb a week later, the man was penitent and duly pleaded guilty but said that the horse was a rather "spirited" animal. He then contradicted himself by saying that the horse was "only trotting".

This was blatant rubbish, and Bailie Lamb noticed that the farmer had a previous conviction for something similar in 1905.

The man was fined £1 with the alternative of ten days imprisonment. £1 in 1907 was a fair amount of money but it had been a fairly serious offence which might have had tragic consequences.

It was very sadly the sort of thing which tended to happen on "mert" or market days, for, as in the case of Tam O'Shanter, deals were often sealed with alcohol!

Lang Strang

May 21 1651

Today in Stockholm, Sweden, Robert Strang died.

Not a great deal is known of Robert other than that he came from Forfar, went to Stockholm on business one day, liked it there and settled becoming very rich.

It is not clear how, but words like "merchant" and "trader" are used to describe him. He may have specialised in campanology, for he bequeathed to the good people of Forfar a huge bell for ringing in the Church, and of course it is still there, commonly known as "Lang Strang".

Strang Street is, of course, named after him, and apparently one of his wishes was that anyone in Forfar called Strang who died should have a funeral knell rung on the bell similar to that when the King dies.

Transporting of the bell to Forfar was a problem — at least the North Sea presented no difficulties — but the magistrates of Dundee turned awkward and first of all wrenched the tongue out of the bell and threw it into the River Tay, then made the Forfar magistrates pay for every bit of land that they transported the bell over.

This was sheer bullying and imperialism, not to mention extortion and vandalism, and those who wonder why it is that, when the half time scores are announced at Station Park, a loud cheer usually rises when Dundee and Dundee United are not doing well, may have their answer here!

In spite of all the efforts of those who say "eh" all the time, the bell was safely transported to Forfar, and has been in action now for over 350 years. Thank you, Mr Strang!

I.A.N Henderson with Forfar Academy Athletics pupils in 1965. Mrs J Dakers is the lady Teacher

May 22 2001

Today Ian "I. A. N." Henderson died. To generations of Forfar Academy pupils, he was simply known as "Henderson", and he was a man whom one would never forget.

He belonged to the tough breed of Physical Education teachers, being particularly interested in sports like rugby and boxing, but he was also very fond of swimming and athletics.

He had no time for idiots or for anyone who thought that they were better than he was, but he was not entirely unsympathetic to those who simply could not do things like climb ropes or walk along beams.

Until 1965, he worked in very difficult conditions at the old school on Academy Street which was frankly inadequate for physical education with only one small gymnasium and a playground!

The rest of the time, the public baths were used for swimming and team games were played on all the public parks of the town.

He was, as we have said, tough but he never had any discipline problems! Occasionally some pupils felt that he went too far with his toughness, but he had the ability to forget and to move on as well.

He lived in Brechin. There was another side to him as well, which some people thought was at odds with his persona. He was a very fine writer.

He wrote many articles for *The Scots Magazine* and *Scottish Field*, and he wrote a superb book "Discovering Angus And The Mearns". This must have taken him several years of research; the end product was one which combines scholarship and humour.

May 23 1952

Forfar Amateur Dramatic Society had another successful performance with a comedy "Sit Down A Minute, Adrian".

The Forfar Dispatch says that the players are always at their best when they know that the drama critics from the local press are there; the critic has to agree with this opinion as they were really very good tonight in the St James's Parish Church Hall.

It was a good three shillings worth. It was a comedy which occasionally looked as if it were going to become a farce but never quite reached that length.

The main characters were the ever popular Fred Milne and Susan Roberts who convinced the audience, Fred as the successful but unworldly husband and Susan as his exasperated wife. They had three daughters — May Anderson, Lynda Whyte and Marjory Tappenden — and a lot of the humour came when one of them went all proletarian to disturb the middle class ambience by falling in love with her Socialist foreman, Harold Adamson.

The humour was sustained throughout, although *The Forfar Dispatch* is a little critical of the playwright for not making more out of some parts.

John Sim, Margaret Copland, Robert Drummond, Jenny White and Harry Ireland completed the cast, and the play was well produced by Walter Cuthbert and Robert Drummond with John Roberts, Bruno Kunkel, David Stewart, Angus Millar, Barbara Rodger, Ann Urquhart, Alison Dalgety, Jean Shiells, Jean Robertson, Helen Small, Vivian Callander and James Sutherland in the backstage team.

"It was a capital show" said *The Forfar Dispatch*.

May 24 1893

The Queen celebrated her 74th birthday today and some of Forfar celebrated with her.

One has to say "some" for although the more enlightened employers took advantage of the fine weather and gave their workers a day off, the jute factories didn't.

There was no legal obligation for Don, Lowson, Craik, Boath and their management team to give their workers a day off, but it didn't really do them any good to be so curmudgeonly and it was bitterly resented.

On the other hand, most shops not only closed for the day but gave their workers a day trip. Messrs JD Boyle, for example, dressmakers and milliners left in two brakes and a wagonette to spend the day at Edzell in the beautiful sunshine, Miss Oram's employees went there as well in their own brake, and Jarvis Brothers took their employees to Balnabooth.

The Literary Institute went to Clova and organised their own entertainment of poetry and dramatic readings in the open air.

Many a glass was raised to the continuing health and well-being of Her Majesty, so much so that there were a few reports of the brakes coming back with a few of their passengers (including some respectable douce Church-going matrons) being what is known in Forfar as "the waur o' the wear" with their refreshment, and a few less respectable songs being heard!

As for the good lady herself, feelings were ambivalent. She frequently passed through Forfar Station on her many trips to Balmoral.

Sometimes she gave orders for the train to slow down so that she could wave graciously at her admiring Forfarians; other times, the train shot through leaving some very disappointed wavers of Union Jacks!

May 25 1967

Forfar was a quiet place at tea time tonight. Cats walked up the road in East High Street wondering where everybody was.

Overtime in the factories, usually much coveted in the 1960s, had been turned down. Curtains were drawn in living rooms, pubs had a few customers, but they were all staring at the TV on the wall.

Just occasionally a house door would open and a noise would be heard. Just what on earth was all going on? It all became clear at about 7.20 pm.

Doors opened to enjoy the bright sunlight, people came out, singing and dancing, cheering and shouting about someone called "Jock" who seemed to have changed the world.

Green was a predominant colour but even those who wore blue were happy as well with "I knew they would do it!" There was no-one left in Forfar who did not know that some Glasgow team had won the European Cup.

Pubs began to notice a huge increase in trade with everyone still on about this chap called "Jock", and even those who did not normally like a green and white jersey suddenly jumped ship and declared that they were happy with the triumph of a Scottish team.

"In fact, my family are actually Catholics..." and other such stuff was heard. Life would never be the same again. Stories abounded, notably the well known local cricketer who raised his arms in triumph — and broke his mother's light bulb! And the veteran supporter who spent the last five minutes in the garden shed, afraid to watch lest the Italians equalised.

The following morning, even the looms in the factory seemed to be chattering excitedly about what had happened in Lisbon last night.

May 26 1952

The death was reported at a very advanced age of Willie Connell, one time Chief Booking Clerk at Forfar Station and a well-known local character, for he was often the first and the last person that visitors saw at Forfar Station.

His fat cheery, chubby, sonsie face was somehow suited to the job. He had retired in 1928 having worked at Forfar Station since 1893 and having served the railway in total 45 years, starting in 1883 with the Caledonian Railway in Perth as a parcel clerk.

In those days the railway was seen as a very important job, and was usually well paid because of the importance that was attached to the railways in the running of the country's economy.

He had, of course, overseen many sombre departures in the years of the Great War and many triumphant and relieved returns to the town.

He had been on duty on the busy days of the Forfar Games, on the day when the mighty Glasgow Celtic arrived in 1914; he always said that the busiest day of them all was the day of the opening of the Reid Park in 1896 when thousands of people passed through the station.

He had seen many changes at Forfar Station — platform extensions, new porters' rooms, enlarged telegraph and parcels offices and the installation of the book and fruit stalls.

He was a member of the Choir of St James's Church and was clerk of the Forfar branch of the London, Midland Scottish Hospital fund. He was survived by his wife and son.

Feeing Market before it moved to the Greens

May 27 1965

As part of the celebrations for the 300th Anniversary of the granting of the Charter to Forfar in 1665, the Scottish Professional Golf Association Championship was held at Forfar Golf Club at Cunninghill.

It was a happy choice, and the course was well praised by several golfers because it was so difficult! The local economy did well also with hotels full, and the town full of visitors.

Taxi firms did particularly well with many people reckoning that the golf course was just a little too far out of town to walk. The weather was not always great with several thunderstorms, but the standard of golf was consistently good.

The Tournament was won today by the ever popular Eric Brown, the professional of Cruden Bay, who had suffered a lean time recently but today's tournament win (his first since 1962) guaranteed him a place in Scotland's Canada Cup team for the autumn, and earned him £250 into the bargain.

His total of 271 equalled the record for the Tournament and he was six strokes ahead of Frank Rennie of Prestwick who finished second. Much of the local money had been on the Downfield professional Bobby Walker but he fell away after a good start, whereas Brown retained his consistency throughout with his scores of 68, 65, 68 and 70.

Forfar's own professional Dave Bell finished on 285. The tournament was well attended but it was generally felt that it would have been better if it had been arranged for a weekend.

Market at the Greens in the 1950s

May 28 1932

The Bowling Season is now in full swing following a somewhat poor start because of the weather.

The weather was not great today but the railwaymen of the Forfar London Midland and Scottish Railway were able to send three rinks to take on their Perth equivalents in Perth today.

Frank Small and Alec Selby did well but it was Harry Rae who won the day for Forfar. The weather was not great but they were able to play between showers as they gave Perth Loco "their licks" as *The Forfar Herald* puts it.

Bowling being a very hospitable game, everyone was well wined and dined and arrangements made for a return match at the Reid Park, next Saturday, weather permitting.

"The bools" were gradually becoming more popular in Forfar, doing its best to shake off the perceptions that it was an all-male sport, an old man's sport or a snobby middle class sport.

Indeed it was none of these three, and even had the advantage over other sports that it was a quiet, sedate, well-behaved sport, so much so that the Churches (apart from the more hysterical, evangelical wing) did not seem to raise any strong objection when the occasional game of bowls seemed to escape the net and to be played on a Sunday.

Perhaps it was because no-one really noticed; apart from the occasional click of the bowls and an even more occasional "Well Done!" there was no real noise emanating from the rinks!

May 29 1906

Today ex-Provost McDougall received a letter from his old friend William Rutherford, late of Forfar and now Managing Director of the California Cotton Mills, East Oakland, USA.

Mr Rutherford had survived the earthquake of a month ago and was writing to tell of his experiences.

Quite a few Forfar people now lived on the west coast of the United States but, as far as could be ascertained, no Forfar person had lost their life. The city of San Francisco was totally devastated with the total casualty list yet to be counted as a result of earthquake and fire.

Mr Rutherford told how shortly after 5 in the morning on the beautiful morning of April 18 1906, an earthquake occurred for 28 seconds throwing furniture about and causing chimneys to implode.

The fire which followed had been all the worse because so much of the water supply had been lost because of fractured pipes and large parts of the city had simply been allowed to burn out, leaving it uninhabitable because of the heat.

Currently about 200,000 people are still living in camps and being fed by the US Army. The paper on which Mr Rutherford's letter had been written was now brown with the fire and he had enclosed a few coins which had been burned and charred by the heat.

There was now a certain doubt about whether San Francisco would ever be habitable again — an unduly pessimistic assessment as it turned out, but everyone in Forfar agreed that it was "an awfa waydain".

204   Advertisement, 1900

May 30 1912

The Market is coming!

The Forfar Dispatch asks the question of the local children "Have you saved up all your pennies for the Market?"

The Market will be on Thursday, Friday and Saturday and of course coincides with the agricultural "term" when farm workers are re-engaged (or not) by farmers for another six months or even a year.

It is a deplorable form of wage slavery, with a few similarities to the Roman Slave Market of classical times, as workers sell themselves to farmers.

But the "term" does of course bring loads of country people into town and a visit to the Market with its show boats and stalls is a pleasant accompaniment to the sometimes difficult negotiations between farmers and their potential workers.

Wise farmers naturally have everything sorted out long in advance, and do their best to retain their best workers by offering them good wages.

The Market of course in 1912 still retained some of its original meaning with hawkers selling their goods at a cheap price. But *The Forfar Dispatch* is very worried about the number of traction engines it has seen coming into the Greens, and worries that they are so heavy on the wet ground (there has been a lot of rain of late) that they might sink and all that will be left will be the funnels!

The writer worries in case the Greens may seem as dangerous as the Atlantic, a poignant reference perhaps to the tragedy there a month ago when *The Titanic* went down after hitting an iceberg, but fortunately, as far as could be ascertained, there were no Forfar people on board!

May 31 1952

Reverend Alfred Wilson of the Forfar Congregational Church in Osnaburgh Church today gave notice of his intention to retire after being a Minister for 53 years.

He had been in Forfar since 1929 and had made a considerable impact in the town since that day as a conscientious and much loved Minister.

He organised concerts in his Church on a Sunday evening, to the annoyance originally of the Sabbatarians, who disapproved of anyone doing anything on a Sunday. But Reverend Wilson stuck to his resolve — "the better the day, the better the deed" — and very soon other Churches began to copy him.

Originally from Dundee, Alfred studied theology in London and as well as serving as a padre in the Great War, was a Minister in Shetland, Glasgow, Liverpool, a village called Swaddlincote, Tillicoutry, Blairgowrie and Rosyth before coming to the town he loved the most.

He felt that it was time to move on and leave his charge to a younger man, but he did not envy him his task, for he felt that the norm of Church going had been broken, and that the Church now had to work harder to get members.

He recalled with fondness the intensity of prayers in his younger day, but did not regret that the days of the God of fire and brimstone had passed in favour of an emphasis on a God of Love.

He would now of course have to leave his Manse at 47 Brechin Road but hoped to get a house in Forfar. He wanted to live here the rest of his life, a remark that, naturally, brought a tear to many a Forfar eye.

June

Forfar Castle Street 1900s

June 1 1895

After an incredibly long period of wrangling which had gone on for well over a decade, at long last the Forfar to Brechin railway line opened to passengers today. (It had been open to goods traffic since January).

The weather was warm and pleasant but not as great a crowd turned out to see the first train come in from Brechin as might have been expected.

The problems had been caused by the geographical layout of both towns, for the train leaving Forfar had to go west first before turning to go north and east to Brechin, and when it reached Brechin it had to almost go past the city before turning into Brechin station.

But the train passed through stations like Justinhaugh, Tannadice and Careston, and for several miles, it ran parallel with the turnpike road from Forfar to Brechin.

The whole run took about 45 minutes, and on a beautiful day like today, there was nothing more pleasant than to enjoy the countryside and the scenery.

Had the Forfar and Brechin people got together a little earlier, this line might have become the main line to Aberdeen, (in the same way as the road would become) but the position of the stations was against them, and in any case the main line was now well established going through Guthrie.

Sadly the Forfar to Brechin railway line was never destined to be anything other than a branch line, and the paucity of numbers saw it closed as early as 1952. It was used by commuters and football teams, however, for it was far more comfortable than the bus.

June 2 1953

This was Coronation Day, and the phrase "chilly for June" seemed to have been specially coined for today.

The predominant feeling was one of anti-climax and disappointment after weeks and weeks of flags flying and "God Save The Queen" being written in flowers on flower beds throughout the town.

In addition ever child in the town was given a cup with "God Save The Queen" and a picture of her, plus, luxury of luxuries, a bar of chocolate! Chocolate was still rare in 1953 only very recently having come "off the ration".

Forfar saw a Parade with loads of pipers, flags and soldiers as they marched past Provost Andrew Smyth at the Town House with Forfar's four surviving veterans from the Boer War standing beside him — JD Clark, R Kerr, J Strachan and J McKinnon.

This was all very well; it certainly attracted a large crowd of people to see it in spite of the bitter cold, but where was the Queen?

We four-year-olds were very disappointed to be told that she was being crowned in London, rather than Forfar, and why that had been decided, no-one knew.

But there was a whisper that some lucky people would be able to see the Queen. These people were the lucky few who had something called TV or television.

Disabled children were given the chance to see TV in a special showing at "the mert", but the vast majority had to wait a few weeks until colour film of the Coronation came to "The Gaffie". A bonfire was lit that night on "Bummie" and that was spectacular.

June 3 1951

The Forfar Amateur Radio Society treated themselves to a weekend away at Lour Hill with two teams, the idea being to get in touch with as many people in as many different locations as possible.

One of the teams had markedly more success than the other one. One of the teams was on the 20/40 band and had R MacFarlane, Gilbert Robertson and Jim Thomson with J Bremner doing the logging.

They managed to get 137 contacts including ones as far afield as Tangier and Malta as well as Sweden, Germany, France, Holland and countless others in all parts of England and Ireland.

The other team of Walter Robertson, John Clark, Willie Lowson with J Patterson and J Gray doing the logging only managed 71; all of them were in the UK, with quite a lot of them in Scotland.

Conditions were not so favourable for their 80/160 meter band. They had spent the whole night living in a tent very graciously loaned to them by the 6th Forfar Scouts, and they had a watch of four hours each.

The weather conditions were slightly on the cold side for camping, but at least it was not cloudy or rainy. Amateur radio was a hobby that had grown in the town since the war.

Clearly the war was where some of them learned about radios, but for a while it was a hobby that was frowned upon by the Government lest it interfere with calls to ambulances and ships etc. However, recent improvements in technology meant that this was less of a problem.

MILLINERY.

* *

For a Choice Selection of Millinery at all Seasons,

VISIT

Miss THOM'S,

130 EAST HIGH STREET, FORFAR.

DAVID ROBERTSON

Boot and Shoemaker,

AGENT FOR

"LOYALTY."	"MARCHIONESS"
—	BOOTS AND SHOES
"ROYAL FEDORA"	(Regd.)
as supplied to and approved	as made for Royalty.
by	—
HER MAJESTY THE QUEEN.	By Special Appointment.

In order to give the variety which is now called for, we stock, in addition to our Royalty Goods, a great many different makes of Walking Boots and Shoes, varying in Style and Price, and Customers can therefore depend upon getting the best Styles put before them, and an Extensive Variety to choose from.

Repairs Carefully attended to at

60 EAST HIGH STREET, FORFAR.

WILLIAM TAYLOR,

Watchmaker and Jeweller,

44 EAST HIGH STREET, FORFAR.

Every Description of Silver and Electro-Plated Goods suitable for Presentation. Engagement and Wedding Rings. Spectacles and Eye-Glasses to suit all Sights.

Repairs promptly and carefully attended to at strictly Moderate Charges.

June 4 1901

The man from *The Forfar Herald* enjoyed his concert and organ recital at the Parish Church in which the main participant was Mr MB Kidd, the organist of that Church.

The weather was fine and the attendance was good considering the other attractions of a summer's evening, and there was quite clearly a large contingent from Kirriemuir.

The programme was mainly classical, perhaps too severely so, for "as yet a promiscuous Forfar audience cannot, without an effort, maintain their interest in the higher flights of musical genius for an hour and a half on end".

There are two interesting points about that comment. One is that the word "promiscuous" means something else in 1901 compared with today — otherwise what on earth was going on in the pews? — and the other point is that this is an extremely patronising or even offensive comment!

"Promiscuous" in 1901 means "of all classes", one assumes, and the implication is that the working classes might find it difficult to enjoy music like this! But he then goes on to say that "only the sacredness of the place restrained the audience from audibly expressing their appreciation of what was from first to last a very fine performance".

The choir performed well and seemed to be much increased in numbers, and the tenor, Mr C Stewart, was much commended as well, particularly for his "recitative and air" from Mendelssohn's "Elijah".

The Reverend Dr George Caie delivered a Vote of Thanks, and this rare musical treat was brought to an end with a hymn, then the Kirriemuir people left to get their train at 9.00 pm.

Forfar Station in the early 1950s.
Ex-Caledonian railway Dunalastair IV Class 54454 was withdrawn from service in 1955.

June 5 1982

Today, a Saturday, saw one of the saddest days in Forfar's history when the last ever train ran from Perth to Forfar Station.

Passenger travel had ceased in September 1967, goods had gone on for a little longer but some of the track further north had already been lifted, and this was a special train which ran from Perth to Forfar and back twice on the same day.

It was as we have said, a very sad day, but it was also a celebration of a service which had been running since January 1839 when Queen Victoria had been on the throne for about 18 months.

Many of the passengers wore Victorian dress, and a piper played old Victorian melodies like "The Road to Mandalay" and "My Grandfather's Clock".

The day was exceptionally hot, and the atmosphere was party-like with people on the train who had travelled frequently on the line, plus quite a number of people from Railway Societies from as far afield as the south of England.

It is now generally agreed that it had been a mistake to close down the Stanley to Kinnaber line, but of course it had been a political decision because Forfar voted the wrong way for the Government of the day in 1967.

Most people now think that there might even be a chance some day of a resurrection of the Forfar railway, given what has happened successfully in the Borders.

None of this detracts from the glorious history of Forfar Station which was, in its heyday one of the busiest per head of the population in Scotland with trains running to Dundee, Arbroath, Kirriemuir and Brechin as well as Aberdeen and Glasgow.

June 6 1944

It was clear from a very early stage today that something important was happening.

Yesterday the Allies had taken Rome, and today, from the time that "the wireless" opened early in the morning, the town was all agog with people coming into the factories reporting news reports that "they have landed".

Every hour the BBC gave news of thousands of British and American soldiers pouring into France from several beaches in Normandy (there was now no point in keeping it a secret).

So far resistance had been minimal, according to the BBC. By dinner time everyone knew with emotions ranging from the deeply anxious (there were many Forfar wives and mothers who knew that their "leds" were involved) to those who were going around predicting that Germany would surrender by the end of the week.

The really difficult part of all this was not knowing exactly what was going on, and it would be some time before anyone would know, while all the time there was the fear of the Post Office red motorbike appearing at your doorstep with a telegram.

In the meantime, life continued in Forfar. Churches were organising special midweek services, and would be open for private prayers throughout the day.

Social life continued with a boxing bout scheduled for the Reid Hall on Saturday night in aid of the "Salute The Soldier" campaign, and of course The Gaffie and The Regal were open for business as usual.

As Forfar braced itself for further news, there was also the funny side as well. Someone shouted to a deaf old lady "Ah see Rome fell!" "Oh, did he hurt himsel?"

June 6, 1841

The 1841 Census for Scotland was taken on the night of 6 June 1841. For the first time, the following information was requested:

Place (name of village, street, square, close, etc.); name of each person that had spent the night in that household; age, sex, profession or occupation, and where born.

The Reverend William Clugston, born in July 1795, lived in the Manse of Forfar with his wife Margaret, born in 1798, and their children George (17), William (15), Janet (12) and Alexander (10).

Elisabeth Cumming was their servant.

James Barclay, a Writer (Solicitor) lived at Hill Park Cottage, Forfar, with his wife Agnes and children James (11) and John (9). Also in the house were Janet Souter (30) and Ann Eassie (19).

James Allan, born in 1801, a hairdresser, was living in the Old Montrose Bothy, Marytown, He had recently been given 5 shillings by the Dundee Destitute Assessors.

He would soon marry; Bell Christie already two children, John and Margaret and would go on to have several more.

His career advanced, by 1851 he was on his way to become a musician of some renown.

June 7 1930

It cannot be very often in sporting history that a Forfar man plays in the same cricket team as two Australian Test Match players.

This was precisely what happened here when Davie McLean was invited to join JM Barrie's Allahakbarries in a game to open officially the cricket pavilion on the Hill at Kirriemuir which JM Barrie had given to the club.

The day was scorchingly hot, and more or less all of Forfar made its way to the Hill. As this was the depth of the economic depression, and many of Forfar's factories were on "short-time", Forfarians, almost en masse decided to walk the six miles to Kirrie to save on the rail fare.

The two Australian cricketers were Arthur Mailey and Charles Macartney, and they were part of the 1930 Australian touring team, although they doubled as journalists as they were only fringe players.

The First Test was due to start at Trent Bridge the following Friday. The Kirriemuir game was between Barrie's side and the West of Scotland, both sides being supplemented by "guests".

Thus it was that when the great Charles Macartney reached his century, his partner was no less a man than Davie or "Dyke" McLean, the hero of Forfar and no mean cricketer for Strathmore, even though he was better known as a footballer.

Macartney himself apparently was impressed and even flattered to hear that his partner was a Scottish international football player. It was reckoned that over 5,000 watched this game.

June 8 1846

An alarming incident occurred today on the Arbroath Road a mile or two outside Forfar. Five men had been at a sale at Burnside in their horse and drosky and were returning home when suddenly the horse bolted.

A drosky

Why it did so, we cannot be sure, but possibly the weight was lighter as the men had sold a heavy item of furniture or it may be that the sun dazzled the horse. It was totally out of control, until it passed the gig of Mr Alexander of Glamis. The back wheel of the drosky came into contact with the gig, and both horse and drosky capsized.

The horse was stunned and easily got under control; two of the men, one them being the driver, escaped unscathed, one had a dislocated shoulder but quickly recovered. Of the other two, one was badly bruised about the head and the chest and other was so seriously bruised that for a while "little hope was entertained for his survival".

Fortunately, just as he was being carried in the drosky to the surgeon's in Little Causeway, he regained consciousness and was able to return to his house, while the other badly injured man also recovered but was not seen about the town for several weeks. It was an alarming occurrence for the five men, and for those who had seen it (the horse had bolted for about 200 yards!) but it was a total accident.

Such things happened quite a lot, and the lovers of the new railway (which had been in existence for seven years now) were not slow to point out that although trains were noisy and a bit frightening to some people and horses, nevertheless their safety record was, so far, really quite good.

June 9 1892

Cynics may say that it had a lot to do with an imminent General Election which was due to take place next month, but there are clear signs that things are beginning to pick up in the jute industry.

The jute industry seemed particularly prone to such variations, and it was a problem for the town because jute employed such a large percentage of the Forfar population, well over 50 %.

Therefore "when jute sneezed, Forfar tended to catch a cold". But this week's *Forfar Herald* contains a certain amount of good news.

There had been a certain amount of short-time working with the "Hauchie" and the "Mull" off on Friday and Saturdays, but now they are to resume Friday working with the only "idle" time being the six hours half shift on a Saturday. (Some revolutionaries were even suggesting that this was no bad thing and that a five day week should be sufficient!)

Laird's and Don's were somewhat similar, whereas the Tails in Academy Street and Jock's in Don Street were back on full time working (56 hours per week) and the only factory still struggling was Craik's who were only working a 45 hour week.

It appears that normally jute workers would work from 6am to 6pm every day from Monday to Friday (with an hour off for breakfast and another for what was called the dietoor (ie the diet hour) or dinner, and from 6 am to 12.00 on Saturday. "Short time" must have seemed like a relief sometimes!

June 10 1940

Today, Mussolini's Italy declared war on Great Britain and France.

It was a cowardly act as the Allies were on their knees after Dunkirk, and rightly did Mussolini earn the name of "that jackal" whose order of the day was "Don't attack unless your victim's back is turned and he is already on the ground".

It led however to one of the saddest notices that *The Forfar Dispatch* ever had to print.

It was from fish and chip man Frank Lorenti who asserted that he was a British citizen awaiting to be called up to the British Army, and that his parents, although Italian born, had not been there for forty years.

Neither he nor his father in law Sandy Iannerelli, whose family had been brought up in Forfar, deserved the opprobrium that was being heaped on them for things that were beyond their control.

Clearly some people who should have known a lot better had been hurling abuse and talking about organising a boycott of "Italian" fish and chip shops, and ice cream sellers.

Sandy, in particular, who ran a chip van, was quite outspoken about his Britishness, even to the extent of having a musical box which played God Save The King and uttering to his male customers a *sotto voce* "F*** Mussolini" as he served them their fish suppers!

It was all to no avail. In one of his less happy wartime utterances, Churchill ordered the police to "Clobber the Lot" and many Italians were interned — not in all truth the worst of fates, but unnecessary, and depriving Britain of many loyal citizens who would have done a good job for them!

June 11 1932

Violence is something that does not very often associate with cricket at Lochside Park, surely one of the most beautiful and peaceful spots in Scotland.

And, to be fair, "violence" is possibly stretching it a little today — it was more like what latterly came to be described as "handbags" where everyone pushes and jostles one another, possibly with threats and certainly with insults ("disgusting epithets" according to *The Forfar Dispatch*), but no-one ever seems to actually land a punch on anyone.

The opposition were Brechin, a superb team in the 1930s and frankly better than Strathie who found the dominance of Brechin hard to handle. But today was a close game. Brechin scored 132 and Strathie were edging towards the total in a tight game.

In 1932, neutral Umpires were not appointed, and the Press protects the identity of the representatives of both teams who had agreed to do this difficult job by calling them "the Forfar Umpire" and "the Brechin Umpire".

Sadly "the Brechin Umpire" gave a few decisions that were not to the liking of the Forfar crowd, including the decision that swung that match, a contentious caught behind. Brechin had won by 6 runs.

This was too much for some Forfar youths who invaded the pitch to shout and swear and jostle "the Brechin Umpire", and some of the Brechin players, although wiser counsel persuaded them not to upset the bigger, more athletic looking specimens.

Strathmore's captain AH Melville was "ferr black affronted" as they say in Forfar, and had to apologise profusely for such unruly behaviour. But the affair was quickly forgotten about, and cricket matches continued!

June 12 1976

The Forfar Games, which were once the mecca for enthusiasts from all over Scotland on the last Monday in July (the start of the Forfar Holiday Week) have long gone, but this Saturday in beautiful weather at Lochside Park, an estimated 6,000 to 7,000 people were attracted to see the Forfar Highland Games.

People arrived from all over the country and the shops, restaurants and ice cream parlours did a roaring trade. The programme at the Lochside was varied and highly enjoyable, according to the writer of *The Aberdeen Press and Journal.*

A particular attraction was the young dancing girls all nicely dressed in Highland costume. The "heavy events" (caber, shot putting etc.) were won by Bill Anderson of Aberdeen with David Edmonds of Rutherglen second and Chris Mathieson third.

The tug of war attracted a great deal of attention and was won by Young Bells, while the 800 metres was won by J Ward of Hillend.

This being Forfar, of course there had to be a certain amount of genuflection towards the landed aristocracy and the Games were opened by the Earl of Strathmore and the trophies were presented by Lt Colonel Leslie Gray-Cheape, chairman of the Angus District Council.

The weather was beautiful — indeed 1976 was looked upon as one of the best summers of them all — and the ground looked nice with all the marquees and flags, and simply because of the sheer amount of people.

The major problem at the moment in the country was inflation, but that seemed to be of no concern to all those spending money.

Forfar Cycling Club 1936

June 13 1887

Provost Doig was a busy man at the Forfar Police Court this morning.

There were the usual fights and drunkenness, a family having what is now called a "domestic" argument on the street outside a house where someone was dying, a case involving a man driving a dog cart far too fast on West High Street, and a rather nasty one involving some boys between the ages of 6 and 12 throwing stones at trains from the Zoar Bridge.

A residenter *(sic)* at Zoar said that they were not necessarily throwing stones at the train, but at another set of boys. He claimed that stone throwing was a frequent occurrence in that part of town, and that the police were seldom seen there.

However, a train belonging to the Caledonian Railway had been hit twice, and action had to be taken. Four boys pleaded guilty and the other didn't. The case against him was dismissed, but of the guilty four, after a lengthy explanation of the seriousness of their crime, the youngest was admonished and released and the other three were fined 2 shillings and sixpence with the alternative of a day in jail.

In another case of stone throwing this time at the junction of North Street and Victoria Street, six boys were found guilty of breaking panes of glass at an empty house, but Provost Doig decided that they were too young to face punishment and they were dismissed after their parents had appeared and promised to look after them a little better in future.

June 14 1931

"An awfa rain the day" "It's no takin' time tae rain!" It's p***in' o rain" — these and all the other Forfar phrases for the downpours of Jupiter Pluvius were heard today, and it was generally agreed by *The Forfar Dispatch* to have been one of the worst downpours this century.

Most of the rain fell this Sunday afternoon and evening, and by early Monday morning there was 2.12 inches registered, more than the whole of June last year! And it was a record since they had started to register such things.

And yet, it was generally agreed that Forfar escaped the worst which tended to fall over Brechin and Montrose, where damage had been done to buildings, houses and bridges. But large parts of Forfar were "hale watter". Saturday had been a fine June day, but early Sunday morning was still, heavy and weighted with clammy moisture.

Everyone got to Church and back (one presumes that the Sermon was not about Noah!) and it was only in the early afternoon that the wind began to blow from the East accompanied by the sound of distant thunder.

Between three and four o'clock it was coming down in a solid sheet, causing devastation to all the Sunday School outings that had been scheduled for that afternoon. Nor did it go off until well past midnight, although it did abate to a certain extent.

Forfar people retained their sense of humour:

"It's stull comin doun, Erchie"

"Just as weel! It wad be a yokie if it was gaen up, Betts".

It was a day that was talked about and reminisced about for the next thirty years, but mercifully the next day was beautiful and hot and the floods soon dried up.

June 15 1903

A rather tragic case came before Bailie Ritchie today at the Forfar Burgh Police Court when an elderly pedlar called Andrew McDonald was asked to plead on the charge of attempting to commit suicide.

McDonald was a well-known character who came in and out of Forfar from time to time, and was generally regarded as a harmless old drunk.

Last week, in the Model Lodging House in Couttie's Wynd, McDonald had said to Mrs Clark, the lodging house keeper, that he was tired of his life and was going to "dae awa wi mysel" pointing to two bottles which he said were full of vermin poison.

As he was in a considerable state of intoxication at the time, Mrs Clark did not take him seriously but a short time later, she heard a noise and found him trying to drink one of these bottles. She managed to take the bottle from him and summoned help.

He was then removed, and in his appearance before Bailie Ritchie, he said he supposed he was guilty of the charge but that he had been in and out of Forfar for the past 45 years and had never given them any trouble.

The wise Bailie concurred that McDonald had never been in trouble before, and when McDonald promised to leave town at once, Bailie Ritchie dismissed him.

This case is interesting from several points of view, not least that no attempt was made to offer counselling to the man nor to find out why he wanted to commit suicide. A promise to "bide awa'" was enough to get him off!

June 16 1926

Tonight the Forfar Presbytery is in jubilant mood (a rare emotion for Presbyterians, perhaps!) because of the recovery of the Records of the Forfar Presbytery 1662-1683.

They had been located at Sotheby's Auction in London but thanks to the action of Reverend Miller of Inverarity Church, the Records had been withdrawn from the sale and returned to Mrs Stirton of Sidlaw House, Newtyle who had returned them to the Presbytery.

The book consisted of 152 pages, folio, in manuscript, bound in calf skin and clasped by thongs of the same material. The book dealt with the distressing events of the Second Episcopacy in Scotland, and in Forfar in particular in the reign of Charles II.

The Presbyterians were compelled to acknowledge the Episcopacy but as long as they kept their heads down, in practice they were left alone.

But there are frequent references to "speaking at conventicles" (illegal religious meetings where presumably the Episcopalians were criticised) and "slaughters" for doing so.

Papists are to be brought to book, while schoolmasters are to be compelled to declare their allegiance to the Episcopalian cause. There are sundry other more mundane matters referring to Ministers' stipends and glebes and details of the visitation of all 10 Churches and parishes in Forfar Presbytery in 1676.

This book had to be submitted every year to Archbishop Sharp just to make sure that the Forfar Presbyterians were behaving themselves under the Episcopacy. It was a fascinating insight into the religious life of Forfar and District in the 17th century.

June 17 710

Give or take a week or two (or possibly even a year or two) this was the day on which St Curitan, sometimes called Boniface, founded Restenneth Priory, although whether it was called that then is a matter of some doubt.

Boniface was working for the Pictish King Nectan who was very keen to bring Pictland (it would be a historical absurdity to talk about Scotland) into line with the rest of Europe and to accept the Ecclesiastical character and the authority of the Pope — something that causes a few feathers to flutter to this day.

Its history since that time is obscured in the mists of antiquity but we are told the Robert the Bruce's infant son was buried there while some claim that Kenneth McAlpine was buried there — hence its name "the resting place of Kenneth" being corrupted to Restenneth.

It is a shame that the medieval history of Forfar and district is not really very well known, but it is hard to imagine that Malcolm Canmore and his Queen Margaret did not at least visit the place on occasion, for Forfar people are never slow to tell everyone that "Malcolm Canmore used tae bide here, ye ken".

It has certainly had a chequered history, the buildings being knocked down and then rebuilt, but it remains a beautiful quiet spot and does a great deal to enhance the tourist attraction of Forfar.

Occasionally religious services are still held there in the open air, and on a nice summer day, it is certainly a good walk.

Restenneth Priory

June 18 1916

It was a lovely Sunday morning in Newmonthill.

Some were preparing to go to Church, others were out enjoying the fresh air and bright warm sunshine, children were playing in the street, one family in particular enjoying telling everyone that a little sister had been born the night before.

Already some of the neighbours had been in to "see the bairn" and a healthy wee thing she was as well with a good pair of lungs. Handshakes were exchanged with the father, relatives were informed, and indeed most of the town shared the joy.

It was one of these mornings when the war seemed so far away, and even one of these mornings when one wondered why there had to be a war. But war there was, and one of the Forfar soldiers had to return from his two weeks leave.

Already he had seen a fair amount of trenches and had developed an understandable dislike of sergeants and sergeant-majors, but he had enjoyed his leave with his wife and children and was reconciled to going back, although he hoped to get more leave by the New Year.

Slowly he walked down Newmonthill with his kilt, kitbag and glengarry with the ribbons blowing in the gentle breeze. His wife didn't want to come to the station because she hated farewells and decided to go in and see the new baby instead. "I'll let ye see the bairn" she said, and a few seconds later she held up the newly born at the window.

The soldier smiled and waved back and continued to the station — sad, and yet proud and happy that he had seen the new bairn. The new bairn lived to a ripe old age ... but they never saw the soldier again.

June 19 1939

A half-holiday at Forfar Academy this afternoon, and one much appreciated by the pupils in this fine weather.

Rector Dr Allardice ("Wee Jimmie" as he was commonly known although not to his face!) was delighted to grant this holiday because of the success of Margaret Mackay Hardie who came out top of the University of St Andrews Bursary Competition, winning a Simson Bursary of £50 for four years, the time required for an MA Honours course.

118 pupils from all over Scotland and England took the examination, and Margaret's three subjects were English, French and German. This was one of the many successes of Forfar Academy in those days, although no-one had ever topped the St Andrews University list since Douglas Black of eight or nine years previously.

Margaret had won the Dux Medal and the medals for English, French, German, Latin and Music the previous year, and was clearly a "clever lassie", as *The Forfar Dispatch* put it.

The award would be a great financial benefit to Margaret and her widowed mother, and everyone wished her a great deal of success when she went to St Andrews University "the College of the Scarlet Gown" in the autumn.

In the 1930s, University could be a financial struggle for many students in the absence of grants, but the Simson Bursary would solve quite a few problems.

1939 was not of course the best year in world history to be starting a University career, but Margaret would go on to do very well at University becoming a teacher of English and eventually a Lecturer in Methods at Dundee College of Education.

June 20 1837

It is easy to imagine the excitement this midsummer evening of the "Drummer" as he went round the town with the news.

Usually he had nothing very interesting to report — a ship or two arriving in Dundee, a landslide in France, a heavy and unexpected flood in Aberdeenshire, an outbreak of illness in Brechin, and no-one really paid any attention to him.

In fact some of the local youths on these summer evenings had nothing better to do than throw stones and mud at him, so much so that he had to ask for the protection of a soldier sometimes.

But tonight, they would listen at the Cross and both High Streets, in the Lappie Dub, the Greens and up by Windmill Hill where they were thinking of building some sort of stopping point for these new railway contraptions that were coming.

Yes, tonight, he had the news that the King was dead! King William IV had died in his sleep at the age of 71 after a lifetime of dissipation and so much stupidity so that he was commonly referred to as "Silly Billy".

But today someone had come on horseback at full gallop from Dundee with the news that the King was dead. And who was going to be the new King? Well, there was the thing! For the first time since before the Highland rebellions, there was no King!

There would be a Queen, a young girl aged 18 called Princess Alexandrina Victoria, a bonny wee girl according to the few people who had actually seen her, now the Queen of Great Britain!

"Aye, they'll lusten to me the nicht!" thought the Drummer as he set out on his trip round the town!

June 21 1918

The Forfar "comb out" continued.

This was the term used to conscript every person that they could to fight in the war with even reserved occupations like bakers now being enlisted.

Tribunals were set up in every town — in the case of Forfar, Bailie Lamb, James Black, Mr JL Alexander the solicitor, and the representative from the military a Lieutenant Gourlay.

The wisdom of the "comb out" was much discussed after the war with even Prime Minister Lloyd George weakening on the policy, (but only after the event).

Surely the war effort would have been better served by men like bakers, blacksmiths, mechanics, loom operators and others doing their jobs on the home front rather than being unwilling soldiers.

At this stage of the war, however, although the news from Europe was now looked upon with suspicion as there had been so much propaganda and sheer lies in the past, advances seemed to be being made.

Yet the casualty list was appallingly high, and more men were needed at the front. Tonight, for example, at the Tribunal in the Town Hall, we had the case of a 35-year-old baker in poor health being conscripted, and a 43-year-old man who already had two sons in the Army being compelled to enlist!

Even though the two Forfar men on the tribunal, Bailie Lamb and James Black did their best to "save" them, the will of Lieutenant Gourlay was sufficient to over-rule them, and thus we had several more Forfar men unwillingly enlisted for what President Woodrow Wilson of the United States described as "the European slaughterhouse".

June 22 1897

Today was Queen Victoria's Diamond Jubilee, much celebrated in Forfar as well as everywhere else.

It was a holiday, and that, if nothing else, made the town happy. She had been Queen for 60 years and there were now very few people around who could recall the time when she was not Queen.

It would be true to say that opinions were divided about the Queen. There were those who "couldna see by her" in term of how good she was.

The Forfar Herald, for example, talks about how great she was, talking about her reign being so "prosperous and beneficent" when a walk round Market Street, Newmonthill and even Castle Street might give a rather different impression, and one wonders whether there is an element of tongue in cheek.

There were others who referred to her in the Forfar vernacular as a "thrawn ald bitch" and recall the times when she went into a prolonged sulk when her husband Prince Albert died in 1861. Her family were strange as well, and she had never ever come to Forfar.

Nevertheless, this was a day to celebrate her with parades, flags and a bonfire on Bummie, even though the weather was not all that good. Some sang genuine patriotic songs, although there were one or two unofficial renderings of "My floppy German sausage" sung when Albert was still alive, and then when she was consorting with John Brown, it became "My floppy Scottish sausage".

What, on earth, were they referring to?

The Parish Church, Forfar.

United Service

ON THE OCCASION OF THE

CORONATION

OF

Their Majesties

KING GEORGE V.

AND

QUEEN MARY.

Thursday, 22nd June, 1911

at Eleven o'clock a.m.

Order of Service for Coronation Service, 22 June, 1911

June 23 1932

A huge crowd at Cunninghill saw local professional Robert Dornan win the Scottish Professional Golfers Association trophy.

He made history by being the first professional to win the trophy on his home course with an aggregate score of 286, the lowest in the history of the competition. His four rounds of 72, 69, 70 and 75 told of an admirable consistency. His worst round was his last in which he started badly and had three 5s on the way in.

The weather was superb on both days, and Dornan was eight ahead after the first day and finished eleven ahead of second placed James Adam of Barassie, while last year's winner Mark Seymour of Crow Wood was well down the list with 302.

The very popular Dornan was chaired off the final green to the Clubhouse. At the close of proceedings, Provost Tom Hanick presented to Robert Dornan the White Horse Cup with a replica and a gold medal as well as a cheque for £32 10 shillings.

Mr JN Strachan, the Club president, expressed pleasure at Forfar being asked to host this prestigious tournament. Mark Seymour, last year's winner, congratulated Robert Dornan and praised the Cunninghill course which provided a very good test for the golfers.

This being 1932, the golf course saw a huge influx of men who had walked out from the town because they were unemployed or on short time working.

They watched as much of the game as they could from the road, and when some of them managed to gain entrance to the course itself, a blind eye was turned to this illegal invasion — quite simply because they clearly did not have the money and it was good, in any case, to see them supporting the Forfar man.

June 24 1920

A clear sign of the new world beginning to appear out of the debris of the old appears today in *The Forfar Herald.*

Contracts have been awarded for the building of the "Lilybank Cottages" to the east of the town. Forfar was ahead of the game in this respect for the municipal building of houses was by no means common until later in the 1920s, but Forfar had fought hard for Government support for this project to the east of the town.

No-one could deny that some of the houses in Forfar were terrible, some of them not even waterproof anymore and the more perceptive were able to point out that the recent flu epidemic had been severely aggravated as much by sub-standard housing and awful hygiene facilities as anything else.

It was intended to build 40 houses in the Lilybank area, not far from the new Lowson Memorial Church, and now the contracts had been awarded for Bricklayers, Joiners, Plumbers, Plasterers, Slaters, Painters and Glaziers at the total cost of £7553 8 shillings and 4 pence.

All this would also provide much needed employment in the town as well, but it was still looked upon as an enormous undertaking.

On these beautiful summer days, it was a fine walk out to the east of the town, to observe the site and to try to imagine the houses beginning to arise. Rumour had it that the houses were going to have indoor toilets which flushed! A brave new world, indeed!

June 25 1930

This Wednesday afternoon saw a very distinguished visitor indeed to present the prizes to Forfar Academy pupils at the Reid Hall.

This was no less a person than Herbert Jennings Rose, Professor of Greek at St Andrews University, invited by Dr J Allardice, whose first year this was as Rector of Forfar Academy.

Rose had been Professor at St Andrews since 1927, and had already produced several fine works of Classical scholarship. He would remain there until 1953.

In 1911 he had married a lady called Eliza Plimsoll, the daughter of the famous Samuel Plimsoll, the man responsible for all ships having the "plimsoll line" to prevent them being overloaded with cargo.

Rose, a Canadian by birth, said that he had never been to Forfar before but had been delighted to come here to see the town from which came so many fine scholars to St Andrews University.

Having met the staff of the school, he could now understand why Forfar Academy produced so many great pupils. He said that the main thing in life was not making money but educational learning. He then presented the prizes, having a particularly long chat with Jeannie Farquharson who had won the prizes in Latin and Greek.

The prizes having been presented, the rest of the afternoon was spent in musical entertainment under the direction of Mr Ross, the Music teacher. It included songs, recitations, violin solos and piano solos, something that Professor Rose clearly enjoyed, as did Bailie Hanick and the rest of the platform party.

June 26 1903

Today's *Forfar Herald* contains a lovely contributed piece about the trip of the Forfar shopkeepers who managed to get to Ayr and back on the one day.

Ayr is a fair bit away at the best of times, but in 1903 it was looked upon as almost the ends of the earth, and a place to go to only if you were very rich and had loads of time to get there and back.

But the intrepid shopkeepers left Forfar Station at 6.00 in the morning (a beautiful morning where "the alluvial plains of Strathmore were seen to their advantage under the radiant light of the rising sun") and their particular railway connection allowed them to bypass Glasgow, as it were. Their route was through Coatbridge and Airdrie, a different part of Scotland, before they reached "Auld Ayr" in loads of time to visit all that they were likely to want to see of the beautiful town and the Burns Country.

This was of course the attraction, because Forfar was famous for the number of lovers of Burns that it had, and the writer expressed his hope that one day, Forfar may produce a man of the stamp of Burns.

Provost McDougall was with the company and while they were enjoying their tea and refreshments, he stood up and praised the Committee of the shopkeepers for arranging this trip.

The train journey home, we can imagine, was a pleasant one with many of the company, no doubt well "refreshed", obliging with a few of the Burns songs. The train eventually arrived home at shortly after 10 o'clock at night, after what was universally described as a wonderful jaunt.

Opening of Reid Park, 1896

241

Tails Weavers before parade in 1896 for the opening of the Reid Park

June 27 1896

Today was one of Forfar's greatest ever days, according to *The Courier,* whereas *The Forfar Herald* talks of little else!

It was the opening of The Reid Public Park by John Morley MP, with Provost McDougall in attendance as well, and it attracted a crowd from all over the county and beyond. When the late Victorians celebrated something, they certainly did it in style.

The main attraction was the GOM (the Grand Old Man) of Forfar, ex-Provost Peter Reid, now 92 and a little frail, but still robust enough to enjoy the celebrations, including a parade of all the trades, actors dressed up as Kentucky Minstrels and various other entertainments, and the occasion was blessed with lovely weather.

From early in the morning, Forfar Station had been a busy place as ex-Forfarians arrived from as far afield as Glasgow and Aberdeen to join in the celebrations.

People had come to see old Peter himself, sitting happily and contentedly in his carriage as he drove round the town waving to all those who loved him.

He had been a great supporter of the Anti-Corn Law League and was a genuine philanthropist and lover of the town in an age when we hear a great deal about grasping capitalists, of whom there were, sadly, not a few in Forfar.

Peter had built his confectionery business and his rock would remain famous long after this death. The Reid Park was a veritable wonder, situated in exactly the right spot on the lower slopes of Balmashanner with a lovely view over the town, and 125 years later, no-one could really argue that it had not proved its value.

John Morley MP opens the Reid Park in 1896

June 28 1941

Today in the midst of the Second World War, Forfar received news that one of its best ever scholars and teachers had passed away.

This was Adam S Thomson, Rector of Forfar Academy for the very long time of 1897 until 1925. He died in Mooroopna, Victoria, Australia at the age of 81.

Forfar Academy had a great tradition of excellence in education when he arrived there, and it continued with the arrival of Adam S Thomson or AST as he was commonly referred to by his colleagues.

A native of Aberdeen and with a BA in Classics from Oxford, Mr Thomson combined great ability as a teacher with a high level of scholarship, and a strong and commanding personality, and under his guidance Forfar Academy became one of the best schools in Scotland.

He had the ability to inspire his teachers to love both their pupils and their subject, and he was famous for the encouragement that he gave even his poorest pupils.

He steered the ship in difficult times of poverty and the horrors of the Great War in which so many of his colleagues and former pupils fell, but how appropriate it was that when a Good Fellowship or "Virtutis Causa" medal was established, it was named in his honour!

AST left an indelible mark on so many of his pupils, that many felt a deep sorrow at his passing even many years after they had left school.

The Forfar Dispatch quotes a very apposite piece of Latin from Horace in "non omnis moriar" — I will not die entirely.

Neither he has! A great man was AST!

June 29 1932

It was early this morning in Dundee that the by-election result was announced, and it was the time that Labour almost made it.

Normally Forfar and Labour are not on speaking terms, but this time they came very close. The circumstances were unusual to put it mildly. There was a National Government in power and this was a by-election, caused by the elevation to the peerage of the previous MP.

There were several other factors — one was the presence of a Scottish Nationalist (unusual for 1932). The Labour candidate, Tom Kennedy, had been an MP before. He had served Kirkcaldy, having won there in a famous by-election of March 4 1921 with the slogan of "March forth on March fourth!"

He very nearly did the same here, charming the electorate with his soft Aberdeenshire accident and his impassioned oratory about the traitorous Ramsay MacDonald, showing clear and genuine concern for the unemployed and the hated "Means Test".

The Scottish Nationalist candidate Douglas Emslie was an amiable eccentric going around with a kilt and a balmoral, but he did enough to sway the result by amassing almost 2,000 votes while Kennedy was less than 1,000 short of Colonel Charles Kerr, the National Government candidate.

Admittedly it was a low poll, but it was also perhaps a certain piece of defiance from Forfar's jute workers, railway workers, bakers and blacksmiths at what the National Government were doing in the name of solving the economic problems of the country by their "Doctor's Mandate" — which involved more unemployment!

June 30 1906

Today in Newmonthill, Forfar business man Alexander Robertson Angus died at the tragically young age of 48.

He was born in Aberdeenshire where he learned to become a blacksmith and then, having married a Dundonian girl, moved to Forfar where he set up a Coachbuilder's Business in Littlecauseway.

His Marriage Certificate in 1880 describes him as a Master Coachbuilder. For a while his business was successful and his family prospered, but in Victorian society, success and prosperity are slender, precarious things.

His family suffered a few bereavements in his children, and the rise of the motor car, the horseless carriage, did not help. It would have required a huge investment to diversify, and it would have been unrealistic to do this in a small town like Forfar.

Depression followed and the all too prevalent availability of alcohol applied the finishing touches. Bankruptcy came soon and the downward spiral continued. Yet he remained a well-known and sociable character in the town with a wide knowledge of Burns poetry until the turn of the year when he was seen less often.

His Death Certificate said that he had been suffering from "mania a potu" (madness from drinking) otherwise known as the "delirium tremens" for three months before lapsing into a coma two days ago.

His funeral was well attended by his fellow townspeople, and he was an excellent and tragic example of what could happen in Victorian and Edwardian times when things went wrong, and when drink took over. It was little wonder that the Reverend Caie of the Old Kirk was so resolutely set against alcohol.

North School, Primary One, 1953

1904

In This Year
Traders in Forfar

W. CALLANDER,

General Drapery Warehouseman,

62 and 64 CASTLE STREET,

- - - FOR - - -

FLANNELS, BLANKETS, HOUSEHOLD LINEN,
FLOCK, HAIR & STRAW MATTRESSES,
LINOLEUM, FLOORCLOTH, CURTAINS, & TABLE COVERS,
DRESS AND MANTLE MAKING. Perfect Fit and Style guaranteed.
SEWING MACHINES of Renowned Makes always on hand, Old ones taken in
exchange. Highest Prices allowed as part payment on New ones.
WRINGERS, MANGLES, BRASS & IRON BEDSTEADS ALWAYS
KEPT IN STOCK.

Drapery and House Furnishing Warehouse,

62 and 64 CASTLE ST., FORFAR.

⇢ THE FORFAR ↢

HAT and CAP SHOP

- - HAS ALWAYS A FINE SELECTION OF - -

SILK AND FELT HATS, CHRISTY'S & TOWNEND'S, LONDON.
MEN'S, AND BOYS' CAPS, TIES, BRACES,
SHIRTS, CUFFS, COLLARS, FRONTS, GLOVES, MUFFLERS,
HOSIERY, UMBRELLAS, WATERPROOF COATS,
TRAVELLING BAGS, TRUNKS, &c., Largest and Best Selection in Town,
MEN'S, YOUTHS', & BOYS' READY-MADE CLOTHING
OF EVERY DESCRIPTION.
SUITS TO ORDER AT MODERATE PRICES.
BUTCHERS' & GROCERS' JACKETS & APRONS A SPECIALTY AT

THE FORFAR HAT AND CAP SHOP,

60 Castle St., Forfar.

W. CALLANDER, Proprietor.

K

Juvenile Highland Costumes.

Stocked in TARTAN and TWEED.
Special sizes made to order.

Sporrans, Brooches, Caps, and other accessories to match either style. Clan Tartan Ties kept in the following Clans:—

Cameron	Leslie	Macdonald
Campbell	Lindsay	Mackenzie
Farquharson	Murray	Mackintosh
Ferguson	Mackay	McNeill
Fraser	Menzies	Robertson
Forbes	Macgregor	Sinclair (green)
Graham	McLaren	Stewart (royal)
Gordon	McLean	Stewart (hunting)
Kennedy	McLeod	Sutherland

THE BEST and THE NEWEST are the characteristic qualities of our stock. To give the best value possible has always been our aim. Our reputation as a Leading Drapery House has been raised, and will be maintained on that principle.

READY - MADE SUITS AND OVERCOATS. — The contracts for our Winter stock of Tailor-made Garments have been placed most advantageously, and we are in a position to maintain our popularity as the leading Clothing House.

NEWEST LONDON STYLES
IN LADIES' AND MISSES' JACKETS AND COATS.
Novelties always added as they appear.

ALEX. DALGETY,

57 EAST HIGH STREET, FORFAR.

TAILORING, DRESSMAKING, MILLINERY, and GENERAL DRAPERY GOODS.

Adam Farquharson

Masonic Hall Buildings

CASTLE STREET (Opposite Post Office)

HAS always on hand a very large and carefully selected Stock of GENTLEMEN'S SUITINGS in Serges, Vicunas, and Tweeds; also, a very fine range of TROUSERINGS at very reasonable prices, and guarantees to every Customer a perfect fit and first-class finish.

DRESS GOODS.

All the newest and best designs made up by first-class Dressmakers.

MILLINERY.

Felt and Straw Hats, Ribbons, Wings, Ornaments, &c., at very Low Prices.

LADIES' and MISSES' JACKETS.

Capes, Fur Necklets, and Muffs, a very large choice at prices that will suit you.

READY-MADE CLOTHING.

For Men, Youths', and Boys', good and cheap. Nothing of a trashy nature kept in stock.

WORKING CLOTHING.

Grocers', Butchers', and Painters' Jackets and Aprons. Dongaree, Serge, and Tweed Jackets, Cord, Mole, and Tweed Trousers, &c.

Flannels, Blankets, Plaidings, Flannelettes, &c.

ADAM FARQUHARSON, Masonic Hall Buildings.

Fenton's Restaurant.

DINNERS.

LUNCHEONS.

TEAS.

SUPPERS.

SANDWICHES.

ONLY THE BEST LIQUORS KEPT.

JOHN M. FENTON,

FORFAR.

OUR THOUSAND
COPIES OF THE
F O R F A R
D I S P A T C H
ARE DISTRIBU-
TED GRATIS IN FORFAR AND
DISTRICT EVERY THURSDAY,
AND ADVERTISERS USING ITS
COLUMNS WILL FIND IT A
CHEAP & EFFECTIVE MEDIUM
FOR PLACING THEIR NOTICES
BEFORE THE PUBLIC EYE

PRINTED AND PUBLISHED BY
O L I V E R   M c P H E R S O N
85 EAST HIGH STREET

JOB PRINTING
of every description

. THE . . .

Forfar Review

Friday Morning. ONE PENNY.

Largest Circulation of any Newspaper in Forfar or District.

PRINTER AND PUBLISHER,

J. MACDONALD,

OFFICE, 10 East High Street, FORFAR.

Printing

The attention of Tradesmen, Merchants, and the general public is directed to the great facilities afforded in the FORFAR REVIEW Office for the efficient execution of Letterpress Printing in all its Departments.

Do you know

KALAC?

If not, be sure you do
before purchasing
a new Cycle, Motor Cycle or Car.

"Swift"
"Triumph"
and other makes.

⟋⟍ KALAC CYCLES ⟍⟋
From £7, with Free Wheel, complete, and Honest Value.

SIDE LINES. ⟍⟋

Gramophones, Phonographs, Records, Footballs,
Golf Clubs, Golf Balls, Golf Bags,
Singer Sewing Machines, Accessories, and Repairs.

JOHN KILLACKY,
NEXT POST OFFICE.

H

D. Mitchell Laing

(*Successor to C. Mitchell & Co.*)

Portrait,

Landscape, and

Architectural

Photographer.

Dealer in Picture Frames and

Photographic Mouldings.

Studios

46 and 48 East High Street, Forfar.

and at Elm Bank, Kirriemuir.

WILLIAM MOFFAT & Co.,

SLATERS,

95 WEST HIGH ST., & 16 NURSERY FEUS, FORFAR.

ROOF LIGHTS, CHIMNEY CANS, CEMENT (best London)—
Large Stock always on hand.

Orders in Town and Country punctually attended to.

James Neill,

Professor of Music and Dancing,

46a CASTLE ST., FORFAR.

Private Lessons given, and Private Classes arranged by appointment.

String Bands supplied to Concerts and Assemblies.
Pianoforte and Violin for Evening Parties.

PIANOS FOR HIRE BY THE NIGHT, MONTH, OR YEAR.

George Guthrie,

Wholesale and Retail Fish and Game Dealer,

58 EAST HIGH STREET,

FORFAR.

Reliable Pianos

A Really GOOD Cheap Instrument.

PATERSON, SONS, & Co.'s

£20 PIANO

Cash or Instalments,
with Iron Frame, Check Action, Full Trichord, and
Latest Improvements—Hand carved panel.

SOLE AGENTS FOR

STEINWAY PIANOS.   SQUIRE PIANOS.
BECHSTEIN PIANOS.   ESTEY ORGANS.
THE "ANGELUS" PIANO PLAYER.

Paterson, Sons, & Co.
PRINCES ST., PERTH
REFORM ST., DUNDEE
And at Edinburgh, Glasgow, Arbroath, &c.

xcvi

Printing
of every
Description

Done Promptly
in the
Best Styles

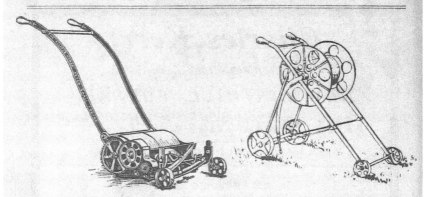

Peter Small,

ENGINEER AND BLACKSMITH,

CASTLE STREET, FORFAR.

Machines of our own Make.

The "ECLIPSE," the SCYTHE," and the "PONY" LAWN MOWERS are light,
   Durable, and Easy to Work, and may be relied upon to give satisfaction.   They are
   equal if not superior to other makes.

The "PERFECTION" PATENT HOSE REELS are now being appreciated, and the
   increasing demand for them is their best testimonial.   Commended by the Royal
   Caledonian Horticultural Society, Edinburgh.

Our PLAIN HOSE REELS are being sought after.

Our GARDEN ENGINES have attained a self-made reputation.

Our "CHAMPION" LIQUID MANURE PUMP, every farmer should have.

MACHINES and LAWN MOWERS of any make Repaired and Sharpened.

REAPERS, BINDERS, and other Machines Over-hauled and repaired.

MATCH PLOUGHS made and Re-mounted.

RAILINGS of all designs made and fitted-up.   All sorts of Jobbing Work done.

HORSE-SHOEING done with care and ability.

All Orders receive Punctual and Personal attention, and are Substantially and Tastefully executed.   ESTIMATES GIVEN.

c

ci

A. D. Strachan,

Wood & Coal Merchant,

Forfar Saw Mill.

 Telephone No. 27.

HOME WOOD OF ALL KINDS,
Also, FIREWOOD, KINDLING, &c.

COAL DEPOT—
Old Railway Station, Victoria Street.

BEST ENGLISH HOUSEHOLD COALS AND NUTS.
SCOTCH CAKING COALS AND NUTS (similar to English).
BEST WISHAW OR HAMILTON HOUSEHOLD COALS AND NUTS.
BEST DUNFERMLINE SPLINT, JEWEL, AND STEAM COALS.
ANTHRACITE, SMALL COALS FOR VINERIES.
BRIQUETTES, COKE, &c.

SALT AND WHITING.

Any of above delivered in Large or Small Quantities at current prices.

ORDERS
which will be promptly attended to, may be sent to
Office, Forfar Saw Mill, or House, 10 Manor Street.

cvi

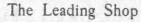

George R. Fowler,

CHEMIST,

38 CASTLE STREET, FORFAR.

Photographic Materials in Stock.

Potatoes, Apples, Carrots, Onions, &c.

Coals, Lime, and Feeding Stuffs, and such like Commodities.

Those wishing a FIRST-RATE ARTICLE, at a MODERATE PRICE,

. . PLEASE APPLY TO . .

David Whyte,

Potato Merchant,

5 STRANG STREET, FORFAR.

C. THOM & SON,

Billposters & Advertising Agents,

5 LITTLE CAUSEWAY, FORFAR.

POSTING and DELIVERING promptly executed in Town and Country. The most Effective Distributors for the District.

THOSE WHO STUDY
. . . ECONOMY . . .

SHOULD use our celebrated BREADS, FRENCH, and (FINE) HOUSEHOLD, PASTRY and FANCY BREADS in great variety—Fresh daily. CAKES of every description, including Plum, Seed, Sultana, Citron, Rice, Political, Sponge, Fruit, &c. MARRIAGE and CHRISTENING CAKES. JELLIES, TARTLETS, CREAMS. DISHES COVERED. FESTIVAL and MARRIAGE SUPPER PARTIES Supplied. . . . .

WILLIAM LOW & CO.
BREAD & BISCUIT BAKERS
THE FORFAR BAKERY. . . . .

House Furnishing Department.

EVERY HOUSEHOLD REQUISITE SUPPLIED.
RANGES, TILED GRATES, TILE HEARTHS, INTERIORS, &c.
BUILT IN AND FINISHED COMPLETE BY EXPERIENCED WORKMEN.
MAKE YOUR SELECTION.   WE DO THE REST.

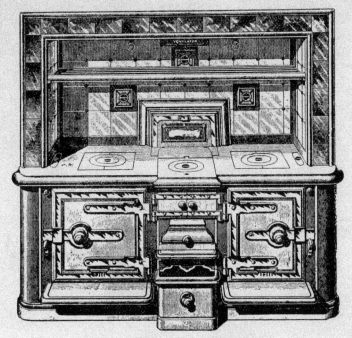

THE "DON" RANGE.

Unsurpassed by anything of its kind. It has no rival. It stands unequalled. Perfect in fit and finish. Can be operated by the most inexperienced. This is a Range of the very highest quality, and is the result of many years close experimental research, and is designed to meet the requirements of those who desire a Range suitable for the best Cooking and simplicity in working. Efficient and economical.

ALL THE NEWEST AND UP-TO-DATE GOODS.

DAVID IRONS & SONS

14 EAST HIGH STREET, FORFAR.

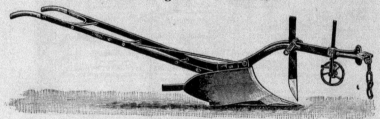

July

July 1 1938

A rather special football match was staged tonight at Strathmore Park in aid of funds for Forfar Infirmary.

£11 was raised from a game staged between Forfar Old-timers and Kirriemuir Old-timers. Forfar won 7-5. Most of them had given up the ghost a good few years ago (or should have!), but some were still active.

There were two Scotland Internationalists in Alec Troup and David McLean, and Troup in particular showed that he still had the touch and the ability to pass a ball, even though the old saying "auld age disnae come itsel" was fairly obvious as well with the pace dropping alarmingly in the second half on a rather warm midsummer night!

But 12 goals were scored and Forfar's goalkeeper Dod Scott saved a penalty kick.

Kirriemuir had four brothers called Newton; the clash between Alec Newton and Davie McLean, both not far off their 50th birthday and more than a little overweight, was the highlight of the night with both of them quite happy to do a little good-natured "bouncing" and "bumping".

At the end of the game, Bailie Inverarity put his hand into his pocket and treated all the players to a fish supper after their strenuous exertions, and, thankfully, the services of the ambulance men on hand were not required!

Forfar's team was Scott, Linton and Soutar; Bruce, Glen and Moir; Black, Menzies, Gerrard, Troup and McLean. Eck Gerrard scored twice, and the other goals were scored by Alec Troup, Walter Linton (with a penalty), Bob Black, Willie Menzies and Alec Glen.

July 2 1875

Today the Reverend George J Caie was inducted to the charge of Forfar Parish Church.

The Revered J Watt of Glenisla "preached him in", there followed a lunch at the County Hotel and then a soiree in the evening at the Reid Hall.

It was a happy occasion and brought to an end a rather unsavoury series of events which reflected little credit on the Church of Scotland.

The previous year the Reverend Caie had been appointed Assistant to the previous incumbent Reverend Stevenson. When Reverend Stevenson took ill with palsy, Caie naturally took over and proved himself popular with the congregation.

On the retirement of Stevenson, Caie naturally applied for the job. Some of the Presbytery objected for reasons best known to themselves, but the recently passed Patronage Act of 1875 now was applied, and as the congregation overwhelmingly "signed the call", there was now little that could be done by Presbytery to stop this happening.

The Patronage Act of 1875 resolved the issue which had caused the Disruption of 30 years previously when so many of the Church of Scotland left because a Minister had to be appointed by "royal assent".

Why Presbytery caused trouble on this issue we will really never find out, although there was a suspicion of "collusion" between the ageing Stevenson and the young Caie.

In any case, it did not really matter because "vox populi" was now important in the Church of Scotland, and Caie proved himself a very able and popular, albeit occasionally strict and unbending, Minister of the Forfar Parish Church for the next 33 years.

Forfar Academy Medal Boards, for Latin, Mathematics and the Dux

July 3 1925

The Prize Giving at Forfar Academy was a remarkable one.

In the first place it was the last Prize Giving of Rector Adam S Thomson, who was now retiring and being replaced by his brother Ben Thomson, both of them excellent Rectors.

The guest of honour and the man who was to present the prizes was a distinguished former pupil, George Duncan, now Professor of Biblical Criticism at the University of St Andrews.

Professor Duncan, the son of a local tailor, had graduated with First Class Honours in Classics in 1906, studied further at Cambridge and various European Universities before being ordained as a Minister in 1915. He became chaplain to Field Marshall Sir Douglas Haig in the Great War.

He was awarded the OBE in 1919, and in later years, he would serve on the panel of theologians and classical scholars who would produce the New English Bible.

Clearly a very humble man and proud to be asked to address his old school, he told them how Forfar Academy was one of the best schools in Scotland, and raised a laugh and a cheer by recalling how he had played in the side which had once "whacked" Arbroath Academy (sic, but he probably meant Arbroath High School) at cricket!

Occasionally lapsing into Forfar dialect (to even more cheers) he said he was losing patience with people who said that they wanted to be lawyers and doctors when they were not really cut out for it.

"They did not go to Forfar Academy to learn to be good at any particular job; what they went to school for was to learn to be good men and good women".

July 4 1895

Lunanhead School had never seen such a crowd all its life as it did this wonderful summer evening.

They all came to hear the Liberal candidate for Forfarshire Constituency in the 1895 General Election. The town of Forfar itself of course voted in the Montrose Burghs constituency, but the landward areas voted in Forfarshire. Politics in the 1890s were strange.

The election was called because, seemingly, Earl Rosebery, the Liberal Prime Minister, was ill and fed up of being Prime Minister, a job for which he was manifestly unsuited.

Yet he was still leading the Liberals, although he was clearly far more interested in his race horses (one of which, Ladas, won the Derby in 1894).

The Liberal candidate for Forfarshire was Martin White. It was the first time that he had ever been to Lunanhead and he listened carefully when someone explained to him the difference between Lunanhead and "the Berricks".

He spoke well, attacking the sitting candidate, the Conservative Charles Ramsay, who had won a by-election last year. Then he embarked on his main plank which was the need to reform and possible even abolish the House of Lords, which was hereditary, totally unrepresentative and a block to progress whether in much needed social reform or in Home Rule for Ireland.

He had already been at the Murroes and was now to progress to Letham. Martin White duly won the seat for the Liberal Party, but in the general picture, it was Lord Salisbury's Conservatives who won, beating the unconvincing Liberals.

The Conservatives would now be in office for another ten years.

July 5 1945

Today Forfar voted in the General Election at the normal polling stations, but it was one of the strangest General Elections of them all.

Held less than two months after VE Day, only very few of the soldiers were home. A few, including some of the wounded, had been repatriated but most were awaiting demobilisation.

Of course, the war was still going on in the Far East; the real fear was that if Japan didn't surrender, all the soldiers who had done so well in Europe would be required for an invasion of Japan, in which the casualties would have been horrendous.

The soldiers were also voting, hence the reason why the results would not be declared for three weeks. There were two candidates for Montrose Burghs — John Maclay, a National Liberal (effectively a Conservative) and Thomas MacNair for Labour.

The Forfar Dispatch is pleased to note that everything in Forfar was very dignified and polite with no mud being slung about (that was not true of everywhere) and tells the story of how last Saturday night at the Cross the Labour candidates for Montrose Burghs and Forfarshire County said their bit, and then asked their crowd to stay and listen to their opponents as well!

The Forfar Dispatch has always been politically neutral but at one point makes an unfortunate comparison between the planned Nationalisation of Labour and the late regime of Germany.

Such partisan behaviour is far more pronounced in the national Press, but everyone seems to think that in three weeks' time, Winston Churchill, the hero of the hour, will still be Prime Minister.

July 6 1871

Today was the annual holiday, and the horse-hirers were making a fortune with hardly a horse left in town, as they were required to pull all the brakes that had been hired.

There was a tendency for works' outings to go to places like Airlie, Clova, and Loch Brandy, which were not served by the railway, although there were as always quite a few who went to Arbroath.

Summer holidays are of course heavily dependent on weather, and this particular Thursday did indeed see a drenching or two.

The Victoria Works (all 900 of the workers!) went to Monikie to visit the Panmure gardens and they were well entertained by their employer Jock Lowson junior while they were there.

The Lowson family may have made their fortune out of the town, but they were generally bright enough to realise that a lot of their wealth depended on them keeping the workers on their side, and this meant paying for the occasional outing for them. In any case, now that the American market had opened up again after their War, business was booming.

The choir of the Established Church with their leader Mr William Dowell went to Craighall in Blairgowrie; being a choir, they sang all the way there and back — although it was rumoured that on the way back, they sang a few songs which they would not have sung in Church including the rather notoriously naughty one about Queen Victoria complaining about "My floppy German sausage" when her late husband was feeling a bit "tired".

But everyone seemed to have enjoyed themselves in spite of a drenching or two in the rain. Life in 19th Century Forfar could be pleasant sometimes.

July 7 1916

These are anxious times in Forfar, and indeed the world. Everyone knows that there was a "push" which started in France about a week ago, but details are scarce about what is actually going on.

The Courier uses headlines like "Hitting Huns All Round" and "British Advance" but phrases like "resisting the counter attack" tend to indicate that all the action at this River called the Somme in France is not a total success, and some of the London papers report large numbers of wounded coming back to England for treatment.

Today *The Forfar Herald* carries stories of three Forfar men who have written to their families in Forfar.

Lieutenant Frank A Ritchie was wounded in the first wave last Saturday (July 1), and his mother received a telegram telling her that, and then a couple of days later she received a letter from Frank himself saying "I was fortunate (sic) enough to be wounded. As we were going forward, I got a bullet from a machine gun in my left ankle. It is not what one would call serious, though the doctors think that one or two bones have been broken. We have done magnificently".

In addition 19-year-old Sergeant George Collie of the Forfar Company of the Highland Cyclist Battalion, whose father is Sergeant Collie of the Forfar Burgh Police, has been "accidentally wounded" but no details are forthcoming.

The wife of James Nicolson of the Motor Transport Corps who lives in East High Street has received word that he has a few broken ribs.

So far no fatalities of Forfar soldiers have been reported, but everyone is living in fear and apprehension.

Forfar Tennis Courts

July 8 1897

The report of Her Majesty's Inspectors was today published after their recent visit to all the Forfar schools, and the general impression was a very favourable one indeed.

The schools visited were Forfar Academy, Forfar East, Forfar West, Forfar North, Wellbraehead and Forfar Burgh School, and the Evening Classes for adults were also inspected.

The Academy is highly praised with "reading in all classes is distinct, fluent and satisfactorily expressive and the pupils show a ready comprehension of their lessons" with only two black marks.

"Better accommodation for cutting out in needlework is required" and "Lower Latin" is singled out for not showing "very accurate and successful teaching".

At the East School, "singing all over the school was done with fine tone and readiness" whereas at Wellbraehead, although the standards are generally very high, the infant classes have a problem in that "their discipline is not up to the mark of the rest of the school".

The Forfar Burgh School shows pupils and the school "in much better order this year" implying that things weren't too great last year, but there needs to be "more general answering" especially from the girls.

And the Inspectors were very impressed by the enthusiasm and standards of the Evening Classes where attendance was good. All this went down well with the Forfar School Board when it had time to digest it all; even allowing for the fact that an Inspector is only there for one day and can sometimes be deceived, education in Forfar does seem to be a satisfactory state in 1897.

July 9 1920

Tennis has made a welcome re-appearance after the Great War. Cricket has as yet failed to come back to Strathmore, but most other sports have — golf, bowls, football etc.

Today at the Reid Park courts, in perfect weather, the Forfar Ladies' Singles were finished with Miss Swinton getting the better of Miss Strachan. A large and interested crowd watched, fellow members of the club, augmented by local people enjoying their walk and curious about a sport that they didn't necessarily know very much about.

Although it was generally agreed that Miss Swinton came a little short of Suzanne Lenglen, "La Divine", the star of the age, nevertheless she played well enough to beat her opponent in straight sets 6-0, 6-4. Miss Strachan seemed off colour in the first set when she was well beaten by Miss Swinton's "effective cutting" but in the second set she was 4-0 up, before Miss Swinton reasserted herself to win 6-4.

It was a sporting and enjoyable contest, but Forfar were not doing so well in the team competitions, losing in the Midlands League to Dundee Stobswell and Arbroath 7-2 and 8-0 (with one game being drawn).

The local tennis players were a spirited bunch, however. They suffered, as most tennis clubs do, from the general perception of being snobby. This they strongly denied, although their subscription was generally agreed to be prohibitive — and like many other such institutions, their female members totally outnumbered their male ones.

Sadly in 1920 there was a very good reason for that.

July 10 1914

Today's edition of *The Forfar Herald* contains one of the great "might have been" stories of Forfar history.

The Labour Party had not put up a candidate for the December 1910 election. Last week — at a meeting in Arbroath attended by many members from Forfar — the Montrose Burghs Labour Party met Mr James Maxton. Their new Prospective Labour Candidate, a school teacher of Barrhead, was for the next General Election which would have to be held before the end of December 1915.

He then met more of his constituents at Glamis Market Muir the following day. Everyone seemed to be happy with the choice, and it was hoped that Labour might now be able to make an impression in Forfar.

After all, Forfar was not without a certain Socialist tradition dating back to the great days of Tommy Roy and the "lockout" of the factories in 1889.

Forfar had been solidly Liberal for some time, but there was a strong opinion in the town that wealth was unequally divided. Maxton looked like a good candidate. He had a slightly cadaverous appearance, but he was a good and impassioned orator on the subject of all that was wrong in the world.

Sadly, it never happened.

There was no General Election in 1914 or 1915, and by the time that a General Election was held in December 1918, the world had changed utterly. But Maxton might have made a difference in Forfar if he had been given a chance.

As it happened he became MP for Glasgow Bridgeton in 1922, having been opposed to the Great War. Talking of which, it is only three and a half weeks away, but *The Forfar Herald* gives not an inkling that there is anything untoward happening or about to happen in Europe!

Willie Bernard, Old Kirk organist and
Music Teacher at Forfar Academy

July 11 1932

Tonight at the Old Parish Church William Ditchburn Bernard LRAM ARCM was appointed as sole nominee to the position of Organist and Choirmaster.

A visiting committee had heard him, and had been pleased with his playing and the congregation accepted their recommendation. He had been born in Chirnside in 1904, but his family had moved to Dunfermline shortly thereafter, and he had been Organist and Choirmaster at Churches in Lochgelly, Auchterarder and Stirling before coming to Forfar.

A few months later he applied for and got the job of Music teacher at Forfar Academy, and so began a long relationship between William Bernard and both institutions.

He was clearly a very talented musician having composed some pieces himself, and he very soon became a well-known local character, universally referred to as "Wullie Bernard" and equally well loved.

He was a great teacher at the school, never failing to remind pupils that a Schools Inspector had told him in 1943 that Forfar Academy was the best for Music in Scotland.

Never a man to suffer fools gladly and certainly more than a little irascible on occasion, there was a story of he had once broken a window in the old Forfar Academy with a chair which had landed in the queue for the Arbroath bus!

This story owed a little to rhetorical exaggeration, one feels, and was hard to reconcile with the gentle, kind and humorous man that his pupils knew him to be.

At Church, he was an organist without peer and organised many musical concerts in the Church. Long into his retirement, he was always willing to come back in an emergency before his death in 1999.

July 12 1902

Tonight at 8.00 pm Major Douglas of Brigton arrived back at Forfar Station from the Boer War.

There had been a few other returns from the war as well, but this one was different. He was met by a flotilla of cyclists from the Angus Cycling Club of which he was the patron. His welcome and escort back to Brigton apparently came as a complete surprise to him.

About 50, with several lady cyclists among them, had assembled at their premises in Osnaburgh Street and, led by the local volunteer band, they cycled towards the station. As the train was somewhat delayed, the band played military airs to entertain the large crowd in front of the station which was gaily decorated in patriotic colours.

The Major got off the train, a few speeches were made and it was remarked that he was certainly looking well in his khaki. He and his wife got into the brake and were escorted along North Street, East High Street, West High Street and Glamis Road with the bands playing "See The Conquering Hero Comes".

Cheering crowds following him on his way to Brigton. A party was thrown for all the escorting cyclists, and dancing went on until late in the night. The occasion was marked with lovely weather.

Although cynics said that nothing was laid on quite on this scale for working class Privates who had also fought well and risked their lives, nevertheless it was right to pay tribute to this brave man who didn't need to have joined the conflict.

July 13 1920

The big argument tonight at the Forfar School Management Committee was whether or not prizes should continue to be awarded at schools on Forfar.

It is of course an age-old argument with whether one won prizes oneself or not being a key factor in one's viewpoint! An exception to this general rule appears to have been Forfar Academy's Rector Adam S Thomson.

An outspoken man and given the credit for the very high opinion in which Forfar Academy was held throughout Scotland, Rector Thomson who himself won cartloads of prizes at Oxford and elsewhere, tonight backed a motion put by Mrs Buchanan that the awarding of prizes should be discontinued and the money used for more educational facilities and excursions which would benefit the whole school.

Mr Thomson's feeling was that prizes bred "conceit and jealousy" and that the study of a subject should not be for any prize but for the sheer love of the subject. In addition, he felt that it was now time for the key word to be co-operation rather than competition.

The counter argument was a strong one as well, not least that the world into which the children were going was a very competitive one, and in any case it would be difficult to do away with prizes entirely because Forfar Academy had been fortunate enough to be endowed with prizes from outside bodies, not least the Edinburgh Angus Club who donated a medal for Latin.

The motion was eventually passed (in an emended form) but it was an argument that was likely to run and run for some time.

July 14 1859

A bizarre and unusual, although in fact rather trivial and petty case came before Forfar Sheriff Court today.

It was a case brought by Mr Pennycook, an auctioneer of Brechin, who was bringing a case against Mr Cooper, the Superintendent of Forfar Police, for wrongful arrest.

It concerned an incident at Forfar Market (presumably the Market at the Cross rather than the Cattle Market) when Mr Pennycook was selling some crockery, and in the course of his marketing said that his crockery was far superior to any crockery from the Mearns.

Mr Cooper, being a Mearns man, took umbrage at this and in what seems to be a gross over-reaction and misuse of his power, ordered the arrest of Mr Pennycook who was "shackled", taken to the Police Station in Chapel Street but nevertheless subsequently released.

It seemed a simple case, but it transpires that there had been "history" between the two of them and Mr Cooper's counter claim was that Mr Pennycook, on a previous occasion, had been found guilty in the Police Court of collecting a crowd and using terms that were injurious to Mr Cooper.

It seemed therefore that what Mr Pennycook had said on the subsequent occasion was a piece of revenge. One might have thought that a piece of advice along the lines of "Grow up, min" might have been more appropriate but the Sheriff himself over-reacted and remitted the case to the Supreme Court!

What happened then we do not know, but we would like to think that wiser counsel prevailed and that the two gentlemen concerned dropped the matter.

July 15 1927

The current medium of communication was "the wireless", otherwise known as the radio.

It had arrived in Scotland in about 1922 and by now most people had been able to listen to this strange device, although they were still ruinously expensive and away out of the pocket of working class families.

They were advertised occasionally by Methven and Simpson of Dundee, and a few wealthy people were able to afford one. Mainly the news and music was what was listened to, but occasionally sport and this year, one could have listened to live broadcasts of the Scotland v England International and both the Scottish and the English Cup finals.

Tonight we had the first ever known broadcast done by a Forfar man — and who else was it likely to have been than the ubiquitous James Black?

James Black,
well known football administrator

He delivered a talk to advertise the forthcoming Forfar Games at the Steele Park.

After talking eloquently about the power of sport to influence lives, he expatiated romantically about the view of the Games at the Steele Park with "a sea of faces eloquent of pleasant anticipation as they watch the brawny, kilt-clad, heavy-weights and lithe-limbed lads o' spring disport themselves in healthy rivalry on the green sward" while the lofty Grampians look on in "their frowning grandeur".

It was good stuff from Jimmy Black, and *The Forfar Herald,* aware that very few of its readers would have been able to hear what he said, printed his speech the following Friday. It read just as well as it sounded.

July 16 1931

Today is the Golden Anniversary of the Wedding of the Earl and Countess of Strathmore who were married in St Peter's Church, Petersham on July 16 1881.

Opinions of course vary about the Strathmores. It is of course an outrage that there is such a disparity of wealth between Glamis Castle on the one hand and those in the town suffering the ravages of unemployment and the depression of 1931 on the other.

And yet, it has to be admitted that there is a human side to the Earl who has been known occasionally to visit the West End Bar while "James" awaits in the carriage outside before "James" too is called inside for a quick "snifter" before driving the horses back to the Castle.

In addition he is a keen supporter of Forfar Athletic and attends frequently and in the summer frequently appears at the Lochside to see the cricket team named after him. (He was a cricketer himself in his younger day).

His wife the Countess is probably less well known and less well loved, and occasionally seems to lack the "human" side of her husband. But of course they are now extremely well connected following the wedding in 1923 of their daughter Elizabeth to the Duke of York.

Their elder granddaughter, Elizabeth, has been seen in Forfar now and again, and of course last year the younger girl, Margaret was actually born in Glamis Castle to great rejoicing.

The Forfar Dispatch sends its best wishes to the Strathmores on the occasion of their Golden Wedding, although the official occasion will be celebrated later.

July 17 1937

It was a glorious summer's day and Arbroath were in town for the derby at the Lochside.

Brechin were probably still the best team in the League, but any contest between Forfar and Arbroath is a mighty one, and today it attracted a great crowd augmented by a few Glasgow holidaymakers who had arrived in town last night and this morning, as this was the Glasgow Fair.

The reporter for the *Forfar Dispatch* reported that he had passed a wedding car on his way westwards through the town and had missed the procession, but today at the Lochside he saw another procession, this time of shame-faced Forfar batsmen walking back to the pavilion as the team were dismissed for 37.

There was no wind and the everything was still and quiet apart from the cheers of the Arbroath supporters whose long walk down from the station had, apparently, been punctuated by a lengthy stop at the Stag Hotel.

Only one man, Forbes, reached double figures, and it was all blamed on the excellent bowling of Arbroath's professional Blakey and their sprightly veteran Bob Sievwright, who had played for Scotland before the Great War!

There was also the "wicked wicket" which was soft after a lot of rain but now in the baking heat was beginning to be a "sticky dog". Even so, 37 was not very many and the tea interval was spent in stunned silence.

It had to be all out attack now, and professional Len Halstead and Jim Young bowled well and took Forfar close but Sievwright's son, young Bobby, scored enough to give Arbroath victory (just) on the "well-kept grave", as the *Forfar Dispatch* writer calls the Lochside wicket.

July 18 2004

Stuart Wilson did Forfar proud at the British Open Golf played at Royal Troon this week.

He was the only amateur to make the cut and earned the right to play on the final day. He thus won the Silver Medal for the leading amateur.

He had been given a place in the Open by virtue of having won the 2004 Amateur Championship at St Andrews earlier in the summer.

He was 27 years old on the day that the Open finished and the very fact that he was able to play in the same tournament as Ernie Els and Tiger Woods says it all.

The Open this year is well remembered for the fact that it went to an exciting play-off between Todd Hamilton, who eventually won it, and Ernie Els.

Stuart Wilson's best day was the first day when he scored 68 at three under par, and he was mentioned among the leaders after the first day in the newspapers and TV.

Hopes were high that he might even do better than he eventually did, but his other rounds, although very respectable were not so good. It was nevertheless a more than satisfactory performance even to play in such exalted company.

Stuart is the son of Neil Wilson, a man who played for Forfar Athletic in the late 1960s, and subsequently became a Director and Chairman.

Forfar has not had very many great golfing occasions — although there was Sandy Saddler in the 1950s and 1960s — but this was one such occasion. Jokes went around that when Stuart was seen with Ernie Els, some said, "Oh, there's that Farfar leddie and somebody else."

July 19 1905

A strange, alarming and rather bizarre case came before Provost Adamson this morning at the Police Court.

It concerned a man called James Samson, described as a labourer of no fixed abode (although it transpired that latterly he had been living with his son) who was charged with "attempting suicide, while in a state of intoxication, in a field at the junction of Brechin Road and Lochside Road to the alarm and annoyance of the lieges".

What was alarming and annoying the lieges was the sight of Samson lying on the ground and apparently drawing a knife back and forward across his throat.

He clearly did not actually kill himself, but his antics upset Mrs Shepherd and Mrs Mavor, who drew the attention of a passing policeman to the incident.

The policeman, Constable Stewart, said that there were a few marks on Samson's body, but he had not damaged himself other than by the consumption of an excessive amount of alcohol.

Mr Samson himself had no recollection of the incident, but Mr Samson's son was in court and said that his father had been drinking very heavily of late, but that he was confident that if his father stayed with him for a couple of days, he "would come to be all right."

Provost Adamson demurred, saying that he knew of a place where he would be well enough looked after, and where the drink "would be properly taken out of his system".

This was prison, and he was given 30 days!

Forfar Cricket Club, 1880s

July 20 1893

Today saw the publication of the results of the University of St Andrews Local Examinations. The girls of the pupils of the Misses Smith School For Girls (commonly known as the Ladies Seminary) in Academy Street, have all done well.

This year, Misses Smith had no pupils for the Senior Certificate (where they were astonishingly successful last year), but this year their pupils in the Junior Certificate have done exceptionally well, and this shows that there are good prospects for them doing better when they come to the Senior section in a year or two.

Pride of place goes to Mary Hill and Nelly Lowson who, out of 130 candidates, came 1st and 2nd in English. In History and Geography, the lowest of the Misses Smith's pupils reached 89%, while in French only one pupil succeeded in doing better than Nelly Lowson, Bessie Wedderburn and Katie Savage, while in German, Bessie Wedderburn came third.

So well done, says *The Forfar Herald* to these clever young ladies, from this Private School run by two sisters. Girls do not seem to have been as yet admitted to Forfar Academy, but this small private school, obviously only for children of wealthy families is an attempt to prove that girls could do as well as boys in education.

It was a small school, and seems to have functioned in a private house in Academy Street, but it had been in existence for a few years now and was clearly an asset to the town as well as perhaps making a point about girls.

July 21 1926

An argument took place at Forfar Town Council tonight about whether dancing should be allowed in the Reid Hall.

Bailie Peffers of the Property Sub-Committee had recommended that no dancing should be allowed in the Hall unless the people running such functions were prepared to wash the place out and to insist on dancing slippers being worn.

The problem was that Games Ball was imminent and they had not agreed to any such terms. The Horticultural Society had already been refused permission. Treasurer Lowson did not really see any problem in dancing. Councillor Chapman invoked the name of the late Peter Reid who gave the Hall to the Town. He did so for community use and would be upset to think that dancing was to be excluded.

The influential Councillor Tom Hanick then joined the argument, saying that the Reid Hall was never intended to be used exclusively as a cinema and that dancing was as appropriate a use of the facilities as anything else.

Provost Lowson then delivered his Solomon-like judgement (with a Forfar accent) that the Games Ball people should get their "shottie", as indeed should the Horticultural Society after the Flower Show, but Councillor Chapman accused them of evasion.

"There is no 'shottie' in it" he intoned. The question should be decided now.

After further discussion, the problem was remitted to the Property Committee to consider the matter once again. They could have another "shottie" at deciding the matter.

In the meantime the Games Ball and the Horticultural Society did indeed get their "shottie", and dancing continued at the Reid Hall.

July 22 1931

One of the unpleasant and painful side effects of the economic depression of this year was the number of Forfar people who felt compelled to emigrate to Canada and the USA.

It was often like jumping out of the frying pan into the fire, but on this occasion we had a Forfar lady leaving for the USA for the far happier reason that she was about to be married!

This was Miss Margaret Milne who was presently working as a draper with Graham Pool in Castle Street, and she was leaving for Detroit on August 11 to marry a Mr McQualter, late of Dundee.

Tonight the St James's Church Women's Guild made her a presentation of a silver tea service, and the Choir, in which she had sung for many years, gave her a set of oxidised silver candlesticks.

The Reverend John Strachan praised her efforts and commitment to the Church and wished her all the best in the new world. There followed a concert and dance in which Miss Milne herself participated.

She was of course a first class pianist and a good singer. Various other members of the Church took part as well, and it was a fine Church concert in the tradition of Church soirees.

Going to America was of course a big step in 1931. Transatlantic communication had improved beyond all recognition since the Great War, and throughout the 1920s it had certainly been a well-trodden path, but it was still a long way. It was sad to see another good Forfar person go there, even though in this case it was for the best of reasons.

Dancers at Forfar Games in Steele Park

July 23 1952

So what was this one all about, then?

A notice appeared this Wednesday afternoon in *The Forfar Dispatch* to the effect that one of the great pieces of entertainment scheduled for tomorrow night in the "Holiday Week" had been cancelled.

A football match had been organised by the Forfar Athletic Supporters Club between Forfar and Kirriemuir at Station Park, the proceeds presumably going to Forfar Athletic.

Ah, but this one was a rather special and somewhat different football match because it was between Forfar and Kirriemuir *Ladies*. It sounded like good fun and a good laugh. Teams had been chosen, and people were looking forward to it, when suddenly on the Monday before the game, Forfar Athletic pulled the plug on it!

The game was cancelled, and Mr Watson of the Supporters Club had no option but to put an advertisement in *The Dispatch* with apologies and regret.

But, why? *The Dispatch* itself refrains from commenting, and that is an eloquent silence, because the local press is usually loyal, to a fault, to local organisations and teams.

It can only be, one supposes, on the grounds of decency because Forfar Athletic in a rare expression of holiness and piety, decided that young Forfar ladies might be showing rather too much in a football strip to young (and old) leering and lecherous loons!

It might not have been so bad if it had been slightly older ladies showing off their more ample girth and varicose veins on their legs to the general public, but no, we cannae hae this!

It is 1952 and we have come far enough with all those legs and lipstick you see at The Gaffie!

Steele Park - Forfar Games 1900s. How on earth do they get an elephant to do that?

July 24 1905

Today was the first day of the new look Forfar Games.

They were now organised by Forfar Athletic Football Club under the energetic leadership of Secretary James Black, and were held at the new Steele Park, adjacent to the Reid Park and affording a wonderful view of the Valley of Strathmore.

The park had been gifted by local man David Steele, and it was an ideal venue for the event, which on previous occasions had been held in the Market Muir.

The weather was by no means propitious early in the morning, but by 12.30 pm when the Games opened, the weather was all that could be desired, and everything went off like clockwork in front of a large crowd of local dignitaries, local people, visitors and with a special enclosure with seats for the inhabitants of the local Poor House.

Events were varied with Dancing, Quoiting, Running, Wrestling, Bagpiping, Cycling and Five A Side Football, and the refreshment tents (Licensed and Unlicensed) doing a roaring trade to make sure that Forfarians and visitors were well catered for.

Particular interest was aroused in the Tug Of War but Forfar's Manor Works lost out narrowly in the final to Dundee Harbour Porters.

Airdrieonians won the Five A Side football, beating Forfar in the final to the distress of the local crowd.

One of the winners of the athletic events catches the eye. The 300 Yards (Handicap) Race was won by W Struth of Edinburgh. This was Willie or Bill Struth who would from 1920 until 1954 become the legendary Manager of Rangers FC.

WR Applegarth, participant in the Forfar
Games in the early 1920s. Applegarth was
a famous runner, and the idea was for the
locals, sometimes being given a few yards
of a start, to race against him.

July 25 1946

This was one of Forfar's saddest days when 10 people were killed and several more seriously injured as a train crashed into a bus at a level crossing at Balmuckety near Kirriemuir.

Seven were killed on the spot and three others died that evening in hospital. The 20-seater Commer bus, owned by Davidson & Smith, of the Zoar Garage, adjoining the Zoar Inn, was 16 years old. It was returning from a trip to Glen Clova with 24 people on board, including three children sharing seats with adults.

Slowing down on the 1 in 20 gradient before the level crossing gates, the brakes did not function sufficiently well and the bus broke through the gates and stuck on the railway line. The 5.08 pm train, hauled by 0-4-4T 15190 running bunker-first, from Kirriemuir to Forfar ploughed into the bus, dragging it for about 40 yards before the train could be stopped.

There was no escape for the poor bus passengers, Although the train passengers came out to offer as much help as they could, it was soon clear that this was a major disaster.

Ambulances were summoned from Kirriemuir, Forfar and Dundee and the casualties taken to Forfar Infirmary or the Dundee Royal Infirmary.

Some people had a lucky escape. David Logan, for example of Wellbraehead was able to jump out of the bus because he was sitting near the door, and his family were only slightly injured, but those sitting in the centre of the bus had no real chance.

The enquiry which reported in October stressed that it was as well that the train was only travelling at 15 miles per hour. No-one on the train was injured, but every one of the ten on the bus who died were resident in Forfar.

July 26 1951

A Forfar man made his debut for England today in the Test Match! Well, almost!

This was Frank Lowson (and with a name like Lowson, you really have to come from Forfar, don't you?) who had played for Yorkshire for a couple of years since he made his debut in 1949 and now he was called up to open the batting with his fellow Yorkshireman Len Hutton.

He was born in 1925 in Bradford (otherwise he would not have been allowed to play for Yorkshire), the son of another Frank Lowson who had indeed come from Forfar and played football for Forfar Celtic, Dundee, Bradford Park Avenue, Exeter City and Barrow.

He was of course a member of the huge and prolific Lowson clan based in Forfar.

Today at Headingley, Frank Lowson junior scored 58 against South Africa and played well enough in the next Test Match to be chosen to go to India and Pakistan in the winter, where he scored 1,000 runs but mainly in the games against the districts rather than the Test Matches.

Generally speaking, Lowson was more of a county cricketer than a Test Match player, and he was unfortunate in that he opened innings a lot with Len Hutton to whom he was inevitably compared.

His best score was 259 not out against Worcestershire in 1953, and he was generally looked upon as one of the best players of spin bowling in the country, being particularly strong on the leg side of the wicket. He played for Yorkshire until 1958 when he took up a career in insurance. He died in 1984.

July 27 1939

It's the Holidays!

The Forfar Holiday Week with its traditional mixture of beautiful and then appalling weather is in full swing, and this year it is impossible not to notice that prosperity is in the air with even "holidays with pay" this year, and even a holiday bonus or two!

Some are away to England and Ireland, there is a wide choice of rail and bus trips to various places, local hotels and restaurants are full with people from Glasgow, Aberdeen and elsewhere, and of course the pubs are doing well.

There is the almost obligatory train trip to Arbroath, a tradition that had been going on now for more or less a hundred years, and the walk along the beach, the cliffs and a look at the Round O. Then fish and chips (naturally, it is Arbroath!) and home again on the train. All great Forfar stuff!

This year there is the spectre at the feast — and it has a moustache and a loud strident voice already making noises about Poland. No-one really wants to talk about him, and how lovely it would be if he just went away!

It was impossible not to take one last look at Arbroath and wonder what it would be like the next time we saw it, or indeed would we see Arbroath again?

But we are still on holiday, and what a choice! Spencer Tracy at The Gaffie, or Edward G Robinson at The Regal! Actually, we have enough money — so one on Friday and the other on Saturday!

July 28 1919

After an interval of four years, the Forfar Games return!

Today at the North Mains field and at Station Park, in perfect weather, over 20,000 (it is claimed!) appeared to celebrate and enjoy the Games, so well organised by men like Dr Lowson, James Black and footballer David McLean, now of Sheffield Wednesday. At one point a gate collapsed and some people managed to get in free.

Since early morning, the Station had been a busy place with trains arriving from Dundee, Glasgow and Edinburgh, and even these new-fangled charabancs were seen to be disgorging passengers in Castle Street.

This was all a great financial boost to the cash-strapped town, and the highlights of the Games themselves was the appearance of Tancy Lee, feather weight champion of Great Britain, who took part in an exhibition match with Sergeant Reilly, the champion of the British Army.

A particular highlight was a display of gymnastics by the boys of the Mars Training Ship based in the Tay, and throughout the afternoon the Forfar Instrumental Band played lovely music under its two conductors John Lamb and Robert Anderson,

There was also dancing, piping, running, cycling and many other sports all enjoyed by the crowd with the lovely background of the Grampian mountains.

But the main thing was that this was a great way to meet old friends and comrades in arms again. One of the sad things, however, was the sight of so many injured and wounded young men, but there was the general feeling that the war was now over.

Yet for so many widows, the war would never be over.

July 29 1891

Rarely has Forfar been so prosperous and looking and feeling so good about itself as it has done this holiday week.

Trade in jute can ebb and flow, but this year, there have been loads of orders and as a result there has been a steady prosperity in the town with most shops doing well for themselves.

The Holiday Week has seen the Station far busier than it has ever been with trips to Glasgow and Edinburgh, as well as the now traditional one to Arbroath, and the railway company having the common sense to keep fares reasonably low and encourage young families.

A particular attraction about Edinburgh is the ability to travel on the new Forth Railway Bridge, a terrifying but rewarding experience according to those who have done it. It has been in operation for almost a year now, and is generally recognised as the best feat of engineering in the world.

Horse hirers and cycle hirers are also doing well in the lovely weather with even the rare sight of a few demure young ladies on bicycles, to the alarm and shock of some.

Less happily, the publicans are also doing well, "judging by the amount of inebriates we see on the street" in the censorious words of *The Forfar Herald.* The shops and cafes are full of working people giving themselves a rare treat of having someone else make a meal for them.

On Monday there were the Forfar Games, as usual, in the Market Muir, and generally speaking the town was a happy and affluent place in the Holiday Week of 1891.

July 30 1966

This was a difficult day in Forfar.

It was the day of the World Cup final between England and West Germany, and who were we going to support?

Even though Scotland were not there, the World Cup had been the highlight of people's conversation for the past month, as more or less every game had been on television.

Television ownership in Forfar was more or less universal unlike in 1958, for example, the last time that the World Cup had been on TV. 1962 in Chile was simply too far away for live television.

In 1966, there was a particular problem in Forfar about how to pronounce the name of the Brazilian footballer called Pele. Some called him Peel, others Peely (as in peely-wally), and even Pell and Pee-el were heard, such is the Forfar feeling that we are entitled to pronounce any name or anything in an idiosyncratic and distinctive way.

But Pele and Brazil were out, largely because "Peel had been crockit", and the Cup final now posed a problem. England or West Germany? Do you back the same team as you did in 1939 and 1914?

Or is the visceral footballing rivalry between Scotland and England just too great? English people living in Forfar had no problem, but what do the local population do?

Had Kenneth Wolstenholme lived in Forfar he would have said "They think it's a' ower. It is noo!"... but he was an Englishman.

There was not much dancing at the Cross or Gallowshade or Easterbank that night, nor did "Bummie" host any bonfires.

July 31 1914

Forfar has been enjoying its holiday week.

The weather started a little cold, but by later on in the week, things improved and Forfarians took full advantage.

The feel-good factor had begun at Lochside on Saturday when Strathie's professional Harry Page had put Arbroath's Bob Sievwright in his place. It was Page's benefit that day as well, and he did well out of it!

Some had left the town to stay with friends at various locations, but for those who stayed at home there were the Forfar Highland Games (as they were called in 1914) in the Steele Park. An estimated attendance of about 8,000 gave total receipts of about £250, with people from all over the county and beyond flocking into Forfar from an early hour.

The highlight was Forfar Celtic winning the Five-A-Side football tournament, beating North End in the final. And then on Tuesday there was a trip to Aberdeen with the Forfar Instrumental Band — a trip which required two trains to take all the Forfarians.

It was a wonderful day, and the rest of the week was spent in almost blissful conditions at Shand's Picture Palace in Roberts Street or simply going for walks round the town.

The Forfar Herald appears this Friday giving a picture of a happy Forfar, although reminding everyone that they would have to go back to the factories soon!

On page seven, going largely unnoticed by everyone is a small sentence to the effect that this war between the Austrians and Serbians might pull other countries like Britain into it. What nonsense!

The Municipal Buildings in the 1900s

August

Strathmore CC 1965. Anyone we know?

August 1 1965

It is not often that one can say of a local cricket match that there were "more spectators than there were runs", but that was undeniably true of the game today at Lochside Park between Strathmore and Blairgowrie.

This was of course the heyday of Strathmore Cricket Club, and it was often felt that they were the best team in Scotland at this time. Certainly they had won the Strathmore Union with a degree of ease over the past three years.

This year Blairgowrie had put a spoke in their wheel in their first encounter in May at Blairgowrie, and this was the return match where it was confidently expected that Strathmore would right the balance.

It was the middle of the Forfar Holiday Fortnight, so a few players, notably fast bowler Neil Prophet, were unavailable. It meant however that, given the good weather, a large crowd moved westwards through the town to see the game.

Strathmore batted first and were, to the discomfiture of the Forfar crowd, dismissed for 42 unable to deal with the pace of Charlie MacPherson who took 7 for 16 including the prize wicket of Nigel Hazel for 2.

Things did not look good for Strathmore, but Strathie fought back. Keen, accurate bowling and enthusiastic, athletic fielding pegged Blairgowrie back.

MacPherson was dismissed for a duck, and runs came slowly with tension tangible among the players and the spectators.

The scoreboard ticked along in singles as Blairgowrie edged to the low total, and eventually Tom Findlay ex-Aberdeenshire saw Blairgowrie home to the loud tooting of Blairgowrie car horns.

It was a rare disappointment for Strathie, but what a game! 86 runs were scored, and the spectators must have numbered well over 500.

August 2 1897

Forfar sports fans had every reason to be proud of their cycling hero John Killacky, mine host of the Queen's Hotel.

Cycling was of course a very new phenomenon in Scotland, and Killacky was an early pioneer.

Today at Celtic Park, the home of Scottish Cycling in those days, John won his favourite event — the 5 mile Professional Sprint Race. He did this in 12 minutes 40 seconds.

Five miles is a long time to keep the attention of the audience as cyclists go round and round a track, when they will naturally hold back and keep all their energy for the final lap.

To counteract this, the organisers had arranged that two shillings and sixpence (half a crown, or 12½ pence in modern currency) should be given to the leader at the end of each lap.

This certainly increased the pace on this hot day, and the last lap of the 20 saw Killacky, Silver and McFarlane all come round "almost in a line".

It stayed that way until the last hundred yards when in circumstances of great excitement, Killacky edged forward and won the race.

One of the first men to congratulate him was Willie Maley, the newly appointed Manager of Celtic and himself no mean cyclist and athlete.

News travelled quickly in 1897 with the telegraph and the story of his success reached the town about half an hour later.

A crowd assembled at the Station to see Killacky and his cycle dismount from the train that night.

He soon earned the nickname "Killacky of the Trackie", and of course, he is commemorated today in the corner named after him.

As Andy Murray is to Dunblane in the 21st century, John Killacky was to Forfar at the end of the 19th century.

John Killacky, Forfar's famous cyclist

KALAC CYCLES

WHERE you see the undernoted Trade Mark you can rest assured it is attached to the high water mark of Perfection in Cycle Construction.

Telephone No. 054.

Motor Repairs

BY

Experienced Workmen.

Motor Spirit in Stock

Symbol of Perfection

Cycle Accessories.

Repairs, Enamelling, and Nickel Plating are Specialties.

JOHN KILLACKY,

KALAC CYCLE WORKS, CHAPEL ST., FORFAR.

Kalac Cycles, Advertisement from 1900

294

August 3 1885

Provost Doig had a rather serious case of breach of the peace to deal with at the Police Court this Monday morning.

It concerned William Grewar, a factory worker of Charles Street. He was accused of breach of the peace while in an intoxicated state at Forfar Station. He was standing on the footboard of a train which was in motion and refusing to desist when requested to do so by Mr Edwards the Stationmaster, and of pushing and jostling the same Mr Edwards to the danger of both himself and Mr Edwards.

Mr Edwards explained to the Court that he was seeing away that the 6.25 pm train and four times asked Mr Grewar to come off the footboard of the train when it was moving.

Not only did Mr Grewar refuse with a certain amount of bad grace, but he then pinned Mr Edwards to the train as it was moving. Mr Edwards was able to push Grewar away but felt the effects of the shock and would do so for some time.

Fortunately no serious damage was done to either man, but the consequences might have been tragic. Grewar admitted what he had done, and it was far from his first offence.

Provost Doig told him that this was a very serious affair, that it was no ordinary breach of the peace, that his conduct was highly dangerous to himself and others, and that he was going to fine him 15 shillings (more than many people's weekly wage in 1885) with an alternative of ten days in prison.

August 4 1914

It was difficult to analyse the mood in the town today.

There had been wars before — in the Crimea, in Africa and recently in South Africa, but now it seemed there was going to be a war in Europe!

It appeared that if Germany did not withdraw from Belgium by 11.00 pm tonight, the country would be at war. There was an air of unreality about it — the King at war with his cousin the Kaiser with another cousin the Czar on our side!

They were all grandsons of the "ald Queen", as Queen Victoria was referred to, and it had all come about so suddenly. Even a week ago, no-one could have predicted it.

But fear mingled with excitement in East High Street, Castle Street, the Cross and all the factories today. What would it all mean? Tonight 50 members of the Cycling Company of the Territorial Army slept in the Drill Hall, awaiting the call to embark on a train, or to go and protect the coast of the North Sea, which was still called the German Ocean.

And there were these new machines that flew in the air called aeroplanes! Someone said that they could carry and drop explosives on the coastal towns!

11.00 pm came and went. Those who were still awake wondered whether the Germans had agreed to terms, or whether Forfar and the rest of Britain were involved in a war.

"Shandies", Shand's Picture Palace in Roberts Street, was going to show on Thursday, Friday and Saturday the Boxing Match between Georges Carpentier and Gunboat Smith which had taken place on July 16. Was the war going to stop that show?

John Morley MP, who resigned from Liberal
Government in 1914 in protest against the war.

August 5 1914

Were there not so many other things going on in the town in this, the first day of war, people would have possibly paid a little more attention to John Morley, one time MP for Montrose Burghs, of which Forfar was a large part.

John Morley had been Forfar's MP from 1896 until 1908 when he had been elevated to the Peerage at the age of 70. He is best remembered in Forfar for opening the Reid Park in 1896, but he was a faithful servant of the town in other respects as well.

He was a Liberal, but an unorthodox one with many ideas of his own. He resigned the Montrose Burghs seat in 1908 when he was elevated to the Peerage by Prime Minister Herbert Asquith, and became Viscount Morley of Blackburn. He still however sat in the Liberal Cabinet, having held important office like the Secretary of State for India when he was Forfar's MP.

He was always however his own man and watched the events of summer 1914 unfold with a certain amount of unease, feeling that the country was being pushed into an unnecessary war that no-one really wanted.

In particular, he felt that the country should not be seen to be in a conflict on the same side as the corrupt and despotic Czar of Russia, and in a war against Germany, he prophesied correctly that there would be no real winners. Now 76, he resigned from the Cabinet and devoted himself to his literary works of which he wrote a great deal. He died in 1923, much respected and missed by everyone, even his opponents, and to his dying day, retained his love of Forfar.

August 6 1848

Big changes in Forfar these days!

A few days ago the new railway station was opened to accommodate the Scottish Midland Junction Railway, which now allows people to travel between Forfar and Perth along a lovely stretch of country.

The idea will eventually be to have the railway line go all the way north to Aberdeen, and west to Glasgow. This is why the Playfield Station and its impressive Hotel across the road ("The Muckle Inn") has had to be abandoned because it would have been impossible to create a direct connection to the west.

The old Playfield Station has served the line to Arbroath very well for almost ten years, but *The Courier* gives a vivid description of what the Market Muir is now like in comparison to a short year ago.

> "Then one would have seen merry groups, in all the buoyancy of youth, kicking the football and shouting for glee; or the more sedate and serious golfers watching, with eager gaze, the ball as it flew towards its goal. Now he can only see the waggon loaded with coals or slates, etc., or the carriage filled with passengers, and only hear the all but omnipotent steam, hissing, as it were, at all such amusements and the ponderous engine snorting out 'mind business' 'go a-head'."

The effect of all this is to make the town go north. North Street will now become a very important area of town and the proximity of the station will encourage the development of the market and hotels in that part of the town.

August 7 1928

In an interesting legal case at Dundee Sheriff Court today, Forfar bus firm McCallum and Graham of West High Street and their driver Donald McMartin of Croft Terrace, Kirriemuir were found not guilty of having faulty brakes.

They were found not guilty on a technicality of police procedure as the policeman concerned admitted, under intense cross examination from defence lawyer Mr Ross of Dundee, that he had no clear knowledge of what exactly he was trying to test.

The bus had been stopped on the Dundee to Forfar road near Middleton in May and the police report said that although the hand brake was in good working order, the foot brake was useless.

Constable Adam, the policeman concerned, was subjected to a rigorous cross-examination by Mr Ross. After the young policeman had clearly been outwitted by the lawyer he was compelled to admit that he didn't even know what the correct procedures were.

The case was dismissed to the great relief of the Forfar bus company, although not necessarily to the Forfar travelling public, who might have been put in some danger.

The leader writer of *The Forfar Herald* is similarly unimpressed. He inveighs with some vigour into the local Constabulary whom he criticises for not having enough to do sometimes and for allowing over-zealous young officers to do jobs that they are not really capable of doing.

The major point of concern however is one of safety. Buses had operated between Forfar and Dundee for the last eight years, and there had been rather too many accidents, faulty brakes on occasion being a cause.

Provost Hanick, third from right, with the Griffin from the Steeple

August 8 1814

The erection of the Steeple was today completed. The griffin was placed on the top, to the accompaniment of three cheers from the men on the scaffolding. The cheers were reciprocated by a large crowd on the ground one hundred and fifty feet below.

The Caledonian Mercury quite rightly goes into raptures about how

"No public undertaking ever gave more universal satisfaction than the erection of this beautiful spire. The excellence of the workmanship, the skill displayed in framing the scaffolding, in short the very superior manner in which every operation has been conducted reflects the highest praise on the professional talents of the architect, Mr Patrick Brown of Lochee; and it is perhaps none of the least of his merits that, owing to his prudent arrangements, no accident whatever to life or limb has happened during the work."

There is no accurate indication of how long the work actually took, but we know that it replaced a previous structure, and the sheer height of the steeple had been a talking point in many circles when the topic of Forfar came up.

The cost to the town was £1000. The architect Patrick Brown, according to one story, was at one point imprisoned for debt during the construction, but the Town Council "bailed him out" and paid the wages of the workmen.

This tale may or may not be true, but in any case it does nothing to detract from the achievement of Mr Brown. The sheer height of the building terrifies most people and it remains a distinctive attraction for the town.

August 9 1902

Forfar's celebrations of the Coronation of King Edward VII and Queen Alexandra were just a little underwhelming today, one feels. There were several reasons for this.

One was that it was the second attempt. The Coronation should have been held in June, but Edward took ill with a form of appendicitis.

Another reason was that this was a Saturday, and there was no special holiday.

Provost Adamson had been invited to London but only at the last minute, and it is not difficult to detect a certain amount of unpreparedness by the other Councillors and even resentment at the Provost not being there but on a freebie in London!

The public buildings were not as well decorated as they should have been, according to *The Forfar Herald*. Such celebrations as there were — with the Volunteer Band playing in the Reid Park — were held in opposition to a cricket match at Lochside where Strathmore played a Lancashire touring team called Heywood.

At night, there was a fireworks display, but bad weather hampered the festivities there as well.

In addition, there was a general anxiety about the King, partly because of his health and partly because of his suitability to be King of Great Britain. He was old, and his life so far had been one of a certain amount of dissipation and hedonism.

The Press had been only partially successful in hiding his exploits with Daisy Warwick, Alice Keppel, Lily Langtree and a few others. Indeed, in some of the Forfar hostelries that night, a few bawdy songs were heard about "Jersey Lil" as Lily Langtree was known!

August 10 1860

The Forfar Games took place today at the Market Muir before a crowd of 5,000 including several local dignitaries.

It was a fine occasion but the aftermath was less so. A paragraph appeared in *The Scotsman* the following day to the effect that at The Forfar Games, William Tait, a gamekeeper of Douglas Castle, had thrown the heavy hammer of 22 lbs the extraordinary distance of 85 feet 8 inches.

It was indeed a mighty feat, but the account was challenged by an Edinburgh man called "WC" a few days later in a letter to *The Scotsman* to the effect that this was not true.

"It was an incredible feat, never yet performed by any competitor, unless the Forfar folk allow the competitors when throwing to take their stand on the brow of a steep declivity"

He went on the say that "the colossal Tait" had thrown the hammer a distance of 64 feet 8 inches at the Edinburgh Highland Society's Gathering a few weeks ago, but the Forfar distance was impossible.

This letter not unnaturally ruffled a few feathers in Forfar with Mr Cowper, the Secretary of the Forfar Games committee, replying that he was convinced of the authenticity of the throw.

It was stated that the ground was flat, or if not perfectly so, flat enough as to make no difference and quite a few people insisted that the distance was marked correctly, although it was conceded that the Forfar "ball" was 21 and a half lbs rather than 22 lbs.

The Edinburgh correspondent was advised to keep quiet about things that took place "50 miles away from him". By an odd coincidence, Tait himself apparently subsequently broke his thigh in a hurdle race at the same event.

The Duke and Duchess of York at Station Park

August 11 1929

Today at Station Park, the Duke and Duchess of York, with Princess Elizabeth, attended a meeting of the St Andrews Ambulance Association in front of 7,000 people.

The function was to present awards for those who helped the injured and the sick; there were also demonstrations by the Scouts, the Cubs and the Rovers with the Forfar Pipe Band in attendance.

It was a very pleasant occasion enjoyed by the town, with everyone remarking how charming the three-year-old Princess Elizabeth was. Her shy but likeable father contrasted with her mother who was anything but shy, being described as "gushing and gregarious".

The only problem was that this was a Sunday, and the Free Kirk of Scotland (not the established Church or even the United Free) saw fit to use words like "sacrilege" and "insult" to describe what occurred in Forfar today on the Sabbath.

Mercifully, God did not seem to agree and Forfar was not visited by any kind of plague, pestilence or flood. Ex-Bailie Hanick replying on behalf of the Town Council and of Forfar Athletic, in a masterpiece of tact and diplomacy, regretted than anyone was offended, but felt that helping the sick and the injured was a very important part of life, even on a Sunday.

In addition many people attended the meeting having been at Church that very morning — and the attendance included many of the Ministers of the town.

Had the Free Kirkers known that Mr Hanick was a practising Roman Catholic, they probably would have concluded that Forfar was definitely in the hands of Satan!

August 12 1870

Today was an important day in the history of the railway in Forfar, for it saw the first day of goods trains of the Caledonian Railway being allowed to travel between Forfar and Dundee.

This had followed several years of hard work both in Parliament to get the idea through and another kind of hard work by navvies and labourers on the line which had involved an awful lot of tunnelling and the loss of several lives in the process.

The line ran through difficult country and would have stations (eventually) at Kingsmuir, Kirkbuddo, Monikie, Wellbank, Gagie, Kingennie, Barnhill, Broughty Junction and Dundee East Station.

Passengers were not yet allowed until such time as certain safety standards could be met — this would happen in November. For the moment, various items of merchandise from the local factories could be transported in both directions, and for Forfar firms, the railway gave quick access to the port of Dundee.

The Dundee train went east to a junction called Forfar North then turned south towards Kingsmuir and Dundee. When it opened for passengers later in the year, it was virtually the only reasonable method of communication between Forfar and Dundee, taking about 45 minutes as distinct from several hours by horse and cart.

Motorised charabancs started in 1920 and they were far more flexible and convenient. The passenger train service to Dundee lasted until January 1955, and goods until December 1958, but road transport was far better, basically because lorries were able to go directly to their destination rather than a railway station.

August 13 1923

We often find it difficult to unravel the attitude of people in the 1920s to tobacco.

On the one hand, it was almost glorified in the First World War with songs like needing "a Lucifer to light one's fag", and we even find evidence of doctors prescribing tobacco as a mild sedative.

On the other hand, there was something almost "infra dig" about it, and it could be even looked upon as "common". And cigarettes were not to be allowed for children, something of course that made it all the more attractive for youngsters.

Today at the Police Court, Provost Moffat had to deal with the case of Archibald McGregor of 124 Dundee Loan, Forfar, who had in his shop at 28 West High Street sold cigarettes to a boy under the age of 16 in contravention of the Children's Act of 1908.

"Erch" McGregor (as he was commonly known) pleaded guilty but in his self-exculpation, he used the somewhat ungallant defence that he was away at the time and that it was all the fault of his wife who had sold the cigarettes to the boy thinking that he had been sent on an errand by a man.

Chief Constable Thomson said that his police force were determined to cut out this practice in Forfar, which had become rather too common, and he called upon Provost Moffat to deliver an exemplary sentence which would deter other shopkeepers.

Provost Moffat agreed and fined Mr McGregor £1, a not inconsiderable amount in 1923.

August 14 1895

Today saw the death of Elizabeth Millar, believed to be Forfar's oldest inhabitant.

She was only a few months short of her 97th birthday and had lived in Forfar all her days, finishing her life in North Street. She married James Lowson in 1819; he had died about 15 years ago. She had a son still alive who himself had "passed the generally allotted span", as *The Forfar Herald,* none too tactfully puts it.

Elizabeth had been born in 1798 when George III was King, William Pitt was Prime Minister, Nelson won the Battle of the Nile and the British put down an Irish rebellion.

She thus lived through Napoleon, the coming of the railway to Forfar, the building of the Peel Monument, Crimea, and the Franco-Prussian War.

The big change in Forfar had been the rapid industrialisation with the building of factories and the coming of jute. She had been active all her life and until very recently had been seen on the streets, although she had been becoming "noticeably more frail of late".

The Forfar Herald reckons that ex Provost Peter Reid is now the oldest Forfarian still alive, certainly the oldest Forfar-born person.

There are two others who are older than Peter — Walter McLean and Isabella Ormond — but they, unlike Peter, were not Forfar born.

Longevity was not common in the Victorian age, but generally speaking if one survived the early years and the dreadfully common childhood illnesses, one was generally strong enough to survive quite a lot!

It is worth stressing that as Registration of Births, Marriages and Deaths only became compulsory in 1855, there was no guarantee that claims about people's births were accurate.

Strathmore Cricket Club, 1971. Winners of the Quaich, the "Scottish Cup"

August 15 1971

It was a red letter day for Forfar when Strathmore won what was effectively the Scottish Cup, although in fact it was a Quaich (called "the Quelch" by the Lochside Park groundsman!) sponsored by a cigarette firm.

For many years, Forfar's cricket fans had argued that their team was the best in Scotland, and now it was true! And they did it without star bowler George Myles!

The game was played against Kilmarnock at Hamilton Crescent, Glasgow. Kilmarnock had as their professional Bob Massie, a man who next year would rip through England at Lord's for Australia. Today however he had less success against Strathmore.

Kilmarnock batted first and reached the respectable but by no means unbeatable total of 177, and most of that was thanks to 67 not out from Alan Simpson.

For Strathie, Alan Guild and Gavin McKiddie took three wickets each, Gavin collecting the prize wicket of Bob Massie when he had him caught by Mike Thornton.

Strathie's progress towards the total did not make for easy watching for the bus-load of supporters from Forfar, nor the many who had come by car, but John Callander, Nigel Hazel, Don Crighton and Ewan Massie all made respectable scores. Effectively a two from the first ball of the last over won the tie for Strathie, and then just for good measure, Gavin McKiddie hit a four.

It was a great triumph and much celebrated by all concerned, and it earned generous praise in newspapers like *The Glasgow Herald* and *The Scotsman* the following day. It also meant that Forfarians no longer living in the town, when asked embarrassing questions about how badly Forfar Athletic were doing, could immediately change the subject to cricket!

August 16 1965

Back to school is always a traumatic and exciting experience for children (and teachers) but today was even more so. It was the first day of the new Forfar Academy in Taylor Street!

It had been long promised, often by local politicians who had not lasted long enough to see the eventual completion of the school, and here it was.

It was a wrench to leave the old Academy, which had a great deal to be proud of, but was frankly too small for the baby boomer generation who had been born in the late 1940s and early 1950s and had thrived and prospered under the National Health Service.

The first day (indeed the first year) was rather chaotic as some things were not quite ready yet. One recalls, for example, that the seats in the library were not very comfortable, and that there were no signs on the toilet doors, something that caused embarrassment on occasion!

There was also the problem of getting around for no-one seemed to know how to get anywhere, and one was particularly sorry for the wee ones who were totally bewildered. There was no point in asking older brothers or sisters for they were similarly lost!

But Rector Mr Alex C Gillespie, a kind and dedicated man, took pains to apologise particularly for the curtains and blinds not always being there, which in a glass dominated building was a considerable disadvantage and disincentive to learning.

Yet the advantages were immense with all the latest equipment and a sometimes breathtaking view of the Grampians. Pupils could now actually watch the weather arrive!

August 17 1908

Football fans and old friends of his were delighted to hear of the appointment of Forfarian Edward M Tarbat (usually known as Neddy) to the job of Manager of Third Lanark.

This was a full time appointment and obliged him to give up his job as a teacher in a Glasgow school. Neddy was born in 1881 and played for Forfar Athletic before moving to Dundee, Airdrie and then Third Lanark for whom he had played for the last two seasons as a forward.

He was remembered by Loons supporters are a useful inside left and clearly had a fine tactical knowledge of how to play the game.

He still intended to play the occasional game for Thirds. They were a fine team in the 1900s, having won the Scottish League in 1904 and the Scottish Cup in 1905 (under a Manager with the unlikely name of Frank Heaven!) and now played at Cathkin Park, previously called Hampden.

They had a good support and were commonly known as "the sodgers" because of course they were originally an army regiment team called the 3rd Lanarkshire Rifle Volunteers.

Neddy Tarbat's finest moment would come early in his career when Third Lanark won the Glasgow Cup on October 28 1908, beating Celtic 4-0 — and this was meant to be Celtic's best ever team!

He stayed at Third Lanark until 1917. As far as football was concerned, he had probably come to a dead end in his career with Third Lanark, and he possibly felt that this was as far as he could go in the game.

He died in Ayrshire in 1933 at the young age of 52, having returned to his profession as a teacher in Saltcoats.

James Allan, famous Forfar musician

August 18 1877

Today was the day that Forfar's fiddler James Allan died at the age of 76.

He was generally looked upon as Forfar's best ever musician and was well known throughout Scotland, even though he seldom left his beloved Forfar apart from when he went on tour.

He was born in 1800, the eldest son of George Allan the barber, and he started to work with his father while also learning how to weave linen at the house of a man who lived in Sparrowcroft.

All his family were musicians of sorts; none of them had the talent of James, or Jamie as he came to be known, but it was his cousin Archie that taught him how to play the fiddle.

In 1840 Jamie married a widow who lived near the East Port and had a small inn there. One of the attractions of the hostelry on a winter night was drinking punch while listening to Jamie playing all the well-known Scottish songs of the Jacobite rebellion as collected by Robert Burns.

In 1856 the Victorian equivalent of a musical agent happened to be in town and invited Jamie to join his touring company.

This he did and he toured all over Scotland and England on several occasions, sometimes making money, sometimes not, but always enhancing his reputation.

Latterly, he made most of his appearances in places like Dundee and Perth, and was always well known for his wit, generosity and good humour. He was generally reckoned to be one of the best Scottish fiddlers of his day, and was much loved in his home town.

August 19 1952

The finishing touches are now in place for tomorrow night's historic occasion. The electric street lights are to be switched on!

They have been in place for some time now, and Forfarians have been promised by the General Electric Company, the providers, that the lighting will be of a superior standard and even fantasy phrases like "fairly wonderland" were used.

More mundanely, and with its feet firmly on the floor, *The Forfar Dispatch* hopes that the "electric shock" will be a pleasant one and that the increase in rates will not be too severe. For the moment, gas and electricity will co-exist until such time as electricity can reach all parts of town.

More and more houses now have electricity, and at long last the debate about gas v electricity (expense, safety, usefulness etc.) seems to be coming to an end. The current belief is that gas cookers will be better than electric ones, but of course electricity in one's house will facilitate television, fridges, washing machines and all the other promised luxuries of the brave new 1950s world.

However that may be, all the electric lights have been checked and all that remains is for Provost Andrew C Smyth to press the switch at the Cross tomorrow night at 9.30 pm when it should be dark enough for all the Cross and Castle Street to resound with the cries of "Ooh!" and "Fut bonny!"

In one respect, however, *The Forfar Dispatch* warns everyone that it will not be like Genesis when God said let there be light, and there was light. There will be a flickering for a while before full power is introduced.

August 20 1899

Tonight, at the meeting of the Town Council there were clear signs that Forfar was preparing to move into the 20th Century, as far as the Police Force were concerned, for Councillor TB Esplin moved that a bicycle should be procured for the use of the Police.

This had followed a recommendation from Captain Munro, Her Majesty's Chief Inspector of Constabulary for Scotland, that all forces should have a bicycle.

This new form of transport had sprouted all over Scotland in the past ten years in particular to the extent that Forfar now had five manufacturers and sellers of bicycles, one of them being the famous cyclist John Killacky.

But Forfar Town Council would not be Forfar Town Council if there were not dissenting views, in this case from Bailie Hanick who wondered if it would not be just as cheap to hire such a machine.

But Councillor Esplin said that by the time you got to the hirer's to procure the machine, the damage would be done, whereas if there were a bicycle handy, a policeman could be at, say, the Station in a matter of "seconds" (Laughter).

Councillor Doig thought that as Forfar had such a small area to cover, a bicycle would be a waste of money, but Provost McDougall said that he wished to second the motion, and the motion was passed to provide a bicycle for the Forfar Police Force. Whatever next?

Someone suggested a motor car to loud laughter! Sometimes a policeman's lot could, in spite of what Gilbert and Sullivan said, be a happy one!

Glamis Castle

August 21 1930

Great news for Forfar tonight with the birth of a Princess at Glamis Castle, and Forfar doctor David Myles was one of the three doctors present when the Duchess of York gave birth at 9.22 pm tonight.

The new Princess was fourth in line to the throne. Her grandfather was the current king, King George V, and the heir apparent was Uncle David (who would become King Edward VIII), then came her father Bertie, then her sister Elizabeth, now four years old, then the new baby who would be called Princess Margaret.

News spread quickly round Glamis, and it reached Forfar a few minutes later by telephone.

Incredibly, though it was a wet night and the hour was late, a crowd gathered at various points on the Glamis Road to greet Dr Myles on his return to the town.

It was nearly 11.00 pm before his car was recognised. On seeing the crowd, Dr Myles, clearly relishing his moment in the limelight, stopped his car from time to time to roll down the side window and shout "It's a girl! Both well".

It was too late to ring the Church bells that night, but they were rung at 11.00 am the following morning and flags hung from appropriate buildings, as the local hotels played host to the world's press, and even, something new, almost sinister and a token of the modern age, a radio crew!

The new Princess, like so many younger siblings in the Royal Family, was destined to have a very unhappy life, and it might have been a kindness to her to give her for adoption to a Forfar family rather than subject her to the stresses and strains of that unnatural existence!

August 22 1911

To the already impressive lists of achievements of 19-year-old Nora Farquharson must now be added the prize of "the best cultivated voice" at the Tonic Sol Fa College of Music in the London Summer School.

Nora, a Forfar girl, a brilliant soprano vocalist, has been attending the college for only two terms, and this competition was open to any student of any year.

When it is taken into consideration that her competitors were already music teachers from other parts of the United Kingdom, the achievement of this young Forfar girl becomes all the more praiseworthy for her part in putting Forfar on the map as far as singing and music are concerned.

She intends to return to Forfar for the winter and to form classes for musical tuition.

She had already impressed Forfarians in her part as a soloist in the "Daughter of Jairus" cantata in St James's Church at the end of February, then in April she had taken part in the Royal School of Arts Concert after the presentation of awards.

She was clearly a young lady of great talent, like so many of the Farquharson family in Forfar at this time.

By the end of the year, the pupils at her classes presented her with her conductor's baton because of the rapid progress they had made under her.

Music attracted a great deal of interest in Forfar in the years before the Great War, but it was often felt that it was an exclusively middle class pursuit.

August 23 1904

In what was possibly Forfar's biggest ever outside event, Buffalo Bill's Wild West Show came today to the Market Muir, and in spite of some disagreeable weather, attracted a barely believable crowd of 16,000, almost twice the population of the town (according to *The Forfar Herald*) over two performances at 2.00 pm and 7.00 pm.

The price for entry was 1/- for the cheapest seat, but for that, you were admitted to the main event and all the many sideshows which filled the extensive area of the Market Muir.

The multi-national company and their horses and other animals had arrived at the Station on three special trains the day before, and today the town was mobbed with people from many miles around.

The crowd was all the more remarkable when one realises that this was a Tuesday! The main attraction was the Red Indians who did all sorts of things on horseback. The Russian Cossacks were similarly impressive.

The highlight of the show was the re-enactment of Custer's Last Stand, made all the more exciting by the fact that the Red Indian parts were actually played by real live Red Indians!

And of course the real Buffalo Bill himself! William Cody made his own appearance, revealing remarkable skill and accuracy in his shooting.

It was an occasion that would be remembered for many years. Often circuses and other shows had proved to be a disappointment for Forfar people, but not this one. It was every bit as good as it was claimed to be.

Forfar Academy, 1900s

322

August 24 1931

Today the Forfar working class are going around astounded by recent events.

Pictures have been torn down from walls, papers have been torn up and a stunned silence reigns in many houses, for they have been betrayed by their Messianic figure, James Ramsay MacDonald, the First Labour Prime Minister.

It is like someone who went to Church all his life discovering that Jesus Christ is really the Devil. MacDonald has abandoned his own Labour Party and formed a National Government with the Conservatives and Liberals to form a Coalition.

To be fair to "the Lossie loon" who had previously been hero worshipped in Don's, Jock's, the Mull and the Hauchie, he had only a minority Government in any case.

The economic depression was an unprecedented one, and the cut to unemployment benefit a severe blow to the already penurious existence of Forfar's hundreds of unemployed, and the many more who are already on or likely to be soon put on short time working in the factories.

Not everyone sees it like this, of course. *The Courier* and *The Forfar Herald* talk about "statesmanship" and "putting the country first" (whatever that specious nonsense means) but it is now clear that MacDonald will still be Prime Minister, but only a nominal one.

And yet, there was a time in 1914 when he was clearly in the right by opposing the war, but the man in the Salutation Hotel who was crying into his pint got it right when he said "Ramsay MacDonald, Ramsay MacDonald, why have you forsaken us?"

August 25 1784

Today James Tytler, a man with very strong Forfar connections became one of the very first men in the world to fly a balloon, and he was certainly the first in Scotland, doing so over Edinburgh, close to Holyrood Palace.

He was the son of the Minister in Fern, near Tannadice, but although a very scholarly and learned man, having learned Latin, Greek and Hebrew from his father, his inclinations were not towards following his father to the Ministry.

Indeed, like a few other sons of the Manse, he went to the other extreme with drink, debt and sexual profligacy which included his writing a Directory of the "Ladies Of The Night" in Edinburgh!

His views of social equality were shared by men like Robert Burns, but not by the Edinburgh establishment! More respectably in the eyes of the Edinburgh bourgeoisie, Tytler compiled many entries for the Encyclopaedia Britannica.

He had spent his youth in Forfar, working as an apprentice to a surgeon — a particularly grizzly job in the 18th century, as one could imagine — but soon tired of the somewhat stuffy and restrictive small town existence, and fled to the bright lights of Edinburgh and London where he became interested in aviation.

Because his attempts were not consistently successful, he was ridiculed and called a charlatan, but it was for his political beliefs that he was exiled.

An outspoken supporter of the American and French Revolutions, and denouncer of King George III and the fairly blatant corruption of the House of Commons, he was exiled for sedition.

He died in January 1804, but his life had not been without its moments, good and bad, and his flying of a balloon was much talked about (and not always believed!) in Forfar.

August 26 1929

The Flower Show in the Reid Hall had been declared open a few days ago by Sir Robert Hutchison MP.

It was, as always, a beautiful sight with "The Drummer" of *The Forfar Dispatch* duly impressed. The MP made no mention of the political situation (a tricky one with a minority Labour Government now in power) but rather complimented all the Forfar gardeners for their hard work in producing such magnificent vegetables and beautiful flowers.

There was a certain air of limited prosperity in the town, certainly since the dark days of the War and its immediate poverty-stricken aftermath, and the town was looking well in the fine weather.

Apparently there were 1,100 entries in all categories, an increase of 400 on last year, which meant that every tenth person in the town put something in the show. (It didn't work out like that, of course, for there were multiple entries!)

"The Drummer", while confessing that he "had nae notion o' gairnerin" nevertheless admired the "patience, skill, optimism and patience" of those who did so. "It took a fell lot o' booin' and sair work" ere Mother Nature was prevailed upon to produce the plentiful fruits that were visible today.

In any case, the Flower Show was a great place for Forfarians to meet and discuss important matters like the price of eggs, holidays, football, schools and of course, the latest love affairs — respectable ones that ended in a marriage, ("She was awfa prutty!") and less respectable ones which were commonly described in terms like "Aye, she's carryin' oan with that led in Castle Street — an they're baith merriet!"

August 27 1920

Today's *Forfar Herald* contains good news for Forfar Athletic fans.

It appears that there will be senior football after all in Forfar this year. It had been feared that the Athletic might either have to play junior football along with Forfar Celtic, East End and others or simply confine themselves to playing friendlies.

There was as yet no resurrection of the Scottish League Second Division after the war, the Central League was too far away for Forfar, the Northern League of before the war had folded, and the Eastern League simply had too few teams to be viable.

Today after a long campaign of lobbying, orchestrated by the energetic Jimmy Black, places had been won for Forfar and Arbroath in the Scottish Reserve League, sometimes called the Scottish Alliance.

The strong point about both Arbroath and Forfar had been the good railway connection with Forfar in particular having a good case as well when Black pointed out that both Alec Troup and Davie McLean were already Scottish Internationalists.

It was a satisfactory outcome for it meant that Celtic Reserves and Rangers Reserves would be seen at Station Park, and the players would have the opportunity to play on the big Glasgow grounds.

There would also be the local attraction of playing Dundee Reserves, and of course there would still be the traditional local derby against Arbroath which could be guaranteed to "pack them in".

The first game would be tomorrow against Aberdeen Reserves and a reasonable crowd could be expected.

Forfar Athletic also announced that admission would be ninepence, fourpence for ladies and children and sixpence extra for the stand. The prices were reasonable, and Black never made the mistake of pricing football out of the market.

August 28 1914

A report appeared today in *The Forfar Herald* of one of Forfar's first casualties of the war.

It was John Johnstone of Don Street. Yesterday his sister Mrs Stormont with whom he lived received news that he had been wounded in Belgium last weekend and that he was in hospital, but she had no indication of exactly where he was, nor of how seriously he was hurt.

John Johnstone worked in the Manor Works before the war, and was well known in local sporting circles, being the trainer of West End Football Club and commonly known as "Sweddie".

When war broke out three weeks ago,"Sweddie" was a Reservist, and enlisted immediately in the 1st Battalion Cameron Highlanders.

As his sister and his friends waited anxiously for further news, this was a salutary reminder that perhaps the war was not going to be quite the picnic that some people thought it was going to be.

But local recruitment continued to go well, with the opportunity of getting to wear a uniform and a kilt and to get away from poor housing and unhealthy jute factories (whose immediate future, in any case, was in some doubt because of the war) a potent factor in the minds of young Forfarians.

Other indications of war came in the call to restrict the sale of alcohol, and the need for the women of the town to knit vests and socks for the troops.

"Sweddie" incidentally survived his wound, and lived to a ripe old age! In that respect, he was luckier than many other Forfarians.

August 29 1940

Tonight, German bombs were dropped on Balmashanner.

The facts are extremely difficult to pin down; newspapers in 1940 were heavily censored lest they gave some important information to the enemy or spread gloom and alarm among the civilian population, although there are a few hints in the newspapers about a town "near the east coast being nearly hit".

Some say that they heard two bombs, others say three but the noise was more like a "puum" rather than a loud explosion. What seems to have happened is that, this being the time of the Battle of Britain in London and Kent, a diversionary attack was made on Scotland, but it was well dealt with by Coastal Command.

The bomber was being chased and had to jettison his bombs to increase his speed. It was fortunate that the bombs were dropped where they were, otherwise serious damage might have been done to the town.

Possibly the German was a humane man who deliberately decided to miss, or possibly he missed because of the blackout. In any event, he seems to have escaped.

The following Sunday, townspeople went up to see the damage. They were not allowed to get all that close, and they were certainly forbidden by police and the Home Guard from taking photographs.

Traces of the bomb crater remain to this day.

Author's note. This entry is incomplete and may even be wrong in terms of the date, but the reasons are explained at the top. Any further elucidation of this event would be welcome.

August 30 1947

Strathmore Cricket Club, already champions of the Strathmore Union for the second year in a row, travelled to Forthill today to play Forthill XI, although some of the players bore a distinct resemblance to men who had played in the full Forfarshire team!

The summer had been a gloriously hot one (after the dreadful winter of February and March) and pitches were dry, but Strathie had enjoyed a good season; although they didn't win today, they were nevertheless competent enough to bat out for a draw.

They thus preserved their unbeaten record in front of a large crowd, particularly good for late August considering that the football season had now started.

Forfarshire batted first and Strathmore soon had three wickets, but crucially fluffed a run out which would have dismissed GH Turnbull, who went on to score 129 not out with one six and several lovely fours.

Forfarshire thus reached 210 for 6 declared, by no means an impossible score on such a dry pitch and with a very fast outfield.

Misfortune dogged Strathie's reply. Professional Ramsbottom played on, JD Henderson was given out caught behind when the ball seemed to hit his pad and Ernie Balfour was given out to a somewhat dubious lbw.

Strathmore were still good enough to eke out a draw with contributions from Davie Robertson, Davie Balfour and Len Halstead, the ex-professional who was now playing as an amateur.

It had been another good season for the men from Lochside, and the consistent good weather meant that the batsmen retained their form throughout the summer and that attendances were high.

August 31 1957

It was a night of good and bad news for Forfar people.

More and more people were beginning to get a television as prosperity began to become obvious with full employment and even scope for overtime in some factories.

So far there had only been one channel — the BBC. Tonight however commercial TV reached Scotland in the shape of Scottish Television which broadcast from the Theatre Royal in Glasgow, and it would of course bring programmes like "Scotsport" and the "One O'Clock Gang" to Scotland.

The problem was that Forfar was just a little too far away from Glasgow and reception was poor, unreliable and patchy. The main problem was "snow" — white lines and dots on the screen, and the joke was that if you bought a TV with STV on it, they gave you a shovel as well to clear up the snow from your floor!

The reception was a little better in the north-west part of town, particularly up the Brechin Road, but if you were watching from one of the new housing schemes in Gallowshade and Goosecroft, it was absolutely dreadful, and BBC was far better.

Sometimes in the middle of the day (not that there were many programmes on during the day in 1957) the reception was a little better, and gradually an improvement was seen, but it was not until Grampian TV arrived in 1961 from Aberdeen, that people in Forfar were able to watch ITV programmes with adequate reception.

The trouble with Grampian TV, however, was that some of the programmes were appallingly amateurish!

September

September 1 1907

The summer outdoor programme of entertainment is coming to an end.

Miss Marie Scott's Merry Magnets have been offering an "Up to Date Programme of Songs, Sketches etc with a Laughable Sketch after every evening performance" in the Steele Park every afternoon and evening at 3.30 and 7.30 at the cost of 4 pennies or 3 pennies per seat and 1 penny for children.

It being in the open, and not enclosed, it was difficult to prevent anyone standing at the back and watching for free but they were duty bound to put a "hie" (halfpenny) in the "boxie" when it came round. If wet, everyone moved to the Reid Hall.

The programme consisted of Scottish songs, music hall songs, a few jokes, impersonations of King Edward VII, politicians, national and local and a few pieces of entertainments with puppets and dolls for the children.

In particular there was a larger than life, pantomime dame sort of character called "Bertha" who could provide entertainment on two levels — slapstick for the children and more subtle innuendo for the adults. Generally speaking they had been blessed with good weather all summer, and it had been much appreciated by the locals.

The Merry Magnets were a small, semi-professional troupe of actors based in Glasgow but supplemented by a few local performers, and of course, the strength of the entertainment was that it varied every day.

So popular were this group that they were awarded a "Benefit Concert" in the Reid Hall, and that was well attended with the Forfar Instrumental Band taking part, and the hope was expressed that the Merry Magnets would return next year.

September 2 1901

At the Police Court today Provost McDougall had a nasty case of assault to deal with.

William Troup, fish dealer, was charged with assaulting Walter Boyle, hawker, in Victoria Street by kicking him, seizing him and throwing him to the ground.

It was a rather cowardly assault on a deaf old man and Troup's only defence was "drunkenness". We are amazed at how lenient the Provost was. Equally amazingly, Troup pleaded "not guilty" and then more or less admitted the charge!

Boyle claimed that Troup had said he would plead guilty and pay all the expenses, but on being told that Troup had pleaded not guilty, Boyle then told the court that he had met Troup in Victoria Street and Troup had immediately assaulted him.

Boyle then said he would report him, Troup tried to dissuade him and offered him a drink but Boyle insisted on telling the police and did so but not before Troup had assaulted him again.

All this had been seen by James Bruce, a gravel merchant of Wellbraehead, who duly gave evidence. Troup then said that he had been so drunk he could not remember what happened.

The Provost found Troup guilty but said that if he had not been under the influence of drink, this would never have happened. He then fined him 7 shillings and six pence with the alternative of five days in prison, and warned him on the evils of drinking to excess.

One assumes that this was a first offence by Troup, and one can also assume that Boyle was no shrinking violet either, but even so, an assault on a deaf old man should really, one feels, have been dealt with a great deal more severely.

September 3 1939

It was far from a normal Sunday in Forfar.

The weather was pleasant enough as the congregations, far more numerous than normal, made their way to Church.

Everyone was pleasant enough to each other, but everyone knew what was going to happen. Some decided to forego Church this morning in favour of listening to the wireless in case there was any news.

This time everyone knew that there would be news, today or maybe tomorrow. *The Sunday Post* this morning quoted Mr Chamberlain the Prime Minister as saying "No Weakening".

This was because on Friday, Germany had invaded Poland as it had threatened to do for months. Great Britain and France had now sent an ultimatum telling Germany to remove her troops by 11.00 am this morning, otherwise a state of war would exist.

Everyone knew that Germany removing her troops was not going to happen. The Territorial Army were already in uniform. At the Old Kirk, the Reverend DM Bell, still quite a young man, who had been in post since the tragic death of his predecessor in the pulpit a few years ago, preached to a full congregation with everyone aware that it was now 11.00 am.

Were we at war? The Service finished soon after noon but just as the last hymn was being sung, a man was seen to enter the Church, whisper something to one of the Duty Elders, who in turn whispered something to Reverend DM Bell.

Everyone knew what it was, even before he announced it. That afternoon some of the Territorials marched from the Drill Hall to the station to catch their train, and no-one knew when or if they would ever return.

September 4 1967

The battle had been lost, and only a few survivors were there to see the corpse being buried.

It wasn't quite the end of the story for the station would be open for goods for several years yet, but tonight was the last passenger train to stop at Forfar Station.

The prevailing mood was sadness, but there was also not a little anger for no community had fought harder than Forfar did to save its station.

Very sadly politics was against Forfar. In the first place there was Dr Richard Beeching. He had been appointed by a Conservative Government to save money and to make the railways pay. The only way that he could do this was by closing "uneconomic lines", and this he proceeded to do and the Stanley to Kinnaber line was one for the axe.

Dr Beeching was much vilified, but was only doing his job.

And then Forfar had more bad luck when the Government changed in 1964. Forfar had never voted Labour, and to the distress of the many Labour voters in the town, not a finger was raised by the Wilson Government to save Forfar's railway.

Possibly had all this happened a few years later when the Conservatives were under pressure from the SNP, it would have been a different story, and in any case by then the Aberdeen oil boom would have started and there would have been stronger arguments for maintaining the rail link.

As it was, Forfar was very unfortunate to lose its railway station, and it is now acknowledged by environmentalists and others to have been a huge mistake. The curse of hell on those who destroyed Forfar's railway!

September 5 2009

In one of Forfar's sadder occasions, a young female Forfar jockey called Jan Wilson was today killed in an arson attack on a flat in Norton, near Malton in Yorkshire.

The following year a man called Peter Brown was found guilty of manslaughter.

The incident happened in the aftermath of a party from which Peter Brown, a man with long term problems involving alcohol, had been excluded.

Jan Wilson and an Irish jockey had been killed in the attack, thus bringing to an end two promising careers in horse racing. Jan had already won some races.

Her first was at Ripon and recently she had won a race at Ayr, her first in Scotland. Jan was a former pupil of Chapelpark School and Forfar Academy, and had been brought up on a farm near Rescobie with her parents Drew and Margaret.

She soon realised that she had a passion for horses, and had started to serve her time as an apprentice jockey. Her racing colours were red and black, and these were the colours that some of the mourners wore, and her saddle in those colours was placed on the coffin at her funeral.

Her funeral was held a few weeks later at the Lowson Memorial Church, taken by the Rev Brian Ramsay of Rescobie.

The Church was full of mourners and many more lined the streets outside as her coffin was taken to the Parkgrove Crematorium at Friockheim.

A "Jockey Jan" Memorial Fund was subsequently set up to help other young people follow their dreams.

September 6 1661

The investigations for witchcraft are in full swung.

Today Joanet Guthrie, daughter of Helen Guthrie, herself a witch, told of how she was carried by Isabel Shyrie to the Inch in the Loch of Forfar to meet the "Satanic majesty" who singled her out as "the Pretty Dauncer" from 13 other witches, and a month later at Muryknowes near Halcartounmill she was kissed by the devil.

Soon afterwards she was "nipped to her great pain" but at a place called Lapiedub about "ane myle be-eist Forfar" the Devil called her his "bony bird" and "did kiss her and straiked hir shoulder which was nipped by his hand, and then presently she was eased of her former paine".

But then at Newmanhill "hardby Forfar" at midnight, she saw "what may not be uttered". The Devil also persuaded her to renounce God.

This confession was extorted from her by overzealous Christians from the local Church, and this particular confession differs in that it does not seek to incriminate or involve any one else, but was simply her own experience.

What really happened here is of course impossible to state but one must never under-estimate the power of the human mind to imagine things, nor should we take seriously what has been extorted through torture and pain.

What is interesting is the place names and the way they were spelt in the 17th century. And we really would like to know what it was that Joanet saw at Newmanhill that "may not be uttered"!

September 7 1900

Today's *Forfar Herald* contains news of the ongoing war against the Boers in South Africa and a rather alarming outbreak of bubonic plague in Glasgow which everyone hopes will not reach Forfar.

In the local news, the imminent General Election campaign included a meeting held by the Unionist Party candidate Mr JB Don at the Reid Hall,

The big discussion in the town and in particular at the School Board was whether Religious Education should be taught at Forfar Academy in the upper reaches of the school.

The Rector, Mr Adam S Thomson, had apparently decided that the subject should not be taught to senior pupils, not from any doctrinal or religious position, but simply because he felt that more time should be spent of teaching children for their certificates.

He also cited the fact that the subject was taught further down the school, and that it was *not* taught to senior pupils in Brechin and Montrose.

The Reverend Paterson objected to all this and wanted 20 minutes per day to be devoted to religious education. The argument was a contentious one, and it was one which would go on for a while, but for the moment it was felt that no action should be taken by the Board. Rector Thomson, who had now been in post for three years, should be left to organise his curriculum as he thought fit, even though some people on the Board felt that he was "defying them".

What really counted in Mr Thomson's favour was that Inspectors regularly praised the achievement of Forfar Academy pupils in their certificates.

September 8 1893

Today's *Forfar Herald* contains a semi-serious but also rather humorous account. A member of the *Forfar Herald* staff took a walk along the Lochside one sultry afternoon recently in the company of a friend from Gloucestershire, when the Englishman suddenly said "There are no boys in Forfar".

This sounded like a bizarre comment since they had just passed and were continuing to pass hundreds of boys enjoying themselves in the water at the Lochside.

It transpired that what the man was complaining about was the prevalence of bad language among the boys.

> "Is there anything charming in that little scamp of five trying to outdo that bigger one of twelve in profane language? And there isn't a boy among the lot of them who is conscious of the evil!"

Apparently, according to the Englishman, there was nowhere else in Great Britain "even in the wildest purlieus of Whitechapel" that such language would be heard.

The fault lay in the older generation and the parents who did nothing to reprimand such youngsters or scold them.

> "Hence your Forfar boy is an imp ... I have been looking for the last three weeks in your town for the average loveable little chap, possessing the ordinary uncontaminated instincts of boyhood and I have not found him".

He then goes on to say that the answer lies in more of the Bible to be drummed into them. One feels that the gentleman in question has blinded himself to some of the truth or has not really lived as much or as widely as he claims to have done, if Forfar is the only place where children use bad language, but nevertheless, *The Forfar Herald* feels that more should perhaps be done by parents to curb such profanity.

September 9 1937

What was loosely referred to by subsequent generations of Forfar children as the "Boiled Park" was today opened by the widow of John Stewart Boyle, who had died a couple of years ago and left money for the purpose.

He had been a Forfar loon who had gone to Glasgow and built up a fleet of trawlers, and had clearly died a rich man leaving £10,000 for the park.

Today in warm sunshine, Mr Boyle's widow was present to open the Pavilion with a huge golden key.

It was the Earl of Strathmore, the father of the Queen, who opened the Park for the "benefit of his fellow citizens of Forfar" saying that it was his "business capacity and Forfar grit" that created the wealth of John Boyle.

It was claimed that about 4,000 people were present, and Mrs Boyle was then entertained by a choir of 90 schoolgirls singing two verses of a song that she herself had composed, and then adding another two verses as well!

Tea was then served for the platform party in a marquee especially erected for the purpose. Mrs Boyle was then taken by Provost Graham to the Town House to be given the Freedom of the Burgh.

The Forfar Dispatch was clearly impressed by the lay out of the park. It was not as large as the Reid Park, but it had facilities for bowls, putting and other recreations and the hope was expressed that the Park would be used for many generations of Forfarians in the future.

Boyle Park at the Opening.

September 10 1951

An indication of the popularity of Scottish Country Dancing as a pastime in Forfar is indicated by the notice on *The Forfar Dispatch* of this where it states that "all the classes of Mrs McKenzie, Miss Nairn and Mrs Sutton are full up, and that unless you have already enrolled, you have 'had it'."

There remain however a few classes for Beginners. There is of course a long tradition of dancing in Forfar since the days of "Dancie" Neill and "Dancie" Kydd. It has been a very popular pastime for Forfar people, particularly women, and would continue to be so for a few years, until the arrival of television in people's households made a huge change to everyone's social habits.

These classes were held in the Masonic Halls and the Castle Rooms under the auspices of the "Scottish Country Dance Society — Forfar Branch" and the cost was 1/6 for members and 2 shillings for non-members to be paid on the night.

Music was provided by the society, usually just one person on the piano or the accordion, and there was usually at Christmas and the end of Session a Concert and Dance to which husbands and wives were invited.

It was normally women who went to such classes, and it was much looked forward to as their night out, away from the demands of work and children!

As often in Forfar (maybe not so much in the rest of the world) dancing cut across social class barriers with factory women mingling happily with farmers' wives!

September 11 1921

Today was a day of solemn pride.

It was the unveiling by the Earl of Strathmore of the War Memorial on Balmashanner Hill, a huge and very impressive tower like structure which still dominates the town to this day, and is arguably one of the best known and best frequented of all war memorials in Scotland.

It is little wonder that the town felt constrained to spend so much on this mighty structure, for the figures are truly shocking.

1,950 served in the war and 439 fell, close enough to 1 in 4, and that takes no account of those permanently disfigured and maimed, and those still undergoing the unseen but no less real mental trauma of it all.

The weather was not great, in keeping with the sadness of the occasion, but it was estimated that about 4,000-5,000 were there, not far short of half the town's population.

For so many of them it was simply impossible to hear the speeches of the Earl of Strathmore and Reverend WG Donaldson of the Old Parish Church.

Many of them could not get any closer than halfway up the hill, and some of them occupied the field behind the Memorial. After the Memorial was unveiled, wreaths were laid by various local organisations who had lost folk.

It was a day on which many people wept, but there had been a little politics involved as well.

Queen Mary had been in the area a few days previously, but for some reason had declined to unveil the Memorial. This did not go down well with some of the ex-Servicemen.

Unveiling of the War Memorial in 1921

September 12 1949

One fears that there are times when there is just not enough news going on in Forfar to keep "The Drummer" of *The Forfar Dispatch* occupied.

Certainly there seems at the moment to be an agreeable lack of crime, suicides and murders, the war has been over for a few years so there are no casualties to report, not enough cars on the road as yet to yield a lot of accidents, very few weddings and not really enough deaths, even by natural causes.

The cycling club, the dramatic society, the operatic society and all the Churches have already given their unremarkable copy for the week. The cricket season is sadly coming to an end, so "The Drummer" has been amusing himself by making up football teams eg a team of all the colours begins "Gray, Black and Gold..."

They could play a team of tradesmen whose forward line is "Woodman, Mason, Shepherd, Carter and Cook" while the mighty half back line of the Birds "Heron, Hawkes and Parrot" would be confronted in the midfield by "Bull, Lyon and Lamb" of the Animals.

It is good entertaining stuff, but "going to press" is fast approaching and still no murders being committed or wars breaking out in Forfar, so he concludes by making up a side of Forfar tradesmen viz." Iannerelli, Ednie and Kinninmonth; Barclay, Ross and Hutchison; MacLean, Lowson, Caird, Dalgety and Son"

Such a side would, one feels, be well fed, well clad, well treated health wise and with no lack of screwdrivers for any agricultural vehicles that were going on the blink.

September 13 1939

And so Forfar, after the initial shock and excitement of it all is adjusting itself to being at war.

The big issue in the town at the moment is that of the Dundee evacuees.

The children arrived in town last week, and were duly billeted at appropriate houses, sometime on people who were less than 100% enthusiastic about the idea, but now some of the evacuees have departed!

In truth it was hard to imagine the Luftwaffe descending on Dundee in the first place, and quite a few of the Dundee children have decided that the quieter life of Forfar is not for them!

Dire warnings are posted in *The Forfar Dispatch* about anyone who claims an "Evacuation Allowance" after their evacuees have gone!

Meanwhile the schools are closed for reasons that escape everyone, senior football is suspended, but the Regal and the Pavilion are still open (but with different hours)

There is a notice telling everyone that Air Raid Shelters are available at 33 Nursery Street, 57 North Street, the Shelter at the top of Albert Street, the Pend at the Cross and the Centre Arch behind the Town Hall.

Everyone is meant to be going around with a gas mask, but it is a rule that, even at this early stage of the war, is honoured more in its breach than its observance.

Volunteers are wanted for just about everything, lectures on First Aid are offered, some men have already been called up and are away, others await their papers and apply for exemptions and deferments.

Forfar is at war, but the weather is excellent.

September 14 1920

Forfar's Council Workers are on strike for possibly the first time ever!

This industrial dispute arose suddenly because the Town Council did not seem to understand that "workers" and "labourers" were both entitled to a wage increase.

Prices in some key commodities like bread and eggs had been rising steeply since the war, and "workers" had been negotiating with the Town Council for some time.

The Town had agreed to a wage increase of 7/6d for its "workers" but seemed to think that this did not apply to the "labourers". As a result, the "labourers" suddenly downed tools on Tuesday September 14 with the Gas Works in North Street particularly badly affected, and threatening to paralyse the town.

But Manager Mr Skea, and a former Manager Mr Harper (now resident in Ayr but by chance on holiday in Forfar) and two Bailies, Lamb and Malcolm who had some knowledge of how the gas supply worked managed to keep the town going for a day or two.

The Town Council which had previously voted by 6-5 with one abstention *not* to pay the increase to the "labourers", suddenly changed its mind, the "labourers" were paid and resumed work immediately with no harm done.

However there may have been another factor at work here. Cynics were not slow to spot a connection with the imminent Royal visit of Princess Mary, the daughter of King George V and Queen Mary on her way to visit relatives in Airlie.

There might have been political demonstrations and the streets would not have been so clean, for the street cleaners were also "labourers"!

The Royal Burgh of Forfar is to
be honoured

TO-MORROW~(Saturday

By Her Royal Highness

Princess Mary

Passing through the town on her way
to Airlie Castle from Dundee.

It is expected that the Royal Car will
arrive in Forfar about 5-30 p.m., and will stop
in front of the Town and County Hall where
the Princess will inspect Detachments of the
local Boy Scouts and Red Cross Nurses and
a contingent of the senior pupils of Forfar
Academy.

The Provost and Magistrates hope that
Citizens will loyally and suitably decorate
their Houses.

JAS. MOFFAT, Provost.
A. MacHARDY, Town Clerk.

Announcement of the visit of Princess Mary

September 15 1996

This Sunday morning the 2nd Forfar Boys' Brigade celebrated their 50th anniversary with a Church Parade of Old Boys to the East and Old Parish Church (as it is now called).

They had enjoyed a Dinner the night before in the Reid Hall, and today, a fine crisp autumn morning saw the Old Boys parade through the town to the Church.

The guest of honour was Founder Captain John Ritchie, now in his 90s. In 1946 Mr Ritchie had founded the Company, based in the East Kirk but meeting for Friday night's parades in the North School until their Hall was built in Green Street in 1961.

Many boys had passed through this company, the highlights being the Camps, the trips to Denmark and the visit of the Danes to Forfar — something that was considered to be very daring in the 1950s and early 1960s.

Today Gordon Forbes and William Nicol, former members of the company took part in the service which was led by the Reverend Graham Norrie and included the presentation of new colours.

The Boys' Brigade, founded originally in Glasgow in 1883, was struggling in the current age.

The ideas of uniforms, marching, pillbox hats, saluting, discipline, patriotism and "muscular Christianity" were more typical perhaps of a previous age, but there was a determination to carry on and adapt to the new world without in any way compromising the old ideals of being "Sure and Steadfast" as exemplified in the BB Hymn of "Will Your Anchor Hold In The Storms of Life?".

2nd Forfar Boys' Brigade 1948

September 16 1902

Today Mr Colin Sinclair Murray Brown, who had at one point been Assistant Minister at the West United Free Church of Forfar, was charged before the Lord Kinross, the Lord Justice General, with the murder of his landlady Mrs McIntosh of Rochester Street, Edinburgh.

He was brought into court by two warders, and it was obvious to anyone that his reason had gone. He was gibbering, pointing at the judge, grinning inanely and muttering incoherently.

He was found to be insane in the opinion of several doctors, and was therefore unable to plead, and was ordered to be detained at an Asylum in Perthshire during His Majesty's Pleasure.

A native of Orkney, Brown, already a graduate of Edinburgh University, had been accepted as a probationer in the Free Kirk and had been Assistant Minister at the West Free Kirk of Forfar throughout 1901 while still studying Divinity.

He had cut a good impression among his parishioners, and had made a few friends in the town. He was described as thoughtful, studious, hard-working and preached a good sermon in the opinion of most of the congregation.

But then suddenly and for reasons not satisfactorily explained, he had suddenly left the Church and left Forfar at the end of 1901. He had gone to Stornoway to preach at one point but was still studying in Edinburgh.

His landlady in Edinburgh had heard him in distress one night and had gone to investigate and without any sort of warning, he had killed her. Naturally, quite a lot of people were distressed and amazed about this in Forfar, but everyone who ever knew Mr Brown said that it was totally out of character.

September 17 1934

The town was shocked to the core to learn today of the death of Provost Tom Hanick, a universally loved figure through the town.

He was 56; it was believed that his early death of a heart attack was caused by his total dedication to the town that he loved and which he had served all his life.

He collapsed on the stairs of the Sheriff Court on his way to preside over the Police Court this Monday morning, having given no indication of ill health, and had died shortly after he was taken to the Infirmary.

Forfar born and bred, he was a bachelor and lived with his sister Jean, having played a large part in the upbringing of the children of another sister who had died when they were young.

There were very few things in the town of which he was not a part, Chairman of Forfar Athletic for example, British Red Cross, the local Liberal Society. He had served on the Town Council since 1910, and had been re-elected any time that he stood, something that says a lot about the high regard in which he was held locally.

He made a point of trying to learn the name of every person in town, and had met Royalty, notably King George V and Queen Mary.

Perpetually cheerful and encouraging, there were very few people who had a bad word to say about him.

A practising Roman Catholic, which might have been a disadvantage in some parts of Scotland, he was very happy to attend the Old Parish Church on Town Council occasions.

Outside the town, he numbered men like Sir Harry Lauder and Willie Maley of Celtic FC as his friends.

September 18 1909

Today the Forfar North School was opened.

Possibly it would be more accurate to say that it had been re-opened for the school had been built on the site of a previous school there, sometimes called the Wellbraehead School, the Wellbrae School or the North Burgh School.

This new school however was large and commodious, and was duly declared open by Mr JM Wattie of His Majesty's Inspection Service as they were then called.

Mr Wattle congratulated the people of Forfar on their school attendance. Over all Scotland, the attendance figures were 87% which meant that, for some reason of another, 13% of children did not attend school.

In Forfar the figures were 90%, even in the winter, and he hoped that this could continue. The first Headmaster of the new school was to be Mr Hamilton, and he clearly took great pride in showing the parents and the pupils his new school which had been built at no little cost.

Indeed the politics of the building of the new school had been going on for several years now, and the hope was expressed that education could now take the place of bickering.

There was one sour note however. A parade had been arranged of all the pupils, going out of one gate down Victoria Road, turning left along Castle Street to the Cross, up East High Street, along North Street and home.

Unfortunately, they turned the wrong way at the bottom of Victoria Street, turned up Carseburn Road and into North Street, thereby disappointing the large crowd of people at the Cross.

The more educated wrote letters of complaint, the less refined shrugged their shoulders and said, philosophically, that "Farfar disnae ken its erse fae its elba"

September 19 1922

One of the features of life in Forfar (and indeed elsewhere) in the 1920s was emigration.

Europe was taking a long time to recover from the war and times were hard as the New World beckoned, although in truth, things were not necessarily a great deal better there.

On this occasion however, it was an older couple who were leaving town, Mr and Mrs Charles Edwards who were leaving with their family to spend their retirement in Calgary, Canada.

The East United Free Kirk with the Reverend Rusk presiding organised a social for them, as Mr Edwards had been an elder at that Church since 1907.

Various musical and dramatic performances were performed for them by members of the congregation, and then Mr Edwards was presented with a walking stick and Mrs Edwards with a handsome umbrella.

Their daughter Jessie (who was going with them) was given a Bible and a lady's handbag for her work in the Sunday School. It was a very emotional occasion, for Mr Edwards and his wife had served the Church in dark and difficult times.

The evening ended with everyone singing "Auld Lang Syne" and "Will You No Come Back Again?" The likelihood, of course, was that they would not come back again, for Canada was a long way away in 1922 — at least five days on the Atlantic and several more days to Calgary with air travel a distant fantasy and another thirty years in the future — and although emigration was common in those days, it was still a huge and more or less irrevocable step.

September 20 1905

A low attendance at the Town Council tonight led to the shelving yet again of what *The Forfar Herald* considers to be a very important matter, namely the building of an underground lavatory at the north end of the Municipal Buildings in Castle Street on the site of the present ugly and not particularly hygienic urinal.

It was the idea of ex-Provost McDougall and presumably it would include accommodation for ladies. Ex-Provost McDougall was disappointed that the current Provost himself and three other members of the Council were not present.

This matter naturally led in 1905 to a certain amount of tee-heeing and embarrassment, but it was nevertheless a real problem, and *The Forfar Herald* roundly condemns Councillor William Michie and those who voted to do nothing about the problem in the meantime.

It has been claimed that visitors to the town have had to go into licensed premises nearby and ask if they could use their facilities, while far too often on a Saturday night in particular those who have been drinking have been known to commit a public nuisance on the streets themselves and the wynds of the town.

The Public Health Committee will have to be consulted on this issue and it is clear that it needs to be addressed with a degree of urgency.

The situation of the lavatory at the place suggested is the obvious answer, although there are those who have suggested elsewhere.

Bailie Peffers brought forward an amendment agreeing that there was a need, but that the decision on the site should be postponed until later. This hardly helped solve the problem.

September 21 1891

A huge attendance of over 1,000 members attended the meeting of the Forfar Factory Workers' Union in the Drill Hall.

It was an astonishing attendance and one wonders how the Drill Hall was able to hold them all, but the idea was to approach the factory owners for an increase given the improvement in the trade.

In the Chair was the President Thomas Roy, a determined character with a great following, sometimes feted with his own song to the tune of "Oh My Darling, Clementine", the current Music Hall favourite with "Tommy Roy" substituted for "Clementine"!

There had been a certain history of militancy in the jute industry and a couple of years ago, Roy had enjoyed a notable success when he broke the owners "lock out" which had almost brought the whole town to its knees until even the local press and the Churches sided with Roy.

On the whole, however, labour relationships were good, although the workers were not well paid, with a particularly Victorian excuse brought forward that "many of the weavers were women".

Roy insisted that the Union was well equipped financially to give strike pay if necessary, although he hoped that matters could be arranged amicably.

Nevertheless, Adam Farquharson, the Secretary was instructed to lodge a claim with the employers, asking for a 5% pay rise. Roy and Farquharson were both confident that the employers were in a position to pay such an increase, and were cheered to the echo by their enthusiastic supporters.

Roy had also received a letter from Miss Routledge of the Women's Trade Union movement saying that she thought that the Women's section of the Forfar Union was "the best organised Women's Union in North Britain".

Drill Hall

357

September 22 1915

Forfar was shocked this morning to hear that Mr Edward Robertson, the proprietor of Burnside Farm had been found by his butler, Mr Bigwood, shot dead in his gunroom.

Dr Peterkin was immediately summoned from Forfar, but Robertson had been dead for hours. It was said that this was an accident caused when he was cleaning one of his guns, but the truth may well have different.

Mr Robertson had been depressed about the way that the war was going. There had been many heavy casualties recently at the Battle of Loos, many of them involving local boys.

This followed what was now acknowledged to be an unmitigated disaster at Gallipoli earlier in the year.

In addition some of his money was bound up in Germany, and it had been frozen by the British Government.

He was a popular and well-liked man, even by his tenants and workers which wasn't always common in 1915.

His well-attended funeral was held in the St John's Episcopalian Church and the Reverend W Magee Tuke praised Mr Robertson's commitment and benevolence.

He was the President of the Local Infirmary, and County Commissioner of the Red Cross. He had been a great botanist, and had given a great deal of money for the erection of a gravestone to Forfar's most famous botanist, George Don.

He was also a very keen golfer and had paid a great deal of money for the relaying and rebunkering of the Forfar Golf course at Cunninghill. It was a great tragedy and he was indeed a casualty of war, albeit an indirect one.

September 23 1933

Forfar's first ever Rugby game was played today at Beechhill, Lour Road when the newly formed Strathmore Rugby Club played against a Midland Union Select XV, based on Dundee High School FP.

The weather was fine and the crowd, although small, was enthusiastic with quite a few rugby fans from other towns keen to see the new club get underway.

The game was, as one would expect, somewhat one-sided and the final score was 40-0 to the Midland Union Select XV for whom Norman Ireland, stand off for the Select, had a field day.

Nevertheless it was a start for the new club in a town which had never before shown any great enthusiasm for the game of rugby in the sense that it obviously did for football and cricket.

It had all started in March this year when some seven-a-side games had been played at Lochside Cricket pitch, Steele Park and then at Station Park at half time in a football match, and the idea had grown.

The first ever AGM had been held at the Meffan Hall a few weeks ago and now 15 guys of reasonable ability had been got together, even though quite obviously they were out classed today.

For the new team IE Fleming from Meigle, J Mackie and Dr GMR Duffus had played well, and best wishes for the new club were extended at the end of the game.

A collection of £1 seven shillings and two pence was raised for the Forfar Infirmary.

Aberdeen Grammar School 3rd XV will be the visitors to Beechhill on Saturday.

September 24 1884

A tough legal case presented itself to the Sheriff Court today.

It aroused strong passions (but also a certain amount of laughter and enjoyment) in the town, highlighting as it did a dispute in the family of William Laird & Company of Canmore Linen Works.

What seems to have happened is that William Doig of Victoria Steet, a Clerk in the firm, was dismissed by John Laird senior and George Laird, two of the three partners of the firm on August 7.

Why he was dismissed we do not know, but in any case, he was re-instated by the other partner of the firm, John Laird junior. The two who had dismissed Mr Doig were now bringing a legal action to prevent him entering the premises of the Canmore Linen Works or the Forfar Power Loom Company (also owned by the Lairds).

The argument of Doig was that his dismissal by only two of the partners was illegal and incompetent, whereas the argument of the two "dismissers" of Doig was that John Laird junior had no right to re-instate Doig.

Public sympathy in Forfar tended to side with Doig, although Doig was almost incidental to the case as the town thoroughly relished the spectacle of the Lairds washing their "dirty linen in public".

The pun was intended, and which of the Lairds paid in how much to the firm and which took out how much was much discussed by the workers of Lairds who were really rather enjoying the whole business, as indeed were Lairds' competitors.

The Sheriff needed a great deal of time to consider this case which was rare, if not unprecedented, in legal history but eventually ruled in favour of John Laird junior and William Doig.

Forfar Academy Staff 1958

September 25 1965

Today saw the official opening of the new Forfar Academy in Taylor Street by the Queen Mother.

It was a day that had been promised for long enough, for it was obvious that the old Forfar Academy in Academy Street, a venerable building which had produced many great scholars and continued to do so, was now really showing its age with pupils for example being taught in a Basement, commonly known as the Dungeon, and with no playing fields of its own at a time when other schools now did.

The school at Taylor Street had opened for business in August but today was the official opening, and it was considered appropriate that the much loved Queen Mother should do the job.

She did, of course, belong to the Bowes-Lyons of Glamis Castle. It was feared that there might be a political demonstration against the closure of Forfar Station (which would happen in 1967), but nothing of that ilk occurred.

Nevertheless security was tight, and only some parents were invited to attend the ceremony conducted by the serving Rector Mr Alex C Gillespie.

No-one really knew exactly how old the original Forfar Academy was — it was certainly in existence in the 1810s — but it would still be used, becoming Chapelpark Primary School with the amalgamation of the North and the East Schools.

Today a bright new future seemed to beckon for education in Forfar and district. Sadly, in a few years' time, the Government would raise the school leaving age from 15 to 16, and the new school would already be obsolete!

September 26 1940

The Battle of Britain seems to be over, and the Luftwaffe have been temporarily removed from the skies of Kent, at least in the daytime, although night time bombing of London's cities is clearly intensifying.

Today's *Forfar Dispatch* is all about the Angus Spitfire Fund whereby the local people are all working together to provide a new Spitfire for the RAF in their ongoing struggle.

Such people have a part to play in this war which affects and involves everyone. Kirriemuir has ruffled a few feathers by trying to say that it can provide a machine on its own, for it has far more wealth than Brechin and Forfar put together.

Maybe this is an attempt to blackmail Forfarians and Brechiners to dip deeper into their pockets, but it does seem to be an unnecessarily provocative piece of one-upmanship.

Far more praiseworthy are the children of John Street who have been organising a series of concerts at their own back greens, free of charge but with a collection being taken for the Spitfire funds.

Most of the entertainment is singing but there are a few acrobats, comedians and some fine impersonations of Harry Lauder and Winston Churchill as well.

A few parents and other adults are involved, and they have been attracting good audiences, including a few men in uniform.

There are hidden depths in John Street, and they are much encouraged by the local population, as the war in various parts of the world continues and intensifies.

September 27 1890

The Forfar Herald reported that today was the biggest day in the history of cycling in Forfar, because never before had there been seen such a large gathering of "wheelmen" as there was today for the Club Road Championship of Forfar.

There were about 300 cyclists in town, many of them having arrived on the morning train with their bicycles from Dundee, and it was estimated that between three and four thousand persons watched the race.

"Football in its palmiest days scarcely ever brought together such a large assemblage of people". The race started at Zoar and finished up at Briar Cottage just outside the town on the Glamis Road, and the route took them through Kirrie and Glamis.

The favourite was Forfar's darling John Killacky, and by the time that the pack reached Padanaram, he was already ahead but had the misfortune to be stopped at Kirriemuir Railway Station to allow a train to go through, and this allowed the rest to catch up.

But by the time they were through Kirriemuir and heading downhill for Glamis, Killacky was again well ahead, being described in the vernacular as "giein them his erse for a looking gless" as he charged for home.

"Killacky's first" was the cry from those who were assembled at Briar Cottage and he finished in 51 minutes and 44 seconds, a good minute and three quarters ahead of Shaw of Kirriemuir who just managed to head off a late challenge from Cant of Dundee.

The other Forfar men did less well — Prophet came in 17th while Coutts had a nasty spill at Padanaram and had to retire with a bruised and lacerated arm, but there was little doubt about who was the hero of the hour.

September 28 1946

Tonight at the Reid Hall, Forfar was treated to a Variety show by the Jolly Jesters Road Show paying a return visit to the town with a totally different programme.

There were two Houses at 6.15 pm and 8.30 pm, and the programme included Hercules, The British Lion who claimed to be "The World's Strongest Man" doing some amazing feats of strength.

A highlight was Macquie Poise, billed as "The Unique and Mysterious Entertainer", who was the "man who completely baffled the American Medical Profession" and who "made a thousand cripples walk".

There were also The Gracie Sisters who "stepped it out" with "grace, pep and personality", Margo "Scotland's Premier Soprano", George Nugent—"Scotland's Star Comedian. Everybody's Favourite" — Tony Lorente the "Ace Accordionist" and George the "Kiddies' Favourite".

Prices were three shillings, two shillings and one shilling. The show was well received, and there certainly was a wide range of entertainment.

One would have to wonder and ask questions about the man who "made a thousand cripples walk". It would have been interesting to know if he had any success with any of Forfar's war wounded who were now home in strength!

The war (even the Japanese war) had been over for well over a year, and almost all the soldiers were back home. The town was making a far better recovery from this war than it had from the last one because the same edition of *The Forfar Dispatch* contained an advertisement for workers being needed in Jock Lowson's!

Unemployment, that scourge of 15 years ago, had gone!

September 29 1933

Today was the last edition of *The Angus Herald,* previously *The Forfar Herald* which had commenced publishing in 1877.

The newspaper itself announces quite curtly that *The Angus Herald* has been "disposed of" mainly due to the recent death of Henry Munro, Managing Director of The Munro Press and "the acquirement of additional publishing interests".

This was a grave disappointment for the town because *The Forfar Herald* had been a great source of news for the past 50 years, and it would be much missed.

It was probably felt that there were three reasons for the demise of the local paper in its Castle Street base. One was it was felt that the writing was on the wall when it became *The Angus Herald* rather than *The Forfar Herald* for it was then spreading itself too thin and the DC Thomson Press already did a great job for Angus.

The other was that *The Forfar Dispatch* was possibly a little better and was a lot cheaper. At one point *The Forfar Dispatch* had been distributed free and paid for by advertisements, but now it was more of a business concern in its own right.

It cost only a "hie" (one halfpenny) whereas the *Herald* was two pence, and *Dispatch* had all the cheery, couthy, gossipy stuff that Forfarians craved.

And the other reason was the worldwide economic depression which affected everything including the payment of staff and the upkeep of machinery. It was impossible not to feel a little pang of sorrow for a Forfar institution which had been an invaluable source of information on things, national, international and particularly, local.

Two Princesses in 1936 with their Grandmother, the Countess of
Strathmore

September 30 1938

Today was the Munich Agreement.

Subsequent historians use words like "betrayal" and "sell out" to describe the day on which Prime Minister Neville Chamberlain ceded the Sudetenland of Czechoslovakia to Hitler in return for "peace in our time".

Now we all know that it merely bought a year and that Mr Chamberlain was a great deal less successful in 1939, but at the time that was not the perception.

The Forfar Dispatch of the following midweek tells of the atmosphere in the factories, cinemas, shops and pubs of the town "shivering on the brink of the mighty maelstrom of war" and how it was only today, Friday 30th that hope came "out of the night that covered us, as black as the pit" when it was confirmed by the 6.00 news on the radio that Europe had been saved!

Ludicrously, "The Drummer" compares Mr Chamberlain to Horatius who defended the bridge and "even the ranks of Tuscany could scarce forbear to cheer" as his political enemies were forced to praise him.

In the meantime, the Air Raid Patrols and the First Aid Services continued their recruitment and the Territorials were not yet "stood down" but remained in preparedness.

There were an awful lot of relieved people going round Forfar, especially when they looked at the sheer amount of blinded and disabled middle aged men going around the town with their injuries a visible proof of what had happened twenty years ago.

That surely must not be allowed to happen again! Sadly, a year later it did!

1910

In This Year
Traders in Forfar

No
dull blades—
and no need for new ones

Smooth, close, quick, comfortable shaving is possible only with a blade that is properly stropped each time it is used. The self-contained stropping arrangement of the Auto-trop Safety Razor enables you to keep a hair-edge on each blade for many months. Remember, no skill or experience is necessary to keep AutoStrop blades in perfect condition. You also avoid the buying of new blades necessary with all non-stropping razors, and thus the

AutoStrop Razor SAFETY

pays for itself in a year. There is no handling of the blade or taking anything apart for either stropping or cleaning. Made in Great Britain.

Don't throw good blades away.

THE COMPLETE OUTFIT INCLUDES AutoStrop Safety Razor, heavily plated, 12 certified AutoStrop Blades, certified Horse-hide Strop, in case, 3½ ins. by 2 ins. Price ..

21/- net.

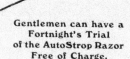

Gentlemen can have a
Fortnight's Trial
of the AutoStrop Razor
Free of Charge.

W. ANDREW & SON,
TOBACCONISTS AND HAIRDRESSERS,
29 WEST HIGH STREET, FORFAR.

JAMES M. ARNOT,

Ironmonger and Seedsman,

11 CASTLE STREET, FORFAR.

(Next to County Hotel Stables).

General and Furnishing Ironmongery.

Fishing Tackle, Rods, Reels, &c.,
GUNS, CARTRIDGES, AND OTHER SHOOTING REQUISITES.

Garden and Agricultural SEEDS and IMPLEMENTS.

OILS, Burning and Lubricating, of Finest Quality.

J. BELL,

General Family Draper,

81, 83, 85, & 87 WEST HIGH ST., FORFAR.

Dressmaking.   Mantles.   Millinery.

Agent for THOMSON Ltd., Dye Works, Perth.

The Best Value in
GENERAL HOUSEHOLD DRAPERY and FURNISHINGS,
including LINOLEUMS, BEDSTEADS, MATTRESSES,
BLANKETS, COTTON and FLANNELETTE
SHEETS, FLANNELS and FLANNELETTES, &c., &c.

. . TRY US WITH AN ORDER. . .

Buy a Cycle built
in Town where Guarantee
can be upheld.

ELITE CYCLES

Prices from
£4-17-6 to £13-13-0.

R. BALLINGALL,

118 East High Street, Forfar.

Billiard Rooms

126 EAST HIGH STREET, FORFAR.

8 FIRST-CLASS TABLES.

SHOOTING RANGES

WAR OFFICE MINIATURE RIFLES, 5 Shots, 2d.
AIR RIFLES, 5 Shots, 1d.

ESTABLISHED in 1853.

The Forfar Savings Bank,

Certified under the Act of 1863.

OFFICE---UNION BANK BUILDINGS.

OPEN—Daily from 9-30 to 10-30 a.m. ;
On Monday, from 9-30 to 11-30 a.m. ;
AND
On Friday Evening, from 6 to 8.

Deposits Received

Of ONE SHILLING up to £50 in One Year; and £200 in all.
The Rate of Interest is £2 10s per cent. per annum.
Amount of Deposits at 20th November 1909, £100,350.

TRUSTEES AND MANAGERS.

JAMES MOFFAT, Provost of Forfar, *Chairman.*
W. T. FARQUHAR, of Pitscandly, *Vice-Chairman.*

John Anderson, Merchant.
Francis Cargill, Bloomfield.
Rev. George J. Caie, D.D.
John B. Don, Manufacturer.
Gilbert W. Don, Manufacturer.
Thomas Henderson, Bank Agent.
Alexander MacHardy, Town Clerk.
William Shepherd, Stationer.
John Strachan, Jeweller.
Dr John Macalister.
David Sturrock, Draper.
Walter G. Laird, Manufacturer.
R. F. Myles, Solicitor.
John A. Grant, Manufacturer.
D. M. Graham, of Pitreuchie.
J. S. Gordon, Solicitor.
William Melvin, Merchant.
R. T. Birnie, Chief Constable.
Thomas Hart, Procurator-Fiscal.

John M. Robertson, Factory Manager.
Dr George Peterkin.
Dr John Cable.
D. J. Carnegy, Assessor.
David Steele, Beech Hill.
Rev. Hugh Macmaster, Dunnichen.
W. Graham Pool, Draper.
Rev. Charles Gardyne.
John S. Whyte, Tanner.
William Warden, Retired Merchant.
Alexander Hay, Solicitor.
Rev. Wm. Adam.
Rev. J. B. Gardiner.
Rev. W. G. Donaldson.
Rev. Alexander Ritchie, Oathlaw.
George R. Fowler, Druggist.
Rev. R. W. Forbes.
Dr Andrew Kerr.
Dr Norman J. Sinclair.

FORFAR BATHS

These Splendid BATHS "through the Pend," are now open at popular prices of admission.

The opportunities for bathing and swimming are unrivalled anywhere.

MEDICATED BATHS

Of various descriptions can be arranged for on application to the Bathmaster. These can be had exactly the same as those supplied at the finest Spas, at a third the price.

ORDINARY HOT BATHS, 4d and 3d.
ADMISSION to Swimming Pond and Spray Room, 2d and 1d.

The Hall and Pond are heated so that all can enjoy a swim at any time of the year.

The Hours during which the Baths are open vary according to Season, and may be found out on application at the Baths.

FOUR THOUSAND FIVE HUNDRED copies of the FORFAR DISPATCH are distributed gratis in Forfar and District every Thursday, and Advertisers using its columns will find it a cheap and effective medium for bringing their Notices before the Public . . . .

. . Printed and Published by . .
. .OLIVER MCPHERSON. .
. 85 East High Street, Forfar .

Job Printing of every description.

CXXXV

GAS--The Ideal Cooker.

Strike a match, turn a tap, and your Cooker is ready. Just think what this means in time and labour saved. Contrast it with all the work necessary in cooking with an ordinary fire.

GAS--The Ideal Heater.

With a Gas Fire you again merely require to strike the match, turn the tap, and your room is comfortably warm in ten minutes. These fires become effective the moment after lighting, and can be immediately turned off when not required. They throw out a remarkable amount of healthy, radiant heat and are **scientifically correct** and **artistically perfect.** The ashes are left at the Gasworks and a clean fuel is delivered to you through pipes.

Users of the latest new pattern fires will testify to the fact that with the foregoing virtues the fires do not possess the vice of extravagance. The useful heat comes into the room. It is not carried up the chimney.

Every one of the difficulties of HEATING UP INTERIOR SPACES, be they Large or Small, will be successfully met by us, and we solicit your Enquiries.

. . THE . .

Corporation Gas Works,

NORTH STREET, FORFAR.

William R. Guthrie,

Grocer, Wine and Spirit Merchant,

82 EAST HIGH STREET, FORFAR.

CHARLES EDWARDS,

FAMILY BUTCHER,

139 EAST HIGH STREET,

FORFAR.

Always on hand a First-class Selection of Prime Butcher Meat at Keenest Prices.
Marriage Parties and others supplied at Moderate Charges.
Orders called for and promptly delivered.

THE FAMED MIXED

PETER REID ROCK

To be had at the Old Address--

51 CASTLE STREET, FORFAR.

ESTABLISHED 1794.

K

cxliii

ESTABLISHED 1877

The Forfar Herald

PUBLISHED FRIDAY MORNING.

EIGHT PAGES.   ONE PENNY.

Oldest Newspaper and Best Advertising Medium.

Full and Reliable Reports of
All Local Meetings, Public Boards, &c.

SPECIAL ARTICLES ON LOCAL TOPICS.

THE HERALD

Can be delivered to Subscribers within the Burgh,
4s 4d per Annum, 6s 6d posted.

GENERAL PRINTING AT THE HERALD OFFICE.

J. & A. McDOUGALL, Proprietors.

HOUSEHOLD WORDS.

BUY

HOOD'S BOOTS

THE BEST VARIETY, VALUE, AND WEAR.
HAND-SEWN BOOTS MADE TO MEASURE.
BRING YOUR REPAIRS.

HOOD'S
96 CASTLE STREET, FORFAR.

D. Irons & Sons,

FURNISHING

AND GENERAL IRONMONGERS,

22 to 24 CASTLE STREET,

FORFAR.

Will show in their new premises the Largest and Finest Selection in the County of GENERAL and FANCY IRONMONGERY in all departments, at prices to suit all requirements.

Large Showrooms.   All Goods on sight.

D. I. & S. invite you to call and Inspect their Stock of IRONMONGERY, CUTLERY, CASED GOODS, ELECTRO PLATE. Travelling Bags, Trunks, Dressing Cases, and Fancy Leather Goods. Brass and Iron Bedsteads and Mattresses, Perambulators and Mail Carts.

SHOPPING A PLEASURE AT
22 to 24 CASTLE ST., FORFAR.

Telegrams--JARMAN, FORFAR.   Telephone No. 18.

Jarman's Hotel

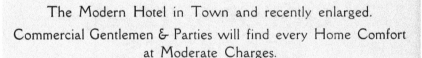

FORFAR.

OPPOSITE THE RAILWAY STATION.

The Modern Hotel in Town and recently enlarged.

Commercial Gentlemen & Parties will find every Home Comfort
at Moderate Charges.

Table d'Hote daily.   Billiards.

Hot and Cold Baths.

ALL LETTERS AND TELEGRAMS CAREFULLY ATTENDED TO.
UNDER PERSONAL SUPERVISION.

BOOTS waits all Trains.   **POSTING** in all its Branches.

DAVID I. KYDD,

TAILOR and CLOTHIER,

79 EAST HIGH ST., FORFAR.

All the Latest PATTERNS in TWEED SUITINGS, OVER-COATINGS and TROUSERINGS.

THE FAVOUR OF A TRIAL ORDER SOLICITED.

SATISFACTION GUARANTEED.

☛ Buy your Groceries, Wines, and Spirits, at

C. Cook & Coy.'s

Where you will get FIRST-CLASS GOODS at Lowest Possible Prices.

Special Value in TEAS, 1/4, 1/6, 1/8, and 2/ per lb.
Very Old HIGHLAND WHISKIES, Finest JAMAICA RUMS,
Pure GRAPE BRANDIES, INVALID PORTS and SHERRIES.
Agents for WINCARNIS, VIBRONA, HALL'S WINE, &c.
Unrivalled Value in Hams, Butter, Cheese, &c.

C. COOK & COY.,

Family Grocers and Wine Merchants,

33 Castle Street, FORFAR.

cl

The Forfar and District
Steam Laundry Company Ltd.

All Kinds of Washing, Dressing, and Cleaning.

Carpet Beating, etc. (by Patent Carpet Beater),

at Moderate Prices.

Good Outside Drying and Bleaching Green.

Works : Easter Bank.

Receiving Office:
Miss J. Ferguson, 71 Castle Street.

clii

James Mackintosh,

Engineer & General Blacksmith,

CANMORE IRON WORKS,

23 QUEEN STREET, 38 CANMORE STREET, and FORFAR AUCTION MART.

LAWN MOWERS.

Our Machinery for this work is the best procurable. Automatic in action, it makes a perfect edge. The amount of work done in this line shows that machines are properly repaired.

HORSE-SHOEING.

Ex-Farrier-Sergeant MACKINTOSH has this important branch under his supervision and clients can rely on first-class workmanship.

PLOUGHS.

The MACKINTOSH MATCH PLOUGH, the "MAC" MOVABLE POINT PLOUGH, and our DRILLING PLOUGH still prove that they are second to none.

Ploughs of any pattern Made, Mounted, and Repaired.
Agricultural Machinery of every description attended to.
Gates and Railings Made and Repaired.
Kiln-Bedding supplied and fitted on.
Jobbing of every description. ESTIMATES GIVEN.

clx

ITALIAN WAREHOUSE.

ESTABLISHED 1835.   Telephone No. 12.

B. & M. MELVIN,

FAMILY GROCERS,
WINE AND BRANDY IMPORTERS,

21 CASTLE STREET, FORFAR.

SPECIALTY—Excellence of Quality at Lowest Market Prices.
FINEST GROCERY GOODS—Selected from the Best Markets. Stock always fresh.
BACON—HARRIS' Wiltshire Bacon in cuts, and sliced by the BERKEL & PARNALL's Patent Slicing Machine.
TEAS—Carefully selected from Best Gardens in INDIA, CEYLON, and CHINA, and judiciously blended—Agents for the MAZAWATTEE TEA COMPANY.
COFFEE—Fresh Ground Daily.
WINES AND BRANDIES—Imported direct from best Shippers.
WHISKY—Our Famous " Old Blend " selected from the Best Distilleries in Scotland, very old and thoroughly matured in Bond in Sherry Casks.
LIQUEURS—Bénédictine, Chartreux, Curaçao, Kümmel, Maraschino, Milk Punch, Noyáu, &c., &c.
MALT LIQUORS—BASS' and ALLSOPP's India Pale Ale. BARCLAY, PERKINS & Co.'s London Imperial Stout. Edinburgh Ale and Table Beer. JACOB's Pilsener Beer. TENNENT's Lager.
ÆRATED WATERS—SCHWEPPES', DUNCAN, FLOCKHART & Co.'s, GILBERT RAE's, &c.

APPOLLINARIS WATERS.   SPARKLING KOLA.

---

*Agents for Dr Penfold's Australian Wines; Max Greger Ltd. Hungarian Wines; " Big Tree " Brand Californian Wine.
Perrier, French Natural Sparkling Table Water.*

Liebig's WINCARNIS. VIBRONA PORT & SHERRY. HALL'S WINE. MALTONA. Agents for " FARMER'S OLIVE MALT," a Nutritious Food, in bottles 1/6 and 2/8 each.

17, 19, and 21 Castle Street, Forfar.

PETER NEAVE & SON,

Plumbers, Tinsmiths,

Gasfitters and Ironmongers,

135½ EAST HIGH STREET, FORFAR.

ALL KINDS OF REPAIRS DONE.
ELECTRIC BELLS FITTED UP OR REPAIRED.
INCANDESCENT LIGHTS A SPECIALTY.

Orders from Town or Country carefully attended to.

UMBRELLAS REPAIRED AND RE-COVERED.

ESTABLISHED 1870.

Norman Craik Guild,

Teacher of Music and Dancing,

100 EAST HIGH ST., FORFAR.

Private Lessons in Dancing by appointment.

Pupils prepared for Trinity College Examinations.
Certificates, Honours, and Prizes have been gained by Violin and Pianoforte
pupils at the above College.

Orchestras supplied for Balls, Receptions, &c.
Professional Men Guaranteed.

FORFAR PUBLIC AND PRIVATE DANCING CLASSES will be re-opened
about the end of January 1911.

All Communications by Post receive prompt attention.

. . T. H. Niven, . .

TOBACCONIST,

94 NORTH STREET, FORFAR.

NORTH STREET SUB-POST OFFICE.

Foreign and British Cigars, Virginia, Egyptian, and Turkish Cigarettes.
Finest Selection of Tobacconist's Fancy Goods in Forfar.

JAMES NEILL,

Professor of Music & Dancing,

46a CASTLE STREET, FORFAR.

Private Lessons given, and Private Classes arranged by appointment.

String Bands supplied to Concerts and Assemblies.
Pianoforte and Violin for Evening Parties.

PIANOS FOR HIRE BY THE NIGHT, MONTH OR YEAR.

George R. Fowler,

PHARMACIST,

38 CASTLE STREET, FORFAR.

Telephone No. 70.

Mrs Petrie,

NEWSAGENT AND STATIONER,
FANCY GOODS MERCHANT,

127 EAST HIGH STREET, FORFAR.

MISS WOOD,

Milliner,

74 CASTLE STREET, FORFAR.

David Masterton,

. . Plain and Ornamental Plasterer. . .

ALL KINDS OF TILEWORK, CEMENT WORK, CONCRETE FLOORING, &c.

AGNES HOUSE, CASTLE STREET.

..The..
Queen's Hotel
Forfar

PROPRIETOR, JOHN KILLACKY

TELEPHONE No. 59
TELEGRAMS: KALAC, FORFAR

FIRST CLASS FAMILY & COMMERCIAL HOTEL. EVERY HOME COMFORT.

CATERING IN ALL ITS BRANCHES.
TABLE D'HOTE DAILY.
POSTING OF ALL KINDS.

BOOTS MEETS ALL TRAINS.   **PERSONAL ATTENTION GIVEN.**

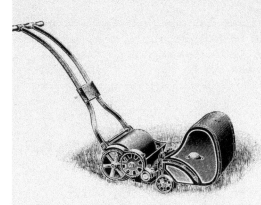

clxxx

Smith, Hood,
& Co., Ltd.,
Largest Colliery Agents
North of the Forth.

Supply all Classes of House and Steam
Coals at Cheapest Prices.

CAKING COALS.
HAMILTON ELL AND WISHAW.
FIFE COALS OF EVERY DESCRIPTION.
SMALL, ANTHRACITE, AND COKE FOR VINERIES.

SPECIAL QUOTATIONS FOR WAGON LOADS.
DELIVERED TO ANY STATION IN SCOTLAND.

Office and Depot,
Old Station Gate, VICTORIA ST., Forfar.

MONTROSE—Hume Street.	BERVIE—N.B. Station.
ARBROATH—Spink Street.	INVERKEILOR—N.B. Station.
CARNOUSTIE—Top of Station Road.	BROUGHTY FERRY—Brook Street.

Registered Office, 48 UNION STREET, DUNDEE.

DUNDEE 'PHONE, 196.   TELEGRAMS—"HOODED."

W. SPARK,

Artistic
Photographer,

85 CASTLE STREET,

~. FORFAR. ~

Telephone No. 54.

*

. . . THE . . .

Station Hotel

⤳ FORFAR. ⤳

This Hotel

Has been thoroughly renovated, re-furnished, and re-decorated.

Hot and Cold Water Baths.

First-class House for Commercial Travellers.

Charges Strictly Moderate.

W. P. HUNTER, Proprietor.

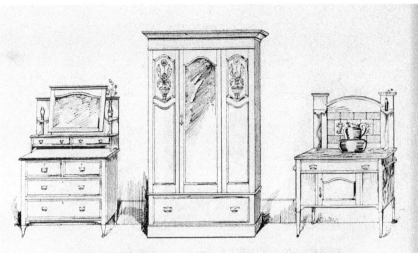

GRAND SELECTION

OF

Furniture

Linoleum, Beds, Bedding, Rugs, &c., from

Alex. Stewart,

CABINETMAKER, JOINER, UPHOLSTERER, and FUNERAL UNDERTAKER.

All kinds of **JOBBING** promptly attended to and carefully executed at

50 East High Street.

BEDROOM SUITES from £7 10/ Upwards.

David Stewart

HOUSE FURNISHER,

23-5 Queen Street, Forfar.

UPHOLSTERY.

All kinds of Upholstery Work. Furniture Re-covered.
Repairs and Renovations carefully executed.

BEDS AND BEDDING.

Only the Best Purified Wool and Hair used. Hair Mattresses
from 30/ upwards. Bedding Cleaned and re-made.

LINOLEUMS.

All Seasoned Goods from Best Makers. Latest Designs. Large
Selection up to 4 yards wide. Prices from 1/4 per square yard.

FRENCH POLISHING.

TELEPHONE No. 3 Y 3.

Showrooms--56 CASTLE STREET.

Alex. D. Strachan

WOOD AND COAL MERCHANT

Forfar Saw Mill

TELEPHONE NO. 27.

HOME WOOD OF ALL KINDS,
Also, FIREWOOD, KINDLING, &c.

COAL DEPOT—
Old Railway Station, Victoria Street.

BEST ENGLISH HOUSEHOLD COALS.
GARTSHORE CAKING COALS AND NUTS.
BEST DUNFERMLINE SPLINT, JEWEL AND KITCHEN COALS.
VARIETIES OF SCOTCH NUTS AND SMALLS.
STEAM COALS, BRIQUETTES, COKE, &c.

SALT AND WHITING.

ORDERS
which will be promptly attended to, may be sent to
Office, Forfar Saw Mill, or House, 10 Manor Street.

The QUESTION

How to Dress .
with good Taste
and Economy .
IS SOLVED.

IF this question hasn't been satisfactorily settled, pay our shop a visit.
While there, notice the many things
on which you can make a Saving.
Our prices are lower; we know it and
so should you. Our quality is better---
you will find this out by giving us a
trial.

Sturrock & Co.

General Drapers & House Furnishers,
145-9 East High St., Forfar.

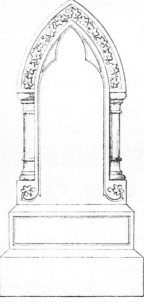

J. F. WILSON,

AUCTIONEER, VALUATOR, AND
LAND SURVEYOR,

20 WEST HIGH STREET, FORFAR.

Telephone No. 77.

JAMES A. WATERSTON, M.P.S.

DISPENSING CHEMIST,

119 EAST HIGH STREET,
ᲙᲒ FORFAR. ᲙᲒ

BUSINESS HOURS—8-30 a.m. to 8-30 p.m. ; Saturday to 10-30 p.m.
Closed on Thursday from 2 to 7 p.m.
SUNDAY HOURS—10 to 11 a.m. ; 12-30 to 2 p.m. ; 5-30 to 7-30 p.m.

A. Esplin,

Fruiterer and Confectioner,

18 CASTLE STREET,

FORFAR.

cxciv

John Crook,

Boot and Shoemaker,

19 SOUTH STREET, FORFAR.

BRING YOUR REPAIRS.   **BRING YOUR REPAIRS.**

David W. Neill,

Organist and Choirmaster Glamis Parish Church,
Visiting Singing Master to Forfar Burgh School Board,

GIVES LESSONS IN

Piano, Harmonium, and Singing,
Theory of Music, Harmony, and Counterpoint,
Also, prepares pupils for all Examinations of the
Tonic Sol-fa College.

PARTICULARS

At the Hall, 46 Castle Street, Forfar.

James Prophet,

PAINTER and DECORATOR,

99 EAST HIGH STREET, FORFAR.

ALL ORDERS CAREFULLY ATTENDED TO AT MODERATE CHARGES.

HIGH-CLASS
DRESS & COSTUME MAKERS

A. Dalgety & Son
57 EAST HIGH STREET.

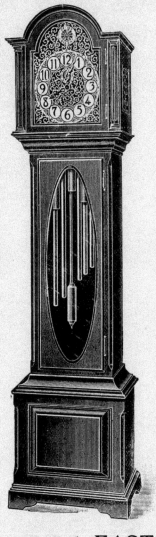

SCOTT

The Jeweller's

FOR

Presentation
Goods

Large Variety.

James Scott,

WATCHMAKER,
JEWELLER,
AND OPTICIAN,

119½ EAST HIGH STREET,
FORFAR.

TELEPHONE No. 21.

THE
ROYAL
HOTEL

 **FORFAR.**

Most Central for Commercial Gentlemen.

BILLIARD ROOM, with First Class Table.

SMOKE ROOM.

**Large Hall and other conveniences suitable
for Marriages, Supper Parties,
and At Homes.**

'Bus meets all Trains.   Charges Moderate.

Headquarters of the C.T.C.

JOHN LICHTSCHEIDEL.

Mrs Prophet,

Family Grocer, Tea, Wine, & Spirit Merchant,

36 PRIOR ROAD, FORFAR.

Liquors of the Best Quality only kept in Stock.

J. & W. LINDSAY,

Drapers, Clothiers,
Dress and Mantle Makers, and General Outfitters.

LINOLEUMS & FLOORCLOTHS in ½-yd., ¾-yd., 1-yd., and 2-yd. widths. CARPET SQUARES, RUGS, MATS, AND MATTINGS.

Specialties of our own Manufacture.
MEN'S AND YOUTHS' SHIRTS of Wincey, Oxford, Grandrill, and Kirkcaldy Shirtings ; also of Army Grey, and Indigo Blue Flannels.

Men's and Boys' Hand-Knit Hosiery.

We are now stocking a Large Selection of MEN'S CAPS, at 1/, 1/6, and 2/6, in popular shapes.   NECK TIES at 6d, 1/, and 1/6. FINGERING AND CASHMERE HOSIERY.

71, 73, 75, and 77 North Street, Forfar.

Charles O. Simpson,

BAKER AND CONFECTIONER,

143½ EAST HIGH STREET, FORFAR.

TEA ROOMS.   Hot Bridies a Specialty.

. . THE . .

Forfar Review

UNRIVALLED MEDIUM FOR PUBLICITY.
WANT ADS. A SPECIALTY.

Friday Morning.   ONE PENNY.

The REVIEW is in every house in Forfar and District.

PRINTER AND PUBLISHER,

J. MACDONALD,

OFFICE, 10 East High St., FORFAR.

Printing

The attention of Tradesmen, Merchants, and the general public is directed
to the great facilities afforded in the FORFAR REVIEW Office for the
efficient execution of Letterpress Printing in all its Departments.

W. Callander,

General Drapery Warehouseman,

60, 62, & 64 CASTLE STREET, FORFAR.

General and Fancy Drapery.

First-class Dress-making at Moderate Charges.

Gent.'s Collars & Cuffs.

Men's and Boys' Ready-made Clothing.

Suits to Order.

Always on hand a fine Selection of FLANNELS, BLANKETS, HOUSEHOLD LINEN, FLOCK, and HAIR MATTRESSES, LINOLEUM, FLOORCLOTH, CURTAINS and TABLE COVERS, also LADIES' JACKETS, SKIRTS, UNDERSKIRTS, and BLOUSES, and all kinds of CHILDREN'S CLOTHING at prices to suit all Purses, at

64 Castle Street.

This is the Leading HAT SHOP in Town. Gentlemen in want of a nice FELT or SILK HAT should ask for CHRISTY'S or TOWNEND'S, London. Also, CAPS, TIES, SHIRTS, BRACES, WATERPROOF COATS, TRAVELLING BAGS and TRUNKS in great Variety. BUTCHERS' & GROCERS' JACKETS & APRONS a Specialty at the

FORFAR HAT & CAP SHOP,

60 Castle Street.

Muir, Son, & Patton

LIMITED,

COLLIERY AGENTS,

Coal, Lime, and Cement Merchants,

and Carting Contractors,

OLD & NEW RAILWAY STATIONS,

 **FORFAR.**

BRANCH AT JUSTINHAUGH STATION.

Every Description of HOUSE and STEAM COAL
Always in Stock.

CHAR, ENGLISH AND SCOTCH COKE, AND BRIQUETTES.

KINDLING.

SCOTCH AND ENGLISH LIME.

CEMENT.

FIRECLAY GOODS of every Description in Stock or to Order.

HAY, STRAW, AND MOSS LITTER.

CARTING of Every Description undertaken.   Estimates Given.

Agents for ALBION FEEDING and DAIRY CAKES and MEALS.

Agents for GUILD & SON, Brick and Tileworks, Glamis.

Orders by Post receive prompt and careful Attention.

Special Quotations for Quantities, and WAGON LOADS of any of
the above at Railway Stations and Sidings.

DEPOT—GOODS STATION.

PRINCIPAL OFFICE—OLD STATION, 35 VICTORIA STREET.

TELEPHONE No. 13.

Representative--GEORGE WISHART.

ccvii

DUNDEE & DISTRICT
HYGIENIC INSTITUTE LTD.

ARTIFICIAL

TEETH

EXTRACTIONS. FILLINGS. &c.
WORK GUARANTEED.
PAYMENTS ARRANGED.

81 CASTLE STREET, FORFAR.

KIRRIEMUIR--Mrs Smith, 27 Kirk Wynd,
Alternate TUESDAYS, 5 to 9.

ARBROATH--211a High Street.

BRECHIN--Mrs Garbutt's, 49 High Street,
Alternate SATURDAYS, 2 to 5-30.

DUNDEE--14 Park Place (1 minute's walk from Queen's Hotel).

Largest and most Successful Business in Forfarshire.

Telephone No. 23.

ANDREW F. SCOTT,

FAMILY BUTCHER,

107 East High Street,

Forfar.

William Strachan,

WINDOW TICKET
and SHOWCARD WRITER,

19 OSNABURGH STREET, FORFAR.

NOTICES, WREATH TABLETS, and all classes of Lettering done.
PICTURES FRAMED.

THE

Grove Dairy Co.
LTD.

"Grovella" Tea, 1/4 per lb.

Fragrant and Refreshing, the Flavour will remind you of the rich
luscious Teas sold at a much higher price.
Try a Sample Qr-lb.

"Grovella" Margarine, 1/ per lb.

There is nothing better, not even choice Butter, for either table
use or cooking. Its delicious creamy flavour is a revelation and
the quality is unsurpassed.
Half-Lb. given free with every Lb.

113 EAST HIGH STREET, FORFAR.

TIES and SHIRTS.

D. P. BOOTH,

Practical Tailor and Clothier,

66 CASTLE STREET,

FORFAR.

HATS and HOSIERY.

L

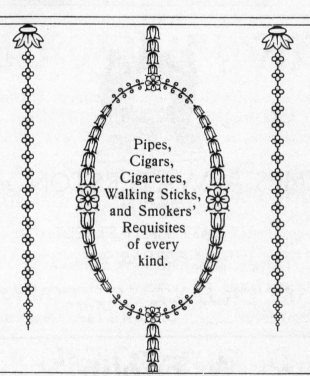

October

October 1 1962

It's tattie time again!

It is a two week autumn break from school and time to help with the potato harvest!

It is a mild form of wage slavery, it would have to be said, but one that is very much looked forward to.

The weather can be a bit dodgy and unreliable, but the wages are good. The work is hard, but there are breaks as well, and it is as much a social occasion as anything else.

You have a wide choice of employers — Renilson's, Mackie's, Heatherstacks, the Baggerton, Butter's and many others. The idea is that you have your "bit" of usually about 15 or 16 yards to gather and you have to gather your tatties before the cart comes round to collect them.

If you fail, you have the disgrace of "stickin' the cairt" and if you are really slow you "stick the digger" meaning that the "digger" is ready to dig up another "dreel" before you have finished the previous one!

"Swickin the peenie" means you have left your neighbour to pick up some of your "bit", and you mustn't leave any "harrows" (nothing to do with any famous snobby school, but simply potatoes that you have missed!).

The real fun however came at dinner time when stories are told over your flasks of soup and sandwiches, romances develop and even the odd sexual experience in a haystack is not unheard of.

("Not unheard of?" They are actually commonplace occurrences and, Forfar being Forfar, well known about and discussed for weeks afterwards!)

October 2 1954

They didn't really know what they were starting when Strathmore Cricket Club announced today that they had signed the Bermudan Nigel Hazel as their professional on a three year contract.

Hazel had played several years for Aberdeenshire, so he wasn't exactly unknown in Forfar, and big things were expected of him.

1954 had not been a great season for Strathie. Since the war, they had been "there or thereaboots" normally, but they hadn't even been thereaboots in 1954, and indeed it would be some time before they rose to pre-eminence.

But not only was Hazel a great batsman and a mighty hitter, he also excelled as a human being, particularly in his willingness to take coaching sessions and bring on the youngsters.

His first season was the glorious summer of 1955 in which he finished up with a Strathmore Union Average of 82.78 as the team won the League (and the Second Division League) with a degree of ease.

Nigel very soon became a local hero, although the myth that he kept hitting the ball into the Loch was indeed just that, a myth. Between 1962 and 1972 Strathmore won the Strathmore Union every year apart from 1965.

It was generally reckoned that the club was the best in Scotland and they proved that in 1971 by winning the Scottish Cup, having reached the final two years before in 1969. The club was lucky in that it had loads of talented local Forfar players, but the man who did so much to nurture that talent was Nigel Hazel.

He stayed in Forfar the rest of his life.

October 3 1920

The Great War undeniably brought many changes to Forfar's social life, not least to how Sundays were spent.

Today was a beautiful autumn day, and it was probably this factor which led to a man calling himself "Colonel Bogey" writing a letter to *The Forfar Herald* asking why golf was not allowed on the Cunninghill on a Sunday.

The man had a fair point as charabanc trips to Dundee had been allowed on a Sunday, and music was played in the Reid Park on a Sunday, so why not golf?

The Churches were naturally opposed to this idea, although already it was obvious that their tyrannical pre-War grip was beginning to loosen, and people were now beginning to ask questions about where God had been in the last few years of the Somme and the flu epidemic, and whether there might just be something in this new creed called socialism?

But for the moment, the traditional Sunday was Church in the morning, then the legendary walk of "east the toon, wast the toon, roond the Spoot and hame" in families.

Except, quite a lot of families were not as they had been.

Far too often did one meet a young widow with three children, a man who used to work in "the Hauchie" but was now blind, or another man who once played for Forfar Celtic or East End but now walked past everyone, suffering from shell shock.

And there was also the undeniable factor of poverty as the jute trade struggled to pick up the markets that had been lost in ruined Germany and revolutionary, war-torn Russia and Ireland.

Nigel Hazel and his Coaching Class

October 4 1910

A great day in Forfar today as the Swimming Baths in Chapel Street were officially opened by the man who had gifted them to the town, the millionaire from Dunfermline, Andrew Carnegie.

Not everyone liked Carnegie. His methods of making his fortune had been unscrupulous and often believed to be an example of 19th century capitalism, both in Great Britain and America, at its worst.

That said, the other side of him was that he was prepared to give away quite a lot of his wealth. He had already made loads of gifts to his home town of Dunfermline, and now gave Forfar their swimming baths because his ancestors had come from these parts.

He arrived by train, and once he had opened the baths formally, and witnessed some "ornamental swimming" demonstrations by Miss Jeannie Veitch of Edinburgh and a display of high diving and "trick swimming" by the Belmont Troup of Dundee, he and Mr Don (who had given the land) were given the Freedom of the Burgh by Provost Moffat.

He was much thanked for his gift, and the phrase "cleanliness is next to godliness" was much bandied about.

It was now up to the good people of Forfar to put the baths to good use.

In 1910, very few houses had any sort of running water, and washing was not always easy, so for these reasons, it was a great boon to the town, and in this respect, Forfar was away ahead of very many towns in Scotland. There was now in Forfar "nae excuse for clort".

Forfar Swimming Baths

October 5 1889

Forfar is in an uproar this Saturday, and excitement stalks the streets with passions rising.

It all concerns a wages dispute at Craik's which has simply got out of hand. Wise owners might have quietly settled the issue and no-one would have noticed, but Craik's seem to have involved the other factory owners, and the end result has been the announcement of a lockout of all Forfar factories!

Industrial agitation was of course not unheard of in Victorian times which was by no means as peaceful and progressive an era as it is often depicted, but this was almost unprecedented, and the objective of the factory owners seems to be little other than the smashing of the Forfar Factory Workers Union.

But they seem to have miscalculated, for *The Forfar Herald*, traditionally a Liberal-supporting but hardly revolutionary newspaper, sides uncompromisingly with the jute workers, talking about "the last extremity" and the attempt to "coerce the workers into silence and obedience by starvation".

Local shopkeepers too are supporting the workers for they need the workers to be earning money so that they can spend it in their shops!

Even the Churches are making noises with Mr Cowper of the Baptist Church openly on the side of the workers.

Reverend George Caie of the Old Kirk (who might have been expected to side with the owners) talked about the need for reconciliation and offered his services for this purpose.

In the meantime the workers' leaders Adam Farquharson and Tommy Roy are going round Angus to Dundee, Brechin, Kirriemuir and Arbroath rounding up support, as Forfar enjoys a few days in the national spotlight.

October 6 1935

The Forfar Dispatch remarked in its next edition that the town was very quiet this Sunday.

Maybe Churches as well noticed a fall in "the plate". The reason was that in the fine weather, the town had decided to treat itself to a holiday this "Fast" weekend, with the railway companies reading this situation well and offering cheap excursions to places like Blackpool.

The turnaround in the affairs of the town was really quite remarkable with short-time working in the jute factories now a thing of the past.

Everything was now working flat out with even overtime not unusual, and all sorts of bonus schemes in operation to ensure maximum productivity.

New housing schemes were springing up all over the town with indoor toilets! This was in great contrast to the bad old days of 1931, 1932 and 1933 when depression was the order of the day.

Of course when the jute factories are thriving, so too are the shops, services, pubs and everything else in the town, and the lovely autumn sunshine contributes to the "feel good" atmosphere at the station and on the buses as people enjoy the good weather.

There is one fly in the ointment, though, and that is the fear of what might happen in Europe. That funny little man with the moustache in Germany says some stupid things now and again, and as for that fat blowbag in Italy... Trying to invade Abyssinia!

No wonder the Italian ice cream and fish and chip men are embarrassed about that! It's like Forfar trying to invade Padanaram!

October 7 1851

Today *The Dundee, Perth and Cupar Advertiser* announces that the monument to the memory of the late Sir Robert Peel MP in the new Burial Ground has now been completed with the exception of two lion figures which are to be placed on the base.

"The work has been executed in a style far surpassing anything in the line of sculpture ever done in this quarter" according to the newspaper report, with the work of David Soutar, "an unassuming mason" singled out for special commendation.

The new Burial Ground had only been acquired in 1849 and opened later that year, and it was felt that something should be done to honour the memory of Sir Robert Peel, the Prime Minister, who had repealed the Corn Laws in 1846 thereby allowing the import of cheaper food and saving thousands from starvation.

It had all been too late for Ireland where thousands were dying in the Potato Famine, but it had at least been an effort.

Not everyone in Peel's Conservative Party agreed with him, for wealthy farmers in Forfarshire and elsewhere liked the idea of expensive food.

The people of Forfar, traditionally a Whig area rather than Tory one, thought Peel was a hero even though (or possibly because!) he had broken the Tory Party and driven it out of office for 20 years.

They erected this monument by public subscription. Sadly Peel had died in 1850 after a fall from his horse.

The monument continues to excite admiration to this day, and in the Great War, it proved its value when the Army erected a platform on the top of it and used it as a watchtower for Zeppelins.

HE WAS G.O.M. OF SCOTTISH FOOTBALL

Mr James Black, president of Forfar Athletic, and grand old man of Scottish football, died in the early hours of this morning. He had been ill for some months, and recently underwent an operation in a Dundee nursing home. He was 85.

There were few better-known figures in the county town. For many years, Mr Black had been closely associated with football.

He started Forfar's first junior club, East End, in 1881, and continued right to the end to take an active interest in the game. He was secretary of the Northern League when it flourished in the nineties, and had been a member of the Scottish Football Association Council for many years.

As a selector, he travelled up and down the country and, even when he was getting very weak, delighted to attend every possible international game.

He served in many capacities, and at one time was chairman of the Referee Committee of the S.F.A. In 1936, he was presented with his portrait in oils as a mark of regard from the Forfarshire Football Association, of which he was president.

In Scottish national sports he was a prime mover. At one time he was president of the Scottish National Sports Association which controlled professional sports.

Games Secretary.

For many years Mr Black was secretary of Forfar Games, to which he brought many famous athletes, including W. R. Applegarth; Mears, the Australian sprinter; Reggie Walker, the South African; Kolehmainen, the Finn, and a host of others.

In 1906, Donald Dinnie was one of the heavy-weight judges at Forfar. The heavy-weights at times included A. A. Cameron, Alex. Morrison, G. H. Johnstone, Matt Steedman. Dancers, jumpers, and cyclists all knew Mr Black.

A native of Forfar, Mr Black at one time was an insurance manager and house factor. He was a J.P., and for many years, a parish councillor.

Famous players he signed for Forfar included Dave M'Lean, Frank Hill, Willie Cook, George M'Lean, Alec Troup, and " Dyken " Nicoll.

A year or two ago, just after he relinquished the post as secretary of Forfar Athletic, he was made life president of the club. He is survived by his wife.

Mr Black's funeral will be to Forfar Cemetery on Monday at 1.30.

1951 Newspaper Obituary for James Black

October 8 1951

The funeral was held this Monday lunch time of James Black, who had died on October 4 at the age of 85.

He was a legendary figure in Forfar Athletic history. He had been ill for some time, and had spent most of 1951 in a Dundee nursing home.

He was in with Forfar Athletic at the very start and basically ran the club from 1884 until his death, proudly boasting that he never took a penny for doing so.

In between times he was a referee, taking charge, for example, of the first game ever played at Dens Park, Dundee and running the line for Scotland on various occasions, notably the Scotland v England international of 1912.

He was commonly known as "Mr Forfar" at SFA meetings and was a great friend of men like Willie Maley of Celtic. He was never universally popular in the town — but that possibly says more about small town jealousy than it does about "Jeem" — but his contribution to town life did not stop at football, for he was a Justice of the Peace and a Parish Councillor.

In the Great War he served on the Tribunals to decide whether men should be conscripted or not, and did his best to save many a Forfar man from the carnage but was frequently outvoted by the military.

He was affable, cheerful and sociable, albeit a shade too dogmatic on occasion, and everything that Forfar Athletic was in 1951 could be put down to James Black.

His funeral in the Old Kirk and the Newmonthill Cemetery was attended by all the dignitaries of Scottish football.

If Willie Maley was "the man who made Celtic", then James Black was "the man who made Forfar". He lived in North Street and was survived by his wife Sarah.

October 9 1886

In one of the best ever games seen at Station Park, Forfar today beat Dundee Wanderers 3-2 in the second round of the Forfarshire Challenge Cup.

It is always good to beat a Dundee team, but it was the manner in which it was achieved that excited most of all the 4,000 or 5,000 spectators round the ropes. They included a large contingent from Dundee.

The day was bright but with perhaps rather too much a breeze blowing in from the west, something that played a disproportionate part in the game, for all the goals were scored in the eastern goal.

Wanderers were two up at half time, but Forfar fought back and won 3-2.

It is clear however that the reporting of football matches in newspapers was still in its infancy, for *The Forfar Herald's* report on the game has simply been lifted straight from *The Courier* and fails comprehensively to mention the name of a single Forfar player, even those who scored the goals!

The first Forfar goal came about when "a long and excitable scrimmage took place and ultimately ended in the sphere getting leave to drop through the uprights", the second goal was scored "with little trouble" and then the third goal was "a soft and lucky point" in the opinion of the gentleman from Dundee who wrote the report.

So Forfar won, but it would have been nice to know who scored the goals at least! The game however was said to be "grandly contested and fast in the extreme" In addition, "there was not a symptom of roughness visible"

October 10 1974

Today Forfar surprised the world and itself, one imagines, but doing something that hardly anyone would have thought possible — namely *not* voting Conservative!

Before World War II, Montrose Burghs (as the constituency was then called) had voted Liberal, but it was the right-wing Liberal, sometimes called National Liberal or Liberal Unionist.

Since 1945 however, the town had been solid Conservative, often baffling political observers who could not understand how it was that jute workers were so solidly behind landowners!

But 1974 was an unusual year with miners' and other strikes, various financial scandals and inflation looking as if it were getting out of control.

There had been a hung Parliament Election in February in which Jock Bruce-Gardyne (a decent chap, it has to be admitted) held off a challenge from the Scottish Nationalists.

But by October, more of the Labour vote was moving tactically to the SNP and the intervention of a Liberal also took votes from the Conservative, and the upshot was that Andrew Welsh, a strong candidate, beat Gardyne by a majority of almost 2,000 for the Scottish National Party.

One still recalls the looks of amazement on the faces of the political commentators in the BBC Election studio, but it was part of a Scottish trend in which the rural, agricultural, farmer vote moved to the SNP while the Labour vote either stayed away or joined them.

It was nevertheless a seismic shock to the lovers of Glamis Castle and the Strathmore families, and a story went around on the following Monday that there "wis a new led started in Dons. He's jiist loast his job lest week. Gardyne or something his name is!"

October 11 1930

A major mystery surrounds a trophy at Forfar Golf Club which has now turned up after apparently being lost for about 20 years.

The trophy was called the Coronation Quaich and was presented to commemorate the Coronation of Edward VII in 1902. It was played for and duly presented every year until shortly before the Great War when the Quaich disappeared.

Then the war came along and everyone forgot all about it. When competitive golf resumed after the war, the competition was still played for but there was no trophy. The winners were always announced but received no trophy!

One member said he had won the trophy, but had not seen it! It was believed that a former winner had failed to return it and *The Angus Herald* made a few enquiries.

Lo and behold, the trophy was found in a Forfar jeweller's shop! Amazingly, and unaccountably, all the winners' names were inscribed including the "lost" years! So, what on earth was all this about?

Clearly someone at the club knew more about this than he was prepared to admit. Another trophy, the Laird Bowl, however, had indeed disappeared, and no-one had any idea where it was.

It was clear that there was a certain amount of incompetence and if not dishonesty, a certain amount of "economy with the truth" at the Cunninghill.

In the meantime, the Coronation Quaich was indeed won by Charles Johnston for the third year in a row, and this year he was looking forward to being presented with it!

October 12 1894

Tonight at the Reid Hall took place the Forfar Factory Workers' Festival.

This annual event was half serious, half fun with proceedings beginning with a "capital tea" served by "numerous stewards and stewardesses".

There then followed the serious side of the evening with speeches from the Secretary Bailie Adam Farquharson and various delegates from other towns who remarked on how well organised the Forfar workers were, and how nice it was to see so many men and women there. Women were, of course, more than half the workforce in the jute industry.

Workers were encouraged to support sympathetic men like Andrew and Hanick in the coming Town Council elections. Then the social side began with a lengthy programme of songs from local sopranos like Miss Clark, Miss Cooper who was particularly good with her rendering of "Kathleen Mavourneen", and Mr Richard, a Forfarian who was now making a name for himself in "Juteopolis", more commonly known as Dundee.

When that part of the evening was over, the ball began with the music from Mr Lowson's Quadrille band, and it all finished in the "wee sma oors" of Saturday morning, even though some of the workers had their half-day shift "starting at six"!

These proceedings faithfully chronicled in *The Forfar Herald* are illuminating in that they show that, contrary to the modern perception perhaps, the Forfar working class were well organised, well enough paid and had a certain appreciation of music and dancing.

The idea that Boath, Craik, Lowson, Don and Moffat kept them all in thraldom, slavery and ignorance is simply not true.

October 13 1920

At the Forfar School Management Committee tonight, Rector Adam S Thomson was far from happy with His Majesty's Inspectors who had delivered an adverse report on the teaching of French in his school without apparently taking the trouble to ascertain all the facts.

The French teacher Mr Dobie had only returned from the war in late February of this year.

It was hardly surprising that the results in that subject had not been as good as English, Latin and Maths, given the fact that French had been taught on a very patchy basis with non-qualified and non-specialist staff until Mr Dobie's return.

Mr Dobie had "not got time to reap his harvest, and was reaping what others had sown". In any case, in the 1920s, oddly perhaps in view of recent events, French was not a particularly highly-valued subject.

For reasons of dark prejudice, German was certainly not encouraged with Mr Thomson himself not unknown to advise pupils against learning "the language of the Hun".

The School Management Committee, whom one suspects of being in awe of Rector Thomson, who had been in position since 1897 and had raised Forfar Academy to being one of the best in Scotland, were generally supportive with Bailie Hanick saying that the school was not a brains factory and could only develop, not manufacture, brains.

If the brains were not there, there was little that could be done. If pupils were "ower dozent", then they were "ower dozent", as another member of the Committee summed it up pithily and epigrammatically.

October 14 1910

A function was held tonight in the Feuars Hall, Letham to mark the "semi-jubilee" of Reverend Hugh McMaster of Dunnichen who had now been with them for 25 years.

The occasion was well attended by members of the Forfar Presbytery and many of his congregation, for he had been a much loved minister since he arrived from Cambuslang in 1885.

Various people spoke, one claiming that he had seen nine incumbents of the pulpit of Dunnichen but that Mr McMaster was second to none.

Mr McMaster for his part said that he had baptised a total of 425 babies in his time, and had made 141 couples "happy in wedlock" and sadly, 140 of this parishioners had passed away in death.

He was presented with a new pulpit gown by his congregation, and his children were given suitable gifts as well. No mention was made of Mrs McMaster, so one assumes that Mr McMaster was widowed.

Mr McMaster spoke graciously and gratefully for his 25 years, adding that he always believed that the Minister existed for the parish and not the parish for the Minister.

He expressed his grateful thanks to all the members of Forfar Presbytery who had helped him in his work, not least Reverend Strachan, now of Cortachy who had grown up a "Letham loon" and who had been very supportive.

The hope was expressed that Mr McMaster would continue to have many years left as a Minister in Dunnichen. 25 years was a long time, but there was more to come yet.

October 15 1964

It was General Election time again.

Amidst all the "a they dae is speak" and "there's no nane them ever dae onything for me" sort of cant that Forfar people are notorious for bringing out now and again, there was a genuine feeling that things were happening, at least in the country at large, if not Forfar.

The result in Forfar was a foregone conclusion. Cynics pointed out that the Conservative candidate had a hyphenated name in Jock Bruce-Gardyne.

The Conservative Prime Minister also had a double barrelled name in Sir Alec Douglas Home (and he had only recently been an Earl), so there really was no doubt who the forelock-touching Forfar people, bred on generations of worship to the Strathmores and the Airlies, were likely to vote for!

On the other hand, there were also more valid reasons for voting Conservative. There could be little doubt that 13 years of Conservative rule, in spite of its occasional silliness like Suez and Profumo, had brought a great deal of prosperity to the town with full employment more or less guaranteed, and people now healthier and living longer.

The Labour candidate was a man called Dick Douglas who tried hard and had a few meetings in the town centre, but he knew he was not going to win.

The Liberal candidate Christopher Scott performed similarly and a few yellow rosettes were seen in town. There was no Scottish Nationalist yet, for they were a party very much still in its infancy.

Although Harold Wilson scraped home for Labour, South Angus voted predictably and dismally for the Conservatives, leaving so many people scratching their heads in amazement about how jute workers could vote for the landed aristocracy?

October 16 1952

The Forfar Rotary Club today were given a talk about the new wonder of life in the 1950s — a thing called a television.

The talk was given by Mr JR Hosie, the proprietor of a successful electrical shop at the bottom of Victoria Street, which sold radios and gramophones and intended to branch into televisions.

Television had only really come to Scotland a couple of months ago with the erection of a transmitter at Kirk o' Shotts in Lanarkshire, and the reception in Forfar was as yet patchy and unreliable, although the north west of the town tended to do better than the east and south.

Mr Hosie explained to his audience the wonders of how it all worked, talking about cathodes and 405 lines and various other things and how an aerial was needed on the roof to attract the signal.

The aerial in future years would very soon become the status symbol of "I've got a TV. Have you?" — something that is very important in Forfar!

Mr Hosie warned about the dangers of untrained people meddling with a television set if anything went wrong, for there were at least 1,600 parts in each receiver.

Inevitably television sets would be expensive, at least initially, but TV was the coming thing, with plans already in place to broadcast next June's Coronation. Mr Whyte of the Rotary Club thanked Mr Hosie for his excellent talk on a very technical subject to a not very technical audience!

Slowly, gradually, over the next few years, television aerials would begin to appear, usually accompanied by a grumble from the spiteful neighbours along the lines of "Ah dunna see hoo she can afford it!"

Plumbers,   Brass

Gasfitters,   and

&c.   Copper Work.

W. Milne & Sons

SANITARY ENGINEERS,

GREEN STREET, FORFAR.

BATHS, LAVATORIES, & OTHER SANITARY FITTINGS.

HOT WATER APPARATUS.

KITCHEN RANGES.   SLOW COMBUSTION STOVES.

GAS FIRES.   GAS STOVES.

WELSBACH INCANDESCENT GAS FITTINGS.

GAS COOKERS.   GAS LAMPS.

GALVANIZED CORRUGATED IRON ROOFING.

TILE GRATES.

**Awarded SECOND PRIZE for PLUMBER WORK at the
Glasgow Exhibition, 1898.**

Address--GREEN STREET, FORFAR.

1900 Advertisement   *389*

October 17 1883

Today in East High Street was born Alexander Sutherland Neill, the famous educator who died in September 1973, just a matter of days before his 90th birthday.

He is best known for the founding of Summerhill School, the famous or, as some would say, the infamous "free" school in which there was no imposed discipline.

Neill's father was the "dominie" at Kingsmuir School, he had a severe Presbyterian background at the Old Kirk under the fierce Reverend Dr Caie and quite clearly went to the other extreme while most people would agree that there is a happy medium between "discipline" and "licence".

Neill and his followers would argue that true freedom comes from a person's ability to choose what they think is best for them. Whether or not one agrees with Neill, one has to admit that he has made a great impact on the educational world, and his writings should not be totally dismissed.

"A Dominie's Log" is about his year at Gretna school at the start of the Great War.

His best book is "Neill! Neill! Orange Peel" which, apart from anything else contains a great account of his early years in Forfar, with his descriptions of his walks in the dark from Forfar to Kingsmuir particularly vivid.

Neill, who was always proud of his Forfar background, returned to the town frequently although no-one recognised him latterly or knew who he was.

He was very happy on occasion to talk to his pupils in broad Forfar, calling the boys "min" now and again!

October 18 1915

Amidst all the casualties of dead, missing and wounded at the Battle of Loos in France, it is nice to report some good news, concerning Sergeant David Mitchell of the Gordon Highlanders, whose parents live at Old Station House, Victoria Street.

He has been recommended for the Distinguished Conduct Medal, a distinction which his brother Corporal Andrew Mitchell of the Scots Guards had already gained.

Sergeant Mitchell is at home on leave at the moment, and the reporter of *The Forfar Herald* was able today to track him down and ask about his experiences.

Understandably reluctant to speak at first, Sergeant Mitchell said that he had served in South Africa but when war was declared, he was a warden at Perth Prison.

He volunteered and was immediately accepted. In the recent battle, he had found himself and a few of his men too far ahead of the rest of the line and was compelled therefore to retreat.

On his way back he found some Gordon Highlanders without a leader, so he took command of them, found a trench then bluffed the Germans into thinking that there were a lot more British soldiers there than there actually were.

There were in fact only 11 all told, but they were able to hold back the Germans for some time before being obliged to withdraw.

It is not all good news for the Mitchell family however for two other brothers are in the Army. Harry has been missing since January and William is in hospital in Manchester receiving treatment for severe wounds.

October 19 1912

Considerable interest and indeed amusement was raised in the town by a case being tried this Saturday morning at the Police Court before Provost Moffat.

It concerned William Paul Hunter, hotel keeper of the Station Hotel, who was charged for keeping open house on Sunday October 6 1912 for the purpose of selling alcoholic liquor in contravention of his seven day's licence.

The law at the time allowed for the selling of drink on a Sunday to *bona fide* travellers, or to people staying in the hotel who could also be allowed to purchase a refreshment for a friend.

The trouble was that the four "customers" were well known Forfar men who were neither travellers nor did they stay in the hotel. The humour lay in how they tried to avoid telling the rather obvious truth that they were undeniably guilty of the mildly outrageous crime of drinking on a Sunday — a "crime" that was widely practised and well known about.

The excuses were various. One happened to be passing and saw a friend inside and went in to talk to him, another went in because "he was dry", (that was at least honest!) another claimed that his drink had been ordered and paid for the night before.

For his part, Mr Hunter claimed that he had left the back door to his premises open while he went down to his cellar to sort out his kegs of beer and was surprised when he came back to find these men on his premises.

There was however no proof, and Provost Moffat had to refer the matter to the Sheriff Court. The incident did however provide a great deal of copy for *The Forfar Herald* and a certain amount of hilarity for its readers.

October 20 1899

This Friday's *Forfar Herald* is far from cheery about the future.

It appears that a state of war now exists in the Transvaal where Paul Kruger has effectively seized power. No doubt British soldiers will be involved sooner or later.

And already there is an indication of it spreading to Forfar, for the children in playgrounds are now playing "British and Boers" rather than the traditional "Cowboys and Indians" or "North and South" dating back to the American Civil War days!

Coincidentally and tragically, at the house of his brother, a Forfar man called George Gordon, back in town on holiday from South Africa, died suddenly.

He had been hoping to return to Port Elizabeth for a spell before coming home to Forfar for the rest of his life, but fate decreed otherwise.

He had told people that he had been very worried about the situation in South Africa and spoke very bitterly of Paul Kruger who was making life for the British intolerable, and this was one of the reasons why he was wanting to come home.

George Gordon had been born in Forfar in 1840, and had been in South Africa for 36 years where he had built up a good business and had also taken part in the various wars which had harassed the colony for the past twenty years or so.

There was a certain division of opinion in the town. Most people believed that the Boers really had to be put in their place, but there were others who feared for the young soldiers who would inevitably be involved in the fighting.

October 21 1935

Dr James Alfred Lowson died today at his home in Kirkton, Academy Street.

He was a much loved and famous man who contributed more to the life of the town than many other people put together. Yet he did not stop at Forfar.

In his earlier life while serving as a doctor, he worked hard to eliminate or at least to mitigate the effects of plague in Hong Kong, India and Japan.

He was born in 1866. His father was the famous "Jock" Lowson of the linen and jute industry and his mother was a member of the Craik family.

James was educated at Forfar Academy and Edinburgh University before going abroad. Ill health in the shape of tuberculosis in 1901 compelled his return to Forfar, but in spite of serious health problems, he never stinted in his service of Forfarians as a doctor — it was widely said that he gave his medical services free to poor families in these pre-NHS days — and as a Councillor, Bailie and Provost (in the difficult economic days of 1925-1931).

He was a Director of Forfar Infirmary and was well known for his determination to get things done, and not to be hindered by bureaucrats and red tape.

He had the ability to grasp the point and to see immediately what needed to be done. In this he doubtless trod on a few toes, but there were very few people who had any lasting dislike of him.

A keen sportsman, a good cricketer and golfer, and a member of the Forfar Burns Club, his funeral was well attended. No-one in Forfar had a bad word to say about Dr "Jeemie" Lowson.

West High Street in the 1900s

October 22 1924

Tonight at the Masonic Rooms, the Labour Candidate for the General Election addressed a packed and enthusiastic meeting chaired by Bailie Peffers.

The Labour Candidate was called Tom Barron and he was from Arbroath, standing against the Coalition Liberal (effectively a Conservative) called Robert Hutchison from Kirkcaldy who had been defeated in last year's election in Kirkcaldy.

The minority Labour Government had lasted less than a year, but according to Mr Barron it had proved itself able to govern, having given, in particular, a great boost to the building of Council houses.

But Mr Barron was clearly aware that the Achilles heel of Labour was its perceived friendship to the Soviet Union to which it had given a loan and negotiated a trade deal.

Mr Barron was at pains to differentiate between the democratic Socialism of the Labour Party and the dictatorship of Russia. Amazingly, from such a large crowd, not a question was asked and a full vote of confidence was passed.

Mr Barron then went on to address the Forfar Women's Citizen Association where he talked mainly about his work for the betterment of social conditions including childcare and nursery education.

He impressed everyone by his charm and obvious concern for the poor and the unemployed, and hoped that everyone would vote for him next Wednesday.

Sadly, the people of Montrose Burghs seemed to feel that a vote for Labour was still a step too far, and Hutchison, who had an impressive military record, won the contest.

October 23 1938

The Forfar Dispatch is pleased to announce that the Forfar Benevolent Society "hit the bullseye" again on Sunday night with a concert from Dr Sarafin's gifted troupe of entertainers from Dunfermline.

The Benevolent Society was a charity much needed in those pre-Welfare State days to help families or people in need, and on this occasion Sheriff McKinnon was able to thank this talented group of people for giving their services free of charge for a charitable organisation.

Dr Sarafin's group had already been in Forfar last March and such was their popularity that the Reid Hall was filled to overflowing with many people unable to gain admission and having to be turned away.

This said a great deal about Sundays in Forfar in 1938, namely that people were craving entertainment now that the icy grip of Presbyterianism was beginning to slacken, and before television (still some 20 years and a world war away) was able to command everyone's attention.

Tonight they had two and a half hours without a dull moment with Willie Wallis, the compère, who entertained everyone by his "stories, witticisms, grimaces and vocal efforts" as he introduced an accordion band which soon had the toes tapping, and a few accordion solos, a few piano solos and several comedians.

Star of the show seems to have been a "versatile little lady" by the name of Betty O'Brien who charmed everyone by her character sketches and musical pieces. The concert was much appreciated and much discussed by Forfar folks in the factories the next day.

October 24 1893

The late Victorian era is often said to be a time of sexual propriety and morality.

We all know of course that it was nothing of the sort with people like Charles Stewart Parnell, Oscar Wilde, not to mention the Royal Family itself, giving loads of material for gossip.

The more that sex is repressed, the more interesting it becomes! Forfar was no exception, and this week we had a juicy salacious story of our own when Mary David or Whyte, 8 Arbroath Road, Forfar successfully obtained a divorce in the Court of Session in Edinburgh before Lord Kincairney.

She had been married since 1883 but she had left her husband in 1890 because of his lazy habits and drinking. Nothing all that unusual there, I don't suppose, but Mr Whyte then went to stay in his sister's lodging house in Kirriemuir with a lady called Margaret Thompson, but they lived "in separate rooms" in the lodging house.

This was stretching credulity more than a little, and Mrs Whyte's brother claimed that he had actually seen Whyte and Thompson in bed together!

The circumstances of how he had managed to see all this was a fertile source of Forfar speculation, but it was enough to persuade Lord Kincairney to grant a divorce.

Behind all the popular dissection of this case, there were two rather more serious issues — one was that it was still very unusual for a woman to bring successfully a case for divorce in the 1890s, and the other was the very tragic one that of the four children the couple had, only one had survived.

October 25 1908

A large congregation gathered this Sunday night in the Old Kirk to hear what the new Minister Reverend W G Donaldson had to say about "When a Woman's Single".

Mr Donaldson had been in post for less than a month — he had been inducted on Thursday October 1 — but he had already made a good impression with his fine clear voice, his ability to talk to his congregation, including children, and his sheer common sense.

As important as anything, his wife Bella had also made a good first impression. For his homily on the role of women, he had chosen as his text Romans XVI 1 which commended Phebe to the Church.

Rev Donaldson was aware that the role of women was changing and stressed the increasing possibilities for women nowadays to be educated.

This would make her more attractive, and would make men also more desirous to get themselves educated for "A pocket full of gold and a head empty of brains, a house full of grandeur and a husband ignorant and uncultured were but poor attractions for an educated woman".

Clearly very progressive stuff this from Mr Donaldson but just in case we are forgetting that this is 1908, we find him then going on to say that "Masculine women were as detestable as effeminate men" as he warned then not to be "mannish" in things like taking an occasional bet or smoking a "harmless" cigarette.

And then most importantly, he warned them against the dangers of being "fishers of men" by dressing, painting, simpering, dancing or flirting with them.

Good stuff, Reverend Donaldson — and, one presumes, it went down well! But did the unmarried ladies follow his advice?

West School pupils, 1927

October 26 1947

Forfar musical fans were treated to a rare treat this Sunday night in the West Kirk with "An Evening With Chopin" — a lecture recital by the talented Cecil Austin with the Reverend D Dewar Duncan an excellent Master of Ceremonies.

The West Church did not always have the reputation of having the best acoustics in town, but on this occasion, there was no problem and everyone heard exactly what was going on.

What was remarkable, apart from anything else, was the fact that Mr Austin managed to bring his own piano with him to counteract the problem, often encountered in smaller towns, of there not being an adequate piano.

It was a fine Challen concert grand, and as much a talking point as any was the curiously shaped van in which he transported it. In a programme which reflected several of the great Polish composer's varied moods, this talented pianist did a great deal to bring Chopin to the people of Forfar, his sympathetic approach to the music being backed up by sound technique and lively interpretation.

The A major and A flat Polonaises were given the right fire and virility, and there was a certain tranquil beauty of the two best loved nocturnes.

There was a good turn-out, something that proves that Forfar has a reasonably high-brow appetite on occasion. The singing was described as "lusty" as far as the congregation was concerned, and "dulcet" in reference to the choir.

"The Drummer" in *The Forfar Dispatch* commended those responsible for suggesting and bringing Mr Austin to Forfar.

October 27 1889

The strike and the lock-out continue with unabated ferocity, but there are signs that Craik's are weakening and preparing to open their factory again on Wednesday because of the losses that they are sustaining.

Remarkably and in contrast to the general perception of Victorian society, the local Press and the Church have sided with the workers who have also been sustained by cash donations from Unions in Alyth, Kirkcaldy, Glasgow and Perth, not to mention kindred jute workers in Brechin, Kirriemuir and Dundee.

In addition, Dr French has an advertisement in *The Forfar Herald* that for the duration of the lock-out he will treat workers and their families for half price, and that every day at 2.00 pm he will have a special "Free Session" for necessitous cases.

Tonight at the Drill Hall, the workers' leaders Tommy Roy and Adam Farquharson were in upbeat bullish mood but warned the workers on two accounts — not to go back to work without the support of the Union, otherwise they might lose their entitlement to alimony, and the other was not to indulge in or even threaten any acts of violence to the Craik family or their property.

Already there had been certain acts of disorder in the town with some stone throwing and attempts to frighten the horses of the hated jute barons, particularly the Craiks whose house and factory were now under police protection.

The meeting broke up to tumultuous cheers for Roy and Farquharson and, alarmingly for some, strains of the French Revolutionary song "Ca Ira" of a hundred years ago were heard as the workers dispersed.

October 28 1923

Tonight was a special night in the life of the West Free Kirk, as the Reverend Peter Diack preached his first sermon.

He had been inducted on Thursday at a special service and ceremony, and this morning he was introduced to his congregation by the Rev Professor JA Selbie of Aberdeen United Free Church before being "unleashed all on his own" to his congregation. He was replacing Reverend McNab who had gone to Paisley.

He spoke with a soft Aberdeenshire accent, having been born in Kemnay, Aberdeenshire. He was a former pupil of Aberdeen Grammar School and a graduate from Aberdeen University. His most recent charge was Grantown-on-Spey and he came with a high reputation of being sociable, sporty and a good preacher.

He was rewarded tonight with a good turnout of well wishers.

It was not the easiest of times to be a Minister, for as everyone said "The war changed a great deal" not least the unquestioning belief in God (for where had God been at the Somme and Gallipoli?) and also the growing belief that God and the British Empire were now not necessarily the same thing!

In addition, in Forfar at least, although the worst of the post-war recession in trade was slowly now passing, there was still a dreadful amount of avoidable misery and poverty and an apparently permanently alienated working class.

How were the Forfar middle class going to cope with the growing Labour party who would soon form a Government, it was believed? On the other hand, Mr Diack had a strong Church, a supportive Kirk Session and Congregation, and his own enthusiasm.

Jim Towns, Dave Stewart and Bill Harvey at Albert Hall 1955

October 29 1955

Today the Forfar Instrumental Band competed at the Albert Hall in London. Last year they had won the Scottish Championships and this was their reward.

They had been there before in 1948 and 1949 when they had been placed seventh, but this time they were really confident of doing better. The trip was a reward for their hard work and the honour that they had brought to the town, and the Town Council and various other organisations in the town made a financial contribution to defray expenses.

The Competition was to be broadcast live on the BBC Light Programme and hosted by Sir Malcolm Sargent.

They had left for London on Wednesday night with all the best wishes of the local press and many jokes about how good Forfar people were at blawin' their own trumpets etc.

The Courier also remarks on how smart the "Loons" looked with their green jackets and red and gold trimmings. They had a professional conductor called Elgar Clayton, and their party included Bob Byars, Ernie Blair, Fred Milne, Bob Waddell (senior and junior) Dave Hill, Frank Hill, George Milne, Sandy Milne, Bill Harvey, Bill Cook, Jim Towns, Dave Stewart, Ernest Milne and Allan Reid.

They did themselves justice, but were unplaced. Nevertheless they had reason to be proud of themselves.

They arrived back on the Sunday evening, and on the Monday, a girl at the North School was telling everyone about how proud she was (and rightly so) of her father.

The teacher concerned expressed disappointment that they hadn't won, and then asked "Where did they come in?" The girl said "Forfar Station"!

October 30 1952

The "Rev Ref" as the sporting press dubbed him, announced his retirement from refereeing today because of his increasing commitments in his day job as Rector of St John's Episcopalian Church, Forfar.

Douglas Noble,
St John's Episcopal Church
and football referee

This was the Reverend Douglas O Noble who had often impressed people by his control of games. He tended to referee Second Division games and run the line at First Division games, but for obvious reasons, he was seldom seen at Station Park except for friendlies and benefit games.

Following his retirement from refereeing, he was a regular attender at Station Park as a spectator. He was born in Aberdeenshire in 1912 and spoke all his life with a soft and charming Aberdeenshire accent. He came to St John's in March 1951 from Alford.

He was looked upon as an innovator, allowing women to sing in the choir and becoming the first Rector of St John's to drive a car, generously provided by his congregation.

He did loads of work as a School Chaplain particularly at the North School where his visits were much looked forward to because of his keen sense of humour including telling the children that there was a job in his Church called a Canon, but he didn't want that job — in case he got fired!

He left Forfar in 1959 to take up a post in Helensburgh, retired in 1975 and spent the last years of his life in Brechin. He died in 1991. He was a much loved cleric and it was generally believed that he could even have made the grade as an International referee if he had continued.

October 31 1956

Tonight is of course Hallowe'en and there were several "dookin for apples" parties in the town, and an awful lot of "gaeysin" as it is called in Forfar.

This a rather quaint Forfar custom of considerable antiquity whereby children dress up in strange garb, visit their friends and neighbours, sing a song or do some other kind of act in return for an apple or a penny.

It was generally tolerated by everyone, but children were usually warned by parents to "just ging tae yer freends". It was harmless stuff, but tonight there was a particular tension in the air.

It was Wednesday night when *The Forfar Dispatch* came out but those who went to the newsagents to get their local paper would have had their attention drawn by *The Evening Telegraph* which had the banner headlines that Britain and France had this morning invaded Egypt.

This was what history has described as the Suez Crisis, and although it soon blew over with total humiliation for Prime Minister Anthony Eden, no-one really knew that at the time.

What made this even more of a fraught time for Forfar girlfriends and mothers was the fact that National Service was in vogue in 1956. This was conscription for a couple of years, and many young Forfar lads were known to be involved in the Eastern Mediterranean.

It was also little more than ten years since the end of the last war, and memories were still sharp about what that was like. It was indeed an anxious time, and "gaeysers" were sometimes ushered out of the door with undue haste so that the news could be heard on the wireless.

All the Year round

. . . WE ARE . . .

"Ready, aye Ready."

In Spring.   In Summer.
In Autumn.   ✸   In Winter.

THE Latest Styles in CLOTHING and PIECE GOODS are
placed in our Fixtures whenever they appear.
We always keep UP-TO-DATE.
The Value and Variety of our Goods are proverbial.
The Selection is the Best at the Popular Depot for
" Hardwear."

DALGETY'S

DRAPERY WAREHOUSE,

57 East High Street, FORFAR.

Established over 30 Years.

November

November 1 1905

Tonight was the "Greetin' Meetin'" as it was called locally when the candidates for the Local Election presented themselves for "examination" before the people of Forfar.

Tonight's meeting was held in the Drill Hall, the Reid Hall not being available, and the smaller Hall lent itself to the sometimes intense atmosphere which occasionally became rather fraught.

The Election was to be held next Tuesday November 7. Five Councillors had to stand down — Bailies Milne and Lamb, Treasurer Lowson, and Councillors Esplin and Whitson.

Milne did not stand again, but the others were joined by Tom Elder (the man with the legendary big feet), Joseph Jarman, Dr James A Lowson and James Rough.

All eight had their chance to speak "trippingly off the tongue" in the words of Chairman Provost Adamson rather than from notes, and then questions could be asked.

But during Councillor Esplin's speech, a man called Smith actually mounted the platform to ask a question before being hissed off the stage by the crowd and compelled to leave the building.

Andrew Stewart, a shoemaker, stood up and repeatedly asked to be heard as the meeting threatened to descend into chaos.

Sergeant Doig of the Police was involved. Provost Adamson at one point left the platform to talk to Stewart who was eventually allowed to ask his question if he promised to behave for the rest of the meeting.

Forfar people clearly enjoyed these occasions, but Election Day itself was peaceful enough with Elder, Rough and Jarman being the unsuccessful candidates. 1093 males and 217 females voted (women being allowed to vote in local government election in 1905 but not yet in Parliamentary ones).

November 2 1920

Today, Forfar voted to stay "wet" in the National Poll on Temperance.

2,107 voted in favour of "No Change" as distinct from 580 who voted for "No Licence" and 48 who had voted for a Limited Licence.

This had followed several weeks of intense campaigning from both sides, the "No Licence" people arguing that alcohol ruins lives (and there was hardly any lack of evidence to back this up in Forfar!) and should be prohibited.

They tended to be supported by Churches and the new factor in the electorate, namely women.

On the other hand, those in favour of "No Change", while admitting that the abuse of alcohol was a bad thing, felt that many people enjoyed a drink in moderation, and that it was draconian to ban it altogether.

It was after all a freedom, and there was a world of difference between Temperance and Prohibition. Prohibition was an American idea and would be very difficult to enforce.

In voting for "No Change" Forfar simply did what the rest of the country did, although there were some towns, notably Kirkintilloch, who voted for Prohibition.

But the Town Council Elections, held on the same day, also produced a talking point, for one of the five Councillors to be elected was an engine driver called William Whitton who, although not an official Labour Party candidate, made no bones about the fact that he would support "the interests of the working class."

Dangerous, revolutionary Bolshevik stuff that for Forfar, but it showed one of the ways that the world was changing since the end of the war.

November 3 1932

The "talkies" have arrived in Forfar with the opening of the "purpose built" Regal in East High Street.

It was opened today, this Thursday afternoon, at 2.15 pm by Provost Hanick in a ceremony and showing attended by various dignitaries and member of the Town Council.

"Regal" was the name of the cinema, and every effort had been made to make the cinema look regal and even palatial.

The balcony was a particular attraction, and it was generally felt that it was worth an extra penny or two to get a good view. Seats could even be booked for the balcony!

It was generally agreed that the acoustics were perfect, and that this cinema would attract people to the town.

It was also a source of satisfaction that so much of the work for this theatre had been done by local firms, something that was very important for the providing of jobs in these times of economic difficulty.

The first film to be shown was to be "Goodnight Vienna" featuring Jack Buchanan, and next week there was to be a real attraction in the appearance of Hollywood heart-throb Lionel Barrymore in "Guilty Hands".

This meant that there were now three cinemas in Forfar, for there was already the Pavilion (opened in 1910 and it too now had a sound system called the Western Electrical) and the Reid Hall Cinema, although the Reid Hall was not exclusively for the showing of films.

It was felt that perhaps three cinemas were just one too many for a town the size of Forfar, although there was no doubt that going to films was now a major part of British social life.

The Regal lasted until it was burned down in July 1987.

PETER SMALL,

✦ ENGINEER, ✦

Horseshoer, and General Blacksmith,

CASTLE STREET, FORFAR.

ENGINEERING DEPARTMENT.

REAPERS and BINDERS and other kinds of Machines Repaired and done up in a tradesman-like manner.

LAWN MOWERS, "**SCYTHE**" "**ECLIPSE**," "**PONY**," made on the Premises.

These Mowers are made of the Best Material, have attained a high degree of excellence, and give universal satisfaction. Numerous testimonials have been received in their favour.

LAWN MOWERS, of any make, repaired, sharpened, and done up. Leave your Order early and your Mower will be called for and returned promptly.

SKATES Hollow-Ground to perfection while you wait.

Horseshoeing & General Blacksmith Department.

HORSESHOEING in all its Branches done with care and ability by experienced Workmen.

AGRICULTURAL IMPLEMENTS made and repaired.

RAILINGS of all Designs made and fitted up, and all sorts of Jobbing Work done.

All Orders receive punctual and personal attention, and are substantially and tastefully executed.

Estimates Given.

1900 Advertisement   *413*

November 4 1920

The Daily Motor Omnibus Service from Forfar to Dundee has begun.

There will be eight buses or charabancs each day in both directions (only six on Sunday). The fare will be two shillings for a single journey, children over four one shilling, under fours go free, children's "go cars" three pence, and dogs eight pence. The Stance is in Castle Street.

Those who were on the trial run yesterday were much impressed, and today even more people decided that it was worth a trial.

The idea came about after a few "Charabanc Tours" in the summer which were a great success. Already, of course, there was a train service to Dundee, but the buses had several advantages over the trains.

In the first place, it was cheaper and also, on the road, there was the plus point that the bus could stop and allow passengers to join. In addition, there was more flexibility in the bus, in that the driver of the last bus to Dundee at night would wait until the "pictures" at The Gaffie or The Reid Hall finished before leaving so that people from farms could now come into town to see films and get home.

The downside was that the Dundee to Forfar road was a very windy one, and was likely to be subject to disruption in winter.

The whole journey took about an hour, but it all depended on traffic because it was sometimes difficult for the drivers of buses to overtake horses and carts. Some buses were still uncovered as well — which was not a great deal of fun on a rainy day!

Forfar To Dundee Bus, 1920

415

November 5 1916

No-one realised it at the time, but the Confirmation Service this grim war time Sunday at St John's Episcopal Church, East High Street, Forfar included a future Queen!

Twelve candidates were presented for confirmation by the Reverend William Magee Tuke, and one of them was Lady Elizabeth Bowes-Lyon of Glamis Castle, daughter of the Earl of Strathmore.

The confirmation of this 16-year-old girl would not necessarily have caused any great stir in the town because although she was of the landed aristocracy, she was not as yet considered to be of any great importance.

Neither *The Forfar Dispatch* nor *The Forfar Herald* mention this event. She only became significant a few years later when she became involved with the second son of King George V.

She duly married him in 1923 and became the Duchess of York. Forfar conversation in 1916 would have been far more likely to centre on the progress or otherwise of the war.

It was now, for example, clear that however much they tried to dress it up, the British had sustained a heavy and prolonged defeat at the place they called the Somme.

Casualties were high, and the battle seemed to be still going on, for wives and mothers were still receiving the dreaded telegram, where "wounded" and "prisoner of war" were actually GOOD news!

Nor were the aristocracy themselves exempt from suffering. Elizabeth's brother The Honourable Fergus Bowes-Lyon, for example, had perished at the Battle of Loos a year ago and his body had not been found. The war affected everyone and Forfar, like everywhere else, was suffering terribly.

November 6 1888

It was local election day in Forfar, and it had been a boisterous campaign with the main issue of the day seeming to be alcoholic drink, as several candidates, notably James McDougall, a shoemaker espoused the temperance cause.

1557 males and 598 females were on the voting list. Women were allowed to vote in certain circumstances in local elections following the Third Reform Act of 1884.

As there were six seats available for ten candidates, each elector was allowed up to six votes, and one could cast six votes for one candidate — what was called a "plumper".

Two candidates withdrew — William Dowell, the painter, on the actual day of the poll, and Mr Rough, the post runner (sic) some time before then.

The doors of the Town Hall opened promptly at 8.00 am but there was only a trickle of voters until the evening when things began to get busy

The animation was augmented when voters went to the Lorne Hotel or the Royal Hotel and came out refreshed! Some amusing political arguments were heard on the street, and they continued even after the Town Hall had closed its doors at 8.00 pm to allow for the counting.

Eventually at 10.00 pm, Provost Doig appeared to announce the results and to declare that John Moffat, bleacher, Robert Craik of Kingston, James McLean, builder, James McDougall, shoemaker, Hugh Greenhill, hotelkeeper and David Whyte, potato merchant had all been elected. The unsuccessful candidates were Peter Tosh, the auctioneer, and John Clementson, the hotel keeper.

November 7 1939

The Forfar School Management Committee is delighted to announce that Continuation Classes will this year go ahead after all.

This had followed a certain panic in the month of September when everything was closed down with much hysterical talk about air raids, blackouts and gas masks.

But wiser, cooler counsel has prevailed and evening classes will take place after all in Forfar Academy. There will be the problems of getting there through the blackouts, and everyone will have to be informed about where the nearest air raid shelters are, but a big take-up is expected.

Ironically, one of the subjects to be offered is German, but then again budding spies will have to know that language! Rationing has not yet been introduced but one wonders how it will affect courses like Cake-Making and Icing.

Other courses include Typewriting, Plumbing, Building and Elocution. Normally the classes will run from 7.00 pm until 9.00 pm at night.

One of the positive aspects of the war is that it has encouraged many people to see that there are possibilities other than staying at home and working in the factories.

No-one as yet knows what exactly is going to be required in terms of manpower and human resources, but already certain young Forfar women have expressed an interest in a career in Nursing.

For young men, there are a huge variety of opportunities in the Armed Forces. There will certainly be a job or an opportunity for everyone, and the bad old days of unemployment and depression have gone for ever. The factories are working full time with loads of overtime.

November 8 1951

Today's *Forfar Dispatch* is full of speculation that Forfar Athletic are considering moving to the new ground called Guthrie Park.

Such a move would not take place for a while, and it would clearly be a big step for the club to take. Station Park has served them well for 67 years, and its obvious advantage is that it is close to the station for visiting teams, supporters and referees.

Its disadvantage is that it is in the north of the town when the town has been gradually expanding in recent years to the south and to the west.

In addition, parking facilities for cars and buses are limited and if Forfar Athletic are to stay at Station Park, they are clearly going to have to build a new stand because the old wooden one is a fire hazard, has some dry rot and is grossly inadequate for any occasion on which a well-supported team is likely to call.

It came as a surprise for supporters in 1951 to learn that the Station Park ground is not their own but is now rented from British Railways. Guthrie Park on the other hand has possibilities.

There is certainly room to build a new stand there and for terracing to go all round the ground. The cost would be quite astronomical however; Forfar Town Council have indicated that they would not be prepared to sell the land, and that they would like the ground to have some "recreational" use (ie not to be used exclusively for professional football).

The arguments raged on for a while but eventually Forfar Athletic decided to stay at Station Park and Guthrie Park came to be used by East End Football Club.

November 9 1963

Forfar Amateur Dramatic Society tonight finished their performance of *Our Town* by Thornton Wilder.

It was a remarkably good performance, but paradoxically watched by a very poor audience in the Reid Hall on all three nights.

The play was different, chosen to reflect a small town in the USA called Grover's Corner in New Hampshire which could just as easily have been Forfar.

It was drama with a difference — possibly too much of a difference for the good people of Forfar to cope with. There was no curtain, no scenery other than a few chairs, all to make people see the universality of all human life in that whatever happens in "our town" could happen in any other town.

Things like adultery, love, alcoholism, death and family arguments happen all the time in Forfar — and everywhere else as well! The small audience enjoyed the performance for the standard of acting was first rate.

The People's Journal was full of praise for the production team of Harry Douglas and Susan Roberts for bravely tackling this play with a strong cast which included Stuart Cameron, Alison Dalgety, Jim Davie, Jack Morgan, James Gardner, June McKenzie, David Potter, Jean Shields and Isobel Miller.

The anchor man was local Art teacher Jack Morgan, who played what was called The Stage Manager, but who was in fact the Narrator. He handled his huge part with panache and distinction.

It was a great play, but it was also clear that Forfar audiences far preferred something more clear-cut, like a murder mystery or a farce. Everyone however agreed that Forfar had a super-abundance of dramatic talent.

November 10 1919

A debate ensued tonight at the School Management Committee about the value or otherwise of corporal punishment.

It concerned a rather sad case of a father being brought before the Committee for failing to ensure that his 12-year-old daughter attended school regularly.

The father (it appeared to be a single parent family as there was no mention of a mother) said that the girl was out of control and had run away from home on several occasions.

Provost Moffat then said rather unkindly and unhelpfully that the man ought to be ashamed of himself for that, but then the man said that the problem was that the girl was not very good at arithmetic and had been strapped for it.

He added that she might be willing to attend another school. Councillor Peffers then wisely said that "You'll never knock arithmetic into a child with a strap".

The headmaster of the school then said that he had "had a word" with the teacher concerned and she had agreed to be more lenient, now that she understood the circumstances of the family.

Councillor Hamilton then said that it was unfair to pursue the matter if the teacher was not there to defend herself.

He added that it was wrong just to depend entirely on the testimony of the girl, and, rather unhelpfully, also said that if parents had more control over their children, less strapping would be necessary.

But the Committee agreed that the girl could go to another school if she wanted to.

East High Street, Forfar, 1912

422

November 11 1918

This was the day that a new word entered the Forfar vocabulary. It was whispered at first, and it being Forfar, it was deliberately and hideously mispronounced into something like "armstish" or "artamis", but eventually people got the word right and it was "armistice".

It appeared that the Kaiser having abdicated, the Germans were wanting peace and they were given an "armistice" — a cessation of hostilities in order to fix up an agreement. And at the three 11s — the eleventh hour of the eleventh day of the eleventh month — the armistice came into force.

Within minutes Provost Moffat had given orders for "Lang Strang" in the Old Kirk to ring out, and very soon the streets were crowded with people and children (the schools were closed because of the flu pandemic) all wondering what had happened.

Eventually Provost Moffat leaned out the Town House and read the terms of the telegram that he had received from the Commander of the Tay Defences.

While cake and wine were disbursed at the Town House, people cheered and sang outside as urchins waved Union Jacks and wondered when "Ma ded'll be hame".

Many of those who had a milder dose of the flu ventured out and immediately felt better. It was a great day for everyone — and yet even today, there was unhappiness for some.

This week's *Forfar Herald* when it came out on Friday would tell us that John Dalrymple, Colville Guthrie, George Stewart, Charles McPhee, Lyndsay Bruce and Stewart Simpson would not be coming home to Forfar again.

November 12 1894

A sad case came to the Police Court today whereby a dog had to be "put down".

The fact that the victim of the dog was a Councillor, Thomas Hanick, of East High Street was not really relevant to the issue, for the matter was a serious one.

Before Bailie Farquharson today appeared Donald Cameron, a brewer of West High Street, who was charged of having a ferocious dog belonging to him at large and not being muzzled.

The dog attacked Mr Hanick, bit his left arm and tore his jacket. The accused pleaded not guilty but it is hard to see what his defence could possibly have been for there were witnesses and evidence.

Bailie Farquharson found the man guilty, fined him 7 shillings and 6 pence with an alternative of 5 days in prison, and ordered the dog to be destroyed.

Dogs attacking people is a serious matter at any time, but in the 1890s there was the added dimension of the possibility of rabies which had not yet been eliminated in Scotland and was of course almost always fatal.

Dogs were also encouraged as a deterrent to burglars in those days, and dogs were commonly kept as pets. Sadly this one had to be put to sleep.

Councillor Hanick did not seem to have any ill effects of this rather alarming experience, but no doubt there were mutterings from the brewer about "Councillors aye stick thegither".

November 13 1901

Mr FG Harvey, Choirmaster of Whiteinch Church, Glasgow was in town tonight to give a talk to the East Free Church in their Church Hall on the subject "Voice Culture and Solo-Singing".

The culture of the voice was too often neglected and too little prized. The important thing was breathing, and on this subject, it was necessary for him to warn ladies about tight garments which would in any way impede their breathing (polite laughter was heard at this point).

For solo singing the important thing was not to strain one's voice by trying to sing too loudly, for this was bad for the voice. Singing should be practised softly with proper attention paid to the tone and the range of the voice.

Music and singing teachers should be very careful that their songs should be "moral, educative and edifying" and that "all vulgar songs should be avoided".

The problem with Forfar people was that they all spoke too loudly. The reason for this was that they had to raise their voices to make themselves heard over the sound of the looms in the factories.

In spite of the raising of voices, there was a tendency for people to be a little deaf, so that everyone, even those who did not actually work in the factories, had to shout even in a shop to make the deafened people hear.

This would not have been conducive, according to Mr Harvey, to good singing of good music. But, of course, anyone walking past a public house on a Friday or a Saturday night would also be aware that there was a distinct lack of "avoiding vulgar songs"

November 14 1662

In what appears to have been the last such execution in Forfar, Helen Guthrie was today burned at the stake, legend has it near the East Greens in what is now called the Staikit Racie.

The crime of "witchcraft" is a difficult one for us to understand three and a half centuries later, but one must allow for the times in which Forfarians lived.

There was, for example, no absolute guarantee that the harvest would produce food, there were frequent outbreaks of plague; "law and order" was a concept that no-one had ever heard of and there was the all-pervasive strength of the Church, itself under pressure from various schisms and arguments and the fear of "popery".

Witches were almost 100% female, and usually suspected of sexual profligacy. Accusing them of witchcraft was a very good way of keeping them quiet, for a man could always say that she was a liar anyway and that the baby he had sired on her was the product of a liaison with the Devil.

In addition, intelligent women or women who were in any way different were often suspected. "I saw her looking at my baby, and a day later the baby died" was often enough to convict someone of witchcraft.

In the case of Helen Guthrie, she had tried to save herself by involving others in the crimes of witchcraft but to no avail, for she met the same fate as those she had denounced.

There seems to have been a general revulsion of feeling against this barbaric practice afterwards, for although other women were arrested and accused of the crime, Helen seems to have been the last to be put to death, as this dark hour of Forfar's history comes to an end,

November 15 1942

Not all casualties in war-time come directly from enemy fire.

Today there was a poignant reminder that a man can be killed in what was an accident not far from his home, and yet in a very real sense, he is a war casualty.

William Pringle of Peffers Place had been a regular soldier before the war, and was involved in the evacuation of Dunkirk in May 1940. He had been "invalided out" of the Army after that, suffering rather severely from shell-shock — a condition which was little understood and little sympathised with in those days.

He resumed his trade as a blacksmith in Forfar for a spell but then got a job as a forester chopping down trees at Wester Cardean near Meigle.

Last night when coming home to his lodgings, he seems to have lost his way in the blackout and was hit by a car, sustaining head injuries from which he succumbed this Sunday morning in the Dundee Royal Infirmary without apparently regaining consciousness.

There was an air of mystery about this, for no enquiry seems ever to be held, and the suspicion lingers that someone was trying to cover something up.

The incident was in any case "buried" under the avalanche of other news, for this was the time when the war slowly turned in the favour of the British at El Alamein and the subsequent advance westwards of the Desert Army.

There were many other Forfar casualties at this time, but Mr Pringle's family are entitled to describe him as a war casualty.

November 16 1977

It was barely believable, but the traffic jam in the Dundee Loan proved it.

It would have been a Forfar totally unrecognisable to anyone who had left Forfar even 10 years ago.

First of all, a floodlight football match, secondly Forfar Athletic actually winning it and reaching the semi-final of the Scottish League Cup.

Yet only two years ago, they were comprehensively the worst team in Scotland, the butt (and not for the first time) of everyone's jokes about a lap of honour when they won a throw in and the two Chinese players they had signed — "Wi Wan Eence" and "Foo Lang Since".

Now, 6,000 were there to see them beat Queen of the South 1-0, and the kick-off had to be delayed because the Queen of the South team bus was caught in that traffic jam in the Dundee Loan!

The stand had to be closed because there was no more room, and there were long queues at all the turnstiles, and the bridies were all sold out before the game even started!

All this was the work of the new Chairman Sam Smith who was enthusiastic, determined and actually knew a little about football — which could not really be said in all honesty of some of his immediate predecessors.

Aided by a very able lieutenant called David McGregor who even produced a programme, the team took off. *The Glasgow Herald* was impressed, saying that "The jokes about Forfar Athletic are over", and now in the semi-final of the Scottish League Cup, they were drawn against some Glasgow team, Rangers or something I think they were called!

David McGregor,
Chairman and Secretary of Forfar Athletic

November 17 1936

The Lowson family are seldom out of the news, and there is always a certain amount of eccentricity about them as well.

Today however Alexander Dickson Lowson, the third son of the late Dr Lowson, one time Provost of this town, lived up to the family reputation by getting married at Gretna Green!

His bride was Olga Valentine Mitchell, daughter of Mr and Mrs Mitchell of Hillside, Montrose.

It is not clear to what extent this was planned in advance but it appears that the couple left the town by car late on the night of Monday November 16, along with a friend William Small of Queen Street.

Apparently Alex phoned his widowed mother to tell her his intentions and Olga phoned her parents as well. What the parental reaction was is not clear, but there was little that could be done in any case, and the wedding party drove all the way to Gretna throughout the night in the incessant November rain.

They reached there very early in the morning, woke the blacksmith up, persuaded him to perform the ceremony and then had a cup of tea with him!

The happy couple then drove all the way back to Forfar (it is not clear whether Mr Small came with them or returned on his own by train lest he be seen to play "gooseberry") and by evening, they reported back to Mrs Lowson senior and Mr and Mrs Mitchell as man and wife.

Naturally this bizarre event was the talk of the town with reactions varying from "an awfa wey tae treat his mither" to "well done, Eck!" but in any case the deed was done and the couple were married.

November 18 1925

The question of the price of meat came before the Town Council again tonight.

There had long been a belief in the town that the price of meat was artificially high and that the Town Council were in collusion with the butchers to keep the prices the way that they were.

A previous meeting had agreed to take no action, but tonight Councillor William Whitton (the "friend of the people" or "agitator" depending on one's own politics) wished the subject to be raised again on the grounds that he and a few others had been unable to attend the previous meeting.

The Food Council, a Government body, had apparently queried why meat was so expensive in Forfar, and according to Mr Whitton, the matter had been disregarded by the Town Council.

Mr Whitton wanted the case to be re-opened and although Bailie Peffers objected to this on a point of order, Provost Lowson felt that Mr Whitton possibly had a point and Standing Orders were suspended to allow Mr Whitton to bring a motion to re-open the question.

Behind all this dispute about procedure etc. there seems to have been a genuine point here about butchers being allowed to charge what they wanted as distinct from what was a realistic price which ordinary working people could reasonably be expected to pay.

Although council politics in Forfar were non-party political, Mr Whitton, an engine driver, had in the past stated that he was a Labour supporter, and there was little doubt that on this issue he enjoyed a wide support.

November 19 1934

This autumn has been a fine dry one with obvious good results in the harvest.

Berries, apples and potatoes have all been gathered in, and are in plentiful supply in the shops at reasonable prices.

But an unexpected and unprecedented side effect has occurred in the shape of a water shortage! In Forfar in November! The Baggerton Reservoir, Forfar's only available water supply, had shown a decrease in two feet on Saturday and a further decrease on the Sunday, enough to panic the Water Convenor into having an emergency meeting on Sunday afternoon in the Town Hall.

As a result of this, various town employees were summoned to make house to house calls on Sunday afternoon, and for the Town Council to ask Ministers of Churches to make an appeal from the pulpit at their Evening Services about the need for households to economise on water.

By today Monday, volunteers were delivering leaflets to every house in the town. Next week saw a few emergency measures taken in the shape of the water being cut off for a spell at the weekend, and the Forfar Fire Engine began pumping water at Glenley from the Noran Burn to the Batternach Burn in order to augment the Baggerton Reservoir.

Arbroath (bless them!) even offered Forfar free water, but the weather soon broke, and by the end of December we read reports of rivers flooding all over Angus.

Little more was heard of water shortages, although it was perhaps unwise to rely too heavily on one reservoir for the town's supply. But on the other hand, water shortage is not really a common problem in Forfar!

November 20 1916

The offensive round about the river called the Somme seemed now to be petering out at long last after almost five months of savage fighting.

The rains of the late autumn had rendered it almost impossible to move tanks and equipment, and there seemed to be a tacit agreement on the part of both sides to stop hostilities until the following spring.

It was hard to say who had won that particular battle, for no-one had made very much ground and the loss of life on both sides had been appalling.

This week had been a particularly terrible week for Forfar as far as casualties were concerned with two men, Private Pearson of the Royal Scots and Private Milne of the Scottish Horse killed outright.

Another two, Private Massie of the Black Watch and Private Stewart of the Gordon Highlanders died of wounds and five more have been reported wounded (three of them from the Royal Naval Division, temporarily drafted in to fight on land).

The wounded are in no great shape, but their families were relieved to hear that they were in hospitals in London and Birmingham where they were safe, and there was even the chance that they might be sent home to recover.

Nothing of course could be said to reassure or comfort the relatives of those who had died, and it was particularly harrowing for those who had heard news that their husband or son had been wounded ... then had died several days later.

The only possible comfort was that they were not alone. There was no monopoly of suffering ... but there was no end in sight.

November 21 1907

Today saw the funeral of James Martin, grocer and wine merchant in Castle Street.

He had been in that shop for more or less exactly 50 years, having set up business in 1857 and having run a successful shop all that time. He was 71 and lived at Lilybank Villa.

He had not enjoyed the most robust of health for some time, but had still been able to attend and work in his shop. He was working late in his shop on Saturday night, and had gone home feeling unwell.

On Sunday morning he took breakfast but then suddenly took ill and died at lunch time.

He was a native of Reswallie and served his apprenticeship with the late William Barrie and then set up business in his own. He was described as being "of a genial disposition" and, although he took a keen interest in town affairs, he had never been persuaded to take part in civic affairs or to stand for the Council.

He was well loved in the town and his funeral was a large one conducted by the Reverend AJ Gossip of the West United Free Church, of which he was an ardent member, according to *The Forfar Herald.*

His wife had died about six years ago, and he was survived by three sons and a daughter. He had built up a good business as a grocer, and specialist in foreign and exotic wines. 50 years was a long time, but groceries and wines tend to stay the same over the years as far as customers are concerned.

November 22 1889

The jute factory dispute is over, and it is a clear victory for the workers, and indeed for common sense!

We have had the rather remarkable spectacle in Victorian Britain of the Provost, the local Press, the shopkeepers and even some of the Churches lining up against the jute factory owners!

It is only really in Forfar that something like that could happen! And little doubt about it, the heroes of the hour are the Union leaders Adam Farquharson and in particular the "workers' darling" Tommy Roy.

A few months ago, some Forfar workers had gone on strike at Craik's because they felt they were underpaid in comparison with Dundee workers.

The jute factory owners had then grossly over-reacted by imposing a lock-out in every factory in the town.

This high-handed and self-defeatingly foolish action had alienated *The Forfar Herald* (a newspaper not hitherto known for any socialist sympathies) and indeed the rest of the town because the loss of earnings had affected everyone in the town while the workers and their families came close to starvation.

But Farquharson and Roy had stood firm, had discouraged their members from any violent action, and had organised soup kitchens to feed poor children.

The owners eventually cracked and this afternoon in the Reid Hall we had the remarkable sight of Provost Doig and Bailie Falconer being cheered to the echo by the workers, as the workers voted to accept the employers' improved offer.

The Forfar Herald heaved a sigh of relief as Tommy Roy told the workers to return on Monday. It was a long time however before the families of Don, Boath, Moffat, Craik and others were not jeered at on the street. They had lost most of all.

November 23 1926

A legal judgement today in favour of Lord Lyell of Kinnordy over fishing rights meant that Forfar people would no longer be allowed to fish for salmon at the Quarry Pool on the River South Esk at Sheilhill, hitherto a favourite spot for Forfar fishermen and the Angus Angling Club.

The case was brought by the guardians of Lord Lyell of Kinnordy against William Pringle of 16 Green Street, Forfar for fishing for salmon.

It was a case which did not show the Kinnordy Estate in a good light, and this being 1926, it did little to alleviate any feelings of class hatred which were undeniably around.

One feels that the Estate might have done well to leave this case alone, for the fishing of a salmon or two was hardly likely to cause them any serious financial harm.

The law, of course, with its predictable propensity to side uncompromisingly with the rich against the poor did not vary its behaviour on this occasion, although it does seem that Sheriff Gordon himself was not entirely without sympathy for the Forfar angler.

The Estate claimed it did not want anything other than £1 12 shillings for its expenses in bringing this case, and Sheriff Gordon fined Pringle that very amount.

It was a hefty fine in 1926 but it could have been a lot worse. As a result, Forfar people were deprived of a way of helping to feed their family, and although Pringle may technically have been guilty of "poaching", the question was asked "Who were the real thieves?"

November 24 1893

The deficiencies of fire fighting in the 1890s were well highlighted by what happened tonight.

A fire broke out between 10.00 pm and 11.00 pm in a stable behind the Finavon Hotel in premises owned by Mr Boath. It is not clear how they got in touch with the Forfar Fire Brigade.

A telephone was still a very rare phenomenon in 1893 and it may be that someone would have had to ride all the way to Forfar on horseback.

In any case by the time that the antiquated horse driven fire engine (which had been in use since the 1840s) got to Finavon, the fire had burned itself out.

It was only by the heroic efforts of Mr Boath himself and a few farm workers that the fire was contained in the stable and prevented from reaching the house and the hotel.

No animals were injured, but a cart and harness were damaged as well as a quantity of hay and straw. It was estimated that several hundreds of pounds of damage was caused.

All that the Forfar Fire Brigade were able to do was to extinguish the burning debris with water drawn from the South Esk. Fire fighting in Victorian Britain was not always easy for reasons that this incident highlighted, and the Forfar Brigade, although often ridiculed and laughed at, were brave unpaid volunteers.

Fires were of course very common at this time, and although running water was never far away, it was not always easily accessible in the quantities required to put out fires.

November 25 1934

Untoward and tragic events in the Old Kirk this Sunday evening service!

The Reverend WG Donaldson, who had been in post since 1908, suddenly collapsed and died in the pulpit.

Ironically the hymn being played was "The Sands of Time Are Sinking". Called "Knockie" for his tendency to thump the front of his pulpit when make a fine rhetorical point in a sermon, Reverend Donaldson was generally well liked and respected in the town.

Occasionally a bit pompous, he certainly would have to be described as a warmonger in the days of the Great War when he kept urging people to do their patriotic duty and enlist.

Nevertheless he had a common touch, and was involved in the Boy Scout movement and the Freemasons. He was also a great speaker at Burns Suppers.

William Galloway Donaldson was now over 70, but still, apparently, in robust health, although his wife had been ill recently. He was born in Pittenweem in 1861 and had come to Forfar via Galashiels, Kelso and St Paul's, Leith.

In 1914, just before the War broke out, he visited the Holy Land on holiday and brought home a canister of water from the River Jordan for the purpose of christening some Forfar babies with the real stuff!

His funeral on November 29 saw strange things happening to "Lang Strang" the bell in his beloved Old Kirk.

In the morning, it pealed out joyously to celebrate the Royal Wedding between Prince George and Princess Marina of Greece and Denmark, but that in the afternoon it changed tone for the funeral of Forfar's much respected and much loved Minister.

WG Donaldson left £15,357.7.7 to his widow, Isabella Thomson Adam, who survived until 1952.

Forfar Minister
: : Dies In Pulpit

REV. W. G. DONALDSON.

Rev. W. G. Donaldson's Collapse

Notable Services To Community

Scot Claims Fortune

Search in Family Bibles

Rev. W. G. Donaldson, of the Old Parish Church, Forfar, died in his pulpit last night.

The evening service was drawing to a close and Mr Donaldson had announced the last Hymn, "The Sands of Time are Sinking." The organist was playing over the verse, and had just reached the words—

"But day spring is at hand,
And glory, glory dwelleth,"

when there was a crash from the pulpit

Rev Who Ran Away

Death of WG Donaldson

November 26 1944

Tonight in Italy saw the death of RAF Warrant Officer David M Bell, elder son of Reverend DM Bell, Minister of the Old Kirk and Mrs Bell.

He was originally reported "missing" on a mission (which is usually a euphemism for "he has been killed") and it was confirmed in early December that he had indeed been killed while on active service.

Not unnaturally his parents and indeed the whole town, and particularly the Congregation of the Old Kirk were distraught by the news.

David was 21 and had joined the RAF on leaving Forfar Academy some three years ago. Although only 21, he was an experienced fighter pilot and had even acted as an instructor in England before going to Italy in summer 1944.

He was six foot four inches, a young man of frank and cheery disposition, a very talented musician and a fine sportsman who had played rugby and tennis and won the junior Sports championship when he was at Forfar Academy.

When home on leave, he returned to Forfar Academy to visit his old teachers, and he was described as a great favourite there, particularly with his old Music teacher Mr Bernard. He won the gold medal for playing the piano at the Arbroath Music Festival, and the Cup for being the best musician in any category.

He had been organist at the East Church before he was called up, and had now been replaced by his younger brother John at that Church. Every war death is a tragedy, but this young man had a particularly bright future ahead of him.

November 27 1905

Under the auspices of an organisation calling itself The Hope Trust, a couple of lectures were given to Forfar people in the Reid Hall tonight.

The first for younger people was on "Martin Luther, The Monk That Shook The World" and it was "profusely illustrated by beautiful limelight views" on the "magic lantern" with lovely pictures of all the places that affected or were affected by his life.

That lecture was delivered by Mr JT Hutton, and was well attended by school pupils, particularly those in the upper reaches of the Academy.

The second, mainly for adults, by Mr JB Cairns of Edinburgh on "Mary Queen of Scots — Her Life, Times, Battlefields and Contemporaries" was well received.

Mary was a romantic character and had many adventures at Loch Leven and elsewhere which were either not well known, or had been forgotten about by so many people.

It was nice to see such a large turnout of Forfar people who were interested in their Scottish heritage. The Hope Trust was a Protestant organisation, and one wonders how Mr Cairns dealt with the uncomfortable but undeniable fact that Mary Queen of Scots was a Roman Catholic!

Nevertheless, in spite of the sectarian overtones of the organisation, The Forfar Herald says that it was a most enthralling lecture well listened to by the Forfar audience, and their journalist was privileged to have an opportunity to talk to Mr Cairns at the end.

Mr Cairns said that the Reid Hall was one of the best in Scotland for acoustics "and the building has such a cosy appearance about it".

November 28 1914

War or no war, the Term was still celebrated in Forfar this Saturday night.

Forfar was today "invaded" (to use a current word in 1914) by loads of farm labourers there to negotiate for the new term with farmers.

Things have taken a turn for the better as far as labourers are concerned because so many men have now joined up, and yet the country will need farm workers to preserve the food supply.

So generally speaking wages took an upward turn with Foremen now able to command up to £30 for six months in addition to their house, potatoes, vegetables, coal etc.

With so many young men in town, recruiting sergeants were there as well trying to persuade everyone that the military life was just the thing for young men. But the weather was not all that great today, and as often happened on a Term Day, the hostelries provided an attraction.

The war was naturally a source of conversation, but there was now a solemn side to discussions. Already there had been some local casualties, and those who had joined up in August in a hurry lest they miss the action because the war might be "over by Christmas", had now discovered that Christmas would probably be spent in these holes in the ground called "trenches".

Although Paris had been saved, Belgium hadn't, and it might even be a "lang waydaein". But the immediate future for some of our young men at the Term was 1 The Vennel, the Police Station, followed by a visit to court on Monday for being "drunk and disorderly".

November 29 2020

The end of The Gaffie!

Today the disused Bingo Hall called The Pavilion went on fire, effectively bringing to an end the entertainment which had gone on in that building over the past 110 years since 1910.

No-one every explained exactly why it was called The Gaffie, but it was believed that a "gaffie" was a word for a low form of music hall in the Victorian age.

At about 2.00 pm smoke was seen issuing from the building, and the Fire Brigade was summoned with flames shooting so high that nearby property was evacuated and the Town Centre was sealed off for a while.

To anyone who had ever watched a film at the Pavilion Cinema, this was a major source of sadness. It had been around for a long time and had shown many films over the years, competing with The Regal in East High Street.

Throughout both world wars, two Forfar cinemas had provided comfort and entertainment for everyone, and its heyday had been in the 1940s and 1950s when films were shown there often only a few weeks after release, and the temptation to price itself out of the market by raising admission was always wisely resisted.

Many, indeed most, Forfar romances began with an invitation to attend a film at either The Gaffie or The Regal! There was one show on Monday, Tuesday and Wednesday and another on Thursday, Friday and Saturday.

However after about 1960, the cinema began to struggle against television and slowly began to surrender to bingo, until the Pavilion was used only for bingo. That too passed however, and the building had been disused since 2009.

November 30 1910

The General Election, the second of the calendar year of 1910, (and the third in three years for there had been a by-election in Montrose Burghs in 1908) was in full swing.

Tonight at the Reid Hall, Robert Harcourt, the sitting Liberal MP (Forfar was a traditional Liberal stronghold) had a very lively meeting, suffering from the attention of hecklers from the Tory opposition.

But it was good-natured stuff with Harcourt, a very experienced politician more than able to hold his own against the "Tory war dogs" as the unashamedly Liberal *Forfar Herald* describes them.

The infant Labour Party had decided not to stand this time, so it was a straight fight between Harcourt and a Tory called William Low who had stood in the January General Election as well.

The Election had been called because the previous one had been a hung Parliament, and the Liberals were wanting a majority to curtail the power of the House of the Lords which had caused them so much trouble over Ireland and latterly finance.

Robert Harcourt was the son of a famous Liberal politician called Sir William Harcourt, and his brother was also a Liberal Cabinet Minister called Lewis Harcourt.

Commonly referred to as "Lou Lou", Lewis was a rather appalling character with an inability to avoid scandal, often juicy sexual ones, something that the Tory hecklers were not slow to remind Robert about.

Robert Harcourt was able to deal with them, and duly won the seat when the election was held in a few weeks' time, but the General Election itself ended up with another hung Parliament.

December

December 1 1890

Limited progress of a sort is being made about the proposed Forfar to Brechin railway.

The Forfar railway connection is generally good — there is no problem about travelling to Glasgow, for example, and the train to Arbroath has now been running for well over 50 years.

The local Traders Association had met on Saturday and had made their opinions known. It is clear that some connection with Brechin is desirable but there is considerable confusion in the town about the route it should take — Finavon or Aberlemno.

Vested interests played a part often disguised under statements like "This route would be quicker", "Better scenery" and other specious arguments.

A sub-committee of Forfar Town Council met tonight under the Chairmanship of the Provost, but rather frustratingly did not seem to take any decision, choosing instead to ask the intentions and feelings of the Caledonian Railway Company and the self-styled Forfar-Brechin Railway Company so that they could make an informed decision at a later date.

This is of course a classic example of buck-passing and local Government in action, but it was annoying nevertheless. There was a clear need to press on with this matter, simply because railway was a far faster method of transport than horse and cart on the road.

Railways had dominated transport in the United Kingdom for many decades now, and there was a danger that towns like Brechin might feel left behind if they did not have fast and reliable communication with the County town.

December 2 1934

The town was saddened to hear today of the death of ex-Forfar Academy Rector Dr Benjamin Thomson at his home at 13 Albert Street Aberdeen.

He was 70 years old and died suddenly. He was a native of Aberdeen, and still spoke with an occasional touch of Aberdonian all his life.

He had been Rector of Forfar Academy from 1925, when he took over from his brother Adam S Thomson, until 1929.

His subject was Mathematics, and he had taught at Montrose Academy and Brechin High School before he arrived at Forfar Academy as Principal Teacher of Mathematics in the first instance.

His tenure as Rector of Forfar Academy was characterised by two things. One was the sustained excellent of the standard of education with Forfar Academy sending a stream of excellent pupils in Latin, Greek, Mathematics, English and French to the Universities of St Andrews, Edinburgh and Aberdeen, and the other was that he travelled daily back and forward to Aberdeen!

This seems to have been a deliberate policy *not* to involve himself in the politics of the town, the better to deal with the problems of the school.

The train service was very good in the 1920s, and only very seldom (if something was happening in the evening involving the school, for example) did he stay the night in Forfar.

The disadvantage of this was that he was not as well known locally as he could have been, but it meant that he was comparatively free from political influences and having his "ear bent".

He was very fortunate in that he loved his pupils, he loved his school and he loved his subject of Mathematics which he still taught occasionally, even when he was the Rector.

December 3 1897

The Victorian Age was a great era of emigration with loads of Forfarians going to Australia, New Zealand and Canada.

There were reasons for this in the shape of poor living conditions and a desire for some people to live in the New World, even though all the grand promises of what seemed to be there did not always correspond to the truth.

However a great many people did go abroad and made a success of it, often coming back to see that had happened to Forfar in their absence.

Today *The Forfar Herald* prints an account from *The Harriston Tribune*, a Canadian weekly newspaper, of Scottish *emigrés* returning to Scotland and Forfar for the Queen's Diamond Jubilee in the summer. One was Mr James Maxwell, whose brother George lived in Helen Street, Forfar and his friend Mr Copland wrote that

> "...we board the train and roll along to Forfar, the home of Mr Maxwell's friends, where I am happy to say he found many he never expected to see after his absence of 42 years. We enjoyed ourselves very much there. The Jubilee bonfire on "balmy Shanner hill" was a great success. The music and the dancing in the Peter Reid Park were "above the average, as nearly the whole of the company round the band and bagpipes joined the making merry".

They then went on to Dundee and to other parts of Scotland before sailing back to Canada from Glasgow. No doubt the Forfar musicians and dancers were delighted to hear that their music and dancing were "above the average".

December 4 1910

This being a Sunday, a few sanctimonious, Presbyterian, Forfar eyebrows may well have been raised at the event of a "Sacred Concert" being held tonight at the newly opened Electric Pavilion in Forfar, commonly known as The Gaffie.

Ex-Provost McDougall and Chief Constable Thomson however had no such scruples because this was a "Boot Fund" for necessitous children.

It was still a matter of considerable distress to see Forfar children without adequate footwear in the middle of winter. There was a General Election campaign going on at the moment, and both candidates said the equivalent of "Awfu' min".

The Churches tended to make a similar reply, but basically not very much was being done about it.

Chief Constable Thomson, however, who had seen a lot of this in his work, and was wise enough to realise that poverty, if not dealt with, could often lead to crime, organised this concert charging threepence to get in and it was such a success that many people had to be turned away from The Gaffie.

The entertainment was of a high standard, with an emphasis on religious songs, all provided freely by local artistes like Miss Mitchell, Mr Strachan, Mr Guild, Mr Beveridge, Mr McLaine and Miss St Clair, while Mr Lumsden showed a few new bioscope films.

A total of over £12 was raised — enough to provide boots for quite a lot of poor families. Ex-Provost McDougall was in the Chair and thanked Forfar people for their generosity and also Fyfe and Fyfe for providing the use of the premises free of charge.

Many Forfar children would now have boots on their feet this winter.

December 5 1918

The war had been over for almost a month.

Princess Mary, the only daughter of King George V and Queen Mary, was touring the battlefields and having lunch at the famous and much battered Cloth Hall of Ypres.

Ypres, of course, often pronounced Wipers, had been at the very centre of the fighting with major battles there on at least three occasions.

Princess Mary was about to leave when she spotted a well-dressed soldier of the 17th Royal Scots. Naturally charming and sociable (unlike her mother and father) she began to talk to the young soldier.

He told her that his name was Corporal Robert Scott from Forfar and that his mother was Mrs Scott, of 84 East High Street, and that in happier, more peaceful times, he had been an apprentice with Dalgety the Draper in East High Street.

The Princess, who was an Honorary Colonel of the Royal Scots, talked to Robert for a spell, mentioning the Strathmores and the Airlies, and decided to cancel the rest of her afternoon engagements in order to watch the march-past of the Royal Scots instead!

Corporal Scott had several interesting incidents in the war, including being wounded once and on another occasion being buried for four hours.

He had been in charge of the snipers and the scouts in his battalion. Like most soldiers, however, he was simply longing to get home.

Princess Mary would in 1920 pay a brief visit to Forfar, but does not seem to have availed herself of the opportunity to call on Corporal Scott!

1900 Advertisement

451

December 6 1920

A considerable amount of undue pressure and moral blackmail is being piled on reluctant young Forfar men to join the Territorial Army.

Advertisements appear in both local newspapers and both newspapers have leaders urging young men to join up, stressing the value of training camps in the fresh air, the wages to supplement the meagre earnings in the recession hit jute works, and how nice young men look in kilts, something that can be guaranteed, apparently, to inflame the sexual urges of young women.

But there are several reasons why the recruiting campaigns are no great success, the most obvious of which is that so many young men have just come back from Army life.

Although the war has now been over for two years, memories linger of what Army life was like, notably in silly stuff like having to salute and to stand at attention, and generally to be patronised by intellectual inferiors.

People have had enough of all that, and of course given the fact that over 400 young Forfar men failed to return from the war, there are considerably fewer young men around to choose from.

In addition, there are persistent rumours that the "terriers" may be deployed to sort out the seemingly insoluble problem of Ireland where even convicts were promised early release if they joined the Auxiliaries, and the newspapers are not slow to report rumours that the Germans are getting uppity again! So "Himeldaeme" (home will do me) seems to be the Forfar response!

December 7 1951

A special meeting of the Town Council was held tonight at the suggestion of the Housing Committee to discuss the layout of the proposed new housing scheme at Gallowshade.

Unlike some other items of Council business which could be a little tedious, to put it mildly, this one excited quite a great deal of interest in the general population.

It would clearly satisfy a need; there being at the moment many sub-standard houses in the town of buildings which had performed an honourable job for a hundred years or more but which now deserved "a decent funeral" by demolition.

In particular there were far too many houses which still had outside toilets shared by several households. The political thrust nationally was for new houses, and this Gallowshade estate (so called because it was in the "shade of the gallows" when criminals used to be hanged at Balmashanner) promised to be huge.

Bailie Selby, the Housing Convenor was not happy about the proposed layout as so many houses would have their backs on Dundee Road, Treasurer Donaldson thought there were far too many triangular corners in the estate and various other objections were raised.

The idea of buying timber houses from Sweden was also mentioned. They could certainly be erected quickly but might not last so long. These matters were delayed pending further investigations, but the atmosphere was certainly one of getting on with it fairly soon as long as funding was available from national government.

The need for getting them built was so obvious.

December 8 1929

"Knockie" was in good form today.

It was often said that the Reverend WG Donaldson was at hjs best at funerals and delivering tributes, and this Sunday morning it was his sad duty to pay tribute to James Lowson Alexander, one of his Elders and partner in the legal firm of McHardy, Alexander and Whyte.

He was also an agent of the Clydesdale Bank, and was well known and much loved in the town. He was 58 and really had never recovered from the death of his wife about a year ago. He had taken ill in his office about a week ago, but it was a heart attack which finished him off.

As well as being an Elder of the Old Kirk, he was involved in the Literary Society, the Horticultural Society, the Operatic Society, the Choral Union and the Cricket Club.

He had lived in Forfar all his life, being the son of Dr Alexander. He was of a kindly and genial nature, according to the Reverend Donaldson, and his willingness to undertake any task that was asked of him meant that he developed a large circle of friends.

He was exactly the person who one would want to help in a crisis, and in recent years in Church circles he had rejoiced greatly in the re-unification of the Established Church and the Free Church.

Similar tribute was paid to him in banking circles and at the Sheriff Court, and his funeral a few days later to the Newmonthill Cemetery was a large and very impressive one.

December 9 1889

The strike and the lock-out have now been settled, and everyone is back working to the satisfaction of all concerned.

There seems to be no other way of looking upon it than as a triumph for the workers, but not according to the *Women's Suffrage Journal* which points to a disturbing anomaly in the settlement of the Forfar dispute, and warns women everywhere to heed the example of Forfar.

What happened was that the Forfar workers, including many women who were specially prized in the jute factories because they had smaller fingers for the looms, had been on strike for nine weeks and the dispute was settled by what was loosely described as a "compromise".

The "compromise" was that men were to receive an advance of wages, but that women were to continue at the old rate. The details were a little more complex than that, but substantially it was true that men received favourable consideration on the grounds, presumably that they were more likely to have dependants.

The Dundee Advertiser tells of "much grumbling" among the female workers to the effect that they had to sacrifice nine weeks ages in order to allow men to get an increase.

There does indeed seem to be a valid point here, but the *Women's Suffrage Journal* is convinced that everything will be sorted out whenever women get the vote.

"Men appear willing to accept everything that women can give or do for them...but when it comes to a division of the spoils, they are very apt to secure the lion's share".

December 10 1936

The story about the newspaper headline "Forfar Girl Becomes Queen" was probably a joke, but there was little doubt that Lizzie of Glamis had now done well for herself!

This was a result of the unprecedented events of the past few days which resulted in the abdication of King Edward VIII. He had been having a liaison with a twice divorced American lady called Wallis Simpson.

That was not in itself a problem as long as things remained discreet, but "David" (Edward VIII) wanted to marry her and make her Queen. The Archbishop of Canterbury said "No", "David" abdicated and "Bertie" became King George VI.

His wife was Lady Elizabeth Bowes-Lyon, daughter of the Earl of Strathmore, who had been brought up at Glamis Castle, and was a frequent visitor to Forfar where she had been "confirmed" as a member of the Scottish Episcopalian Church at St John's in East High Street.

She was now, surprisingly, Queen and apparently a strong support to the stammering, shy and neurotic King George VI.

Opinion in Forfar was divided about the Abdication. Religious and royalist folk tended to be appalled at his "dereliction of duty" in favour of this disreputable American commoner, coarsely referred to as "the Yankee hoor".

But there were those, mainly men, who said "Good for you, Eddy!" and thought that the Archbishop of Canterbury should mind his own business.

One could sympathise with "Eddy" or "Davie" to a certain extent, but sympathy tended to evaporate when he began to consort with Hitler. Now, there was a man who would have been very happy to make Wallis Simpson Queen of the British Empire!

December 11 1935

A rare treat for boxing fans in Forfar tonight at the Reid Hall to see the Scottish Bantam Weight Championship final between Jim McInally of Glasgow and Mickey Summers of Dundee, the holder of the title.

The presence of Summers meant that there was a huge crowd from Dundee with a few special buses being noticed in the Greens.

It was a closely matched fight and went the distance with neither boxer "kissing the boards" or "assuming the horizontal position" as *The Forfar Dispatch* put it.

The reporter could not make up his mind who was better, but in the end the referee awarded the match to McInally of Glasgow, a decision that did not go down very well with the Dundee supporters for the difference was "infinitesimal".

In the supporting bouts, the one involving the Forfar boy Ian Nicoll was far more clear cut, for he had already "made acquaintance with the canvass" four times before the referee awarded the fight to William Ewing of Cowdenbeath.

Nevertheless the local "loon" had fought well, had held his own in the early stages of the fight and was clearly disappointed and willing to carry on when the referee stopped the fight, lest he sustain further damage.

There were six bouts in all and the occasion was very much enjoyed by the local audience.

The Master of Ceremonies was Councillor Andra Smyth and he performed his job brilliantly, Provost Graham was in the Chair and the Honourable Bruce Ogilvy presented the trophy to the new Champion.

December 12 1918

Today *The Forfar Dispatch* appears with instructions on how to vote in the General Election on Saturday.

The only polling station will be the West School, and there will be seven booths. The Presiding Officer is very keen to avoid congestion, so asks electors to remember their number which appeared on all election literature.

These precautions are necessary because this will be the first election since 1910 and there will be many new voters, notably women who have now been allowed to vote in Parliamentary elections — but only if they are over 30 and are householders.

It is a step in the right direction, at least, for women and in this vein, the Labour candidate Mr HN Brailsford is to be supported at an election meeting tonight in the Meffan Hall by Miss Maude Royden, described as an Assistant Pastor in the City Temple, London and one of the most influential speakers in the Fabian Movement.

It was probably the first time that people of Forfar had been addressed by a woman at a political meeting.

Once all the whistles and the filthy remarks died down, she talked intelligently and perhaps convincing a few of the sceptics that the cause of Women's Suffrage was not the bogey that it was portrayed.

In the event Labour were well defeated by the Coalition candidate, Mr Leng Sturrock, probably because so many potential Labour voters were still overseas and the postal vote system was not as efficient as it could have been.

In addition, Labour were perceived as being "soft" on the defeated Germans who, according to Mr Sturrock, really had to be made to pay for what they had done.

John Leng Sturrock (1878-1943),
Coalition MP 1918-22, National Liberal
MP 1922-24

December 13 1745

It is not always easy to work out whose side (if any) Forfar was on in the Jacobite Rebellions of the 18th century.

Indeed it is possible and even likely that the rebellions passed over the heads of most Forfarians who simply did not know what was going on. This was, after all, in the era before the mass media took over.

They would have been aware of loads of soldiers passing to and fro, being quartered sometimes in the town and a few people shouting about the "rightful king" and so on, but the rebellion did not affect Forfar in the way that it did Perth, Stirling and Edinburgh.

Angus generally, and in particular the important port of Montrose, was considered to be pro-Jacobite. Today however in *The Caledonian Mercury,* a pro-Government newspaper, we find a reference to the effect that "the Main Body of Highlanders are not yet in Motion" but are "Cantoned [quartered] in several places such as Perth, Dundee, Forfar, Brechin, Montrose, Aberdeen and Banff."

The troops who were billeted in Forfar, one hopes, behaved themselves better than the troops of William of Orange in 1689 who generally wrecked the place.

The Jacobites did not know that their Army was already in retreat, having changed its mind in Derby, and that when they did join forces with their allies, it would be for a march northward before the eventual cataclysm at Culloden in April 1746.

It would be interesting to know more about Forfar in those turbulent times, but such sources as do exist are scant, often contradictory and usually written by impassioned men with strong feelings on one side or the other.

George Henderson, Rangers

December 14 1922

The Forfar Dispatch today has the rare and possibly unprecedented chance to discuss who Scotland's centre forward should be with two possibilities — and they are both Forfar men!

At the moment Andy Wilson of Middlesbrough is out injured, so the way is open for either Davie McLean of John Street or George Henderson of Green Street to take over at Hampden next April.

It is an interesting choice. Henderson is currently with Rangers, and McLean has now returned from Sheffield Wednesday and Bradford Park Avenue to join Dundee.

The writer muses. It is a difficult choice. Clearly he must not offend the relatives of either candidate, but he comes down in favour of McLean who had more dribbling ability than Henderson.

Henderson is as good a goal scorer as anyone but it is mainly through vigour and bustle, whereas McLean can dribble through a defence as well. McLean has also "originality" of tactics to a greater extent than Henderson does.

It is often felt that Henderson is certainly getting the goals, but then again, he is receiving quality service from Tommy Cairns and Alan Morton, whereas McLean has more idea of how to make a goal out of nothing.

Both would serve Scotland well, however, it was felt.

In the event Andy Wilson (who of course had been seen at Station Park when he played for Dunfermline) recovered from his injury and duly played for Scotland next April.

Henderson never did get a cap for Scotland and McLean had to be content with the one that he earned in 1912.

December 15 1845

Sad news came today that William McLeish had been found dead in the well of Hillpark in Hillside Road.

This had followed several days of feverish activity to rescue him after the well had collapsed. His fellow worker William Brown had been rescued, although badly injured, a couple of days previously.

The operation had begun on Wednesday December 10 when James Barclay, a Forfar Solicitor, had engaged the two men to repair his well which had frequently become choked with moss and was producing brackish water.

The well was sunk to a depth of 60 feet. McLeish had apparently expressed some apprehension about going down, but the kindly Mr Barclay gave him and Brown a dram to give them some "Dutch courage".

They duly descended, but their descent had disturbed the earth and previous fittings of the well, and everything collapsed on top of them, not unlike a mining disaster.

For a while, the helpers at the top were able to send down a tube through which they could send some food, but there was no clear or obvious way of clearing the debris. On Friday December 12, another shaft was sunk some 15 yards to the side with the idea of tunnelling through to the stricken men.

This idea worked as far as Brown was concerned and he was brought out to great cheers, but McLeish could not be reached in time and died of his injuries (mainly to his foot and leg) and suffocation.

His funeral was held a few days later and he was buried in the Forfar Parish Churchyard. It remains one of Forfar's blackest days.

December 16 1925

Relationships remained poor between the Town Council and the town (particularly *The Forfar Herald*) about the lack of transparency in the matter of the building of new Council houses — an urgent need given the amount of dreadful housing in the town.

This evening, at least the Town Council meeting began on a pleasant and light-hearted note when Provost Lowson accepted on behalf of the town a porridge pot once, allegedly, used by Robert Burns.

It was presented to the town by Mrs JB Don of Maulesden, the mother of Councillor Don of Bankhead. It was a small three-legged pot with a straight out handle and it had a capacity for two breakfast cupfuls.

The straight handle was a recent replacement of a broken round handle. It had been inherited by Elsie Burns, a cousin of the poet and her great-granddaughter Anne Mearns had given it to Mrs Don.

It was to be placed in the Meffan Museum for public viewing. Cynics and pedants, of course, were not slow to point out that the connection with the poet was somewhat tenuous.

In fact there was no strong evidence to prove that he ever used this pot at all, but nevertheless it would be an addition to the Museum and one could at least fantasise that the poet had a cup of porridge out of this pot before sitting down to write Tam O'Shanter or setting out to visit one of his lady friends.

Provost Lowson accepted the gift with gratitude.

December 17 1896

Tonight was the great social event in the Reid Hall of the Forfar Railway Employees Annual Festival, called simply "the railway".

This event had been going since 1875 and was much looked forward to by the many people employed on the Forfar Railway.

The Railway was of course a major source of employment in the town, second only to the jute factories perhaps. There were drivers, guards, ticket collectors, ticket sellers, and "p-way" (permanent way) men who kept the railway operating.

The Reid Hall was well laid out and decorated with pictures and motifs of locomotives, bridges and railway lines on the walls. The President was Mr JS Adamson of Careston. Other luminaries at the top table included Station Master Mr Irons, Provost and Mrs McDougall, Mr Craik the jute manufacturer, Mr Graham of Pitreuchie and Dr Peterkin.

Following a meal "quickly and expeditiously served by a large staff of stewards and stewardesses", the gathering moved on to the speeches and entertainment.

The speeches were brief, but Mr Adamson said that "there were few more efficient staffs in the whole network than Forfar". This was met with much applause, and then Reverend Dr Grieve gave a talk on "Duty" which was not so pompous as it might have been.

After this, there was a varied programme of entertainment, particularly old favourite songs such as "Afton Water" "Jock O Hazeldean", "Comin Thro the Rye" and "The Flowers O The Forest" sung by Madam Annie Grey.

This was followed by dancing to the music of Mr Lowson's Quadrille Band. It was a fine night, in the tradition of such things, and much appreciated by everyone connected with the railway.

December 18 1908

A rather strange sounding event took place in the Reid Hall tonight. It was called the Bachelors Dance.

The local Bachelors club invited about 100 people, including local dignitaries to come to this occasion, presumably with the long term intention of ceasing to be bachelors!

The event is described as being the most popular of the local dances, and certainly no effort was spared by the Secretary Mr David J Prophet of Prior Road to make it a success.

The interior of the hall was tastefully decorated "and the effect was very pretty". The music arrangements were well carried out with an efficient quartet of MCs in Robert Graham, James McKay, George Cumming and William Walker and the music provided by Mr Hollingworth of Brechin.

The "purveyor" (ie caterer) was Mr Lichtsheidel of the Royal Hotel and a good time was had by all.

One would like to know a little more about this group, for there is mentioned a list of Matrons, which may very well be the mothers of the bachelors when one would have thought that there would have been more need of Spinsters (young ones of course!) to complement the Bachelors!

It would certainly be interesting to know the "success rate", if one may use so crude a term! A strange omission (to Twenty First Century eyes at least) is of anything to do with Christmas.

This is a week before Christmas Day, but then of course in 1908, Christmas, although now recognised in Scotland, was nothing like as lavish or as all-embracing as it is now.

Brechin Road, Forfar

December 19 1871

The Free Church of Forfar held its Annual Soirée in the Reid Hall for the first time, and it was a great success.

It was a mixture of business and pleasure. Tea was served by the ladies of the congregation, and the accounts were presented by the Treasurer — a Mr Lowson (there were plenty of Lowsons in Forfar in those days!).

A series of speeches, by a collection of clergymen led by Reverend Alexander Cumming, the pastor of the congregation, was followed by a pleasant talk by Mr Dryburgh of Dundee on how well the Forfar Congregation was doing, and how the Free Church was progressing throughout Scotland.

The choir then, under the leadership of Thomas Barclay performed a wide selection of sacred songs with Mrs McLaggan at the harmonium and the pianoforte.

Then in a rather unfortunate turn of phrase which would not be used in modern times, the members were given half an hour in which to have "free intercourse" [sic] with each other, before the meeting was closed with prayer.

This being the Free Kirk, there was no alcoholic refreshment. More surprisingly, given the time of year that it was, there was no mention of the imminence of Christmas, but then again, Christmas was no big deal in Victorian Scotland, certainly not in the Free Kirk.

The late Charles Dickens had made a great deal of Christmas in England, but in Scotland it was just another day. More was made of the New Year, but even that earned a little disapproval as it often involved alcoholic extravagance.

December 20 1953

No-one, not even the most geekish of Forfar cricket fans, would have noticed it at the time; in truth it had very little to do with Forfar.

Today in Hamilton, Bermuda, the great Len Hutton was out lbw for ten runs to the Bermuda captain, one Nigel Leroy Hazel.

Len Hutton, later Sir Len Hutton, was generally recognised as being the greatest batsman of the age, and was the captain of the England team currently *en route* to the West Indies for a tour which would start early in the New Year.

Bermuda, of course, was not technically part of the West Indies, but it was a fine place for the "banana boat" (as it was called) to stop to allow the MCC tourists to play a few games.

Hutton, who scored 364 against the Australians at the Oval in 1938, also broke a tradition when he became the first professional to captain England.

This would have horrified people like Lord Hawke, who said "pray God that no professional would ever captain England", but fortunately died before this unthinkable thing happened!

Today however Hutton was out lbw to Nigel Hazel. In years to come Hazel would strongly deny in the Lochside pavilion that the Umpire was his relative, although *The Yorkshire Post* does concede that the umpiring was "not great".

The game ended in a draw, Hazel returned to Scotland to play the 1954 season for Aberdeenshire before joining Strathmore for the 1955 season. And he was quite a success in Forfar!

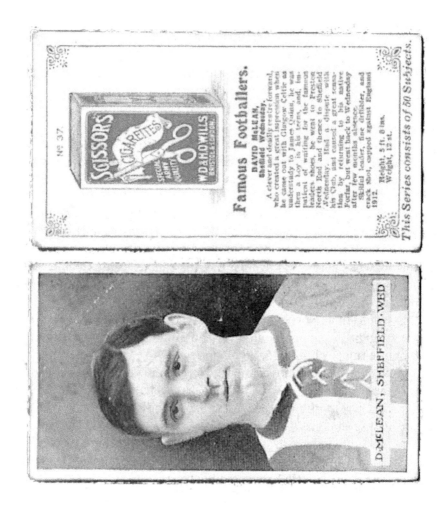

David McLean, great Forfar football player who played for many teams between 1906 and 1922.

December 21 1967

Today David Prophet McLean died peacefully in his sleep at his house in Craig O'Loch Road. He had just celebrated his 77th birthday.

He was a well-known character not least for his professional football career which had lasted from 1907 until 1932 and involved him playing for Forfar Athletic, Celtic, Preston North End, Sheffield Wednesday, Bradford Park Avenue, Third Lanark, Rangers, and Dundee before he eventually finished his career with Forfar again.

He was a centre forward, a prolific goal scorer with a tremendous shot which actually yielded him more goals than Jimmy McGrory of Celtic, although some of Davie's goals were during the Great War, and then for Forfar in the Second Division at the end of his career.

Amazingly he won only one cap for Scotland, against England in 1912. He was "mine host" of the Strathmore Bar for a spell and also played cricket with distinction for Strathmore.

He was probably best remembered for his years at Celtic where he won the Glasgow Cup with them, and also played in their famous eight games in 12 days in 1909 to win the Scottish League.

His brother Geordie, the well-known Fish and Chip man at the East Port, also played professional football.

In his later years, Davie was a keen attender at Forfar Athletic's games, occasionally at Dens Park; now and again he was invited to Celtic games as a guest of honour for he was the last survivor of their great team of the Edwardian era.

His funeral at Forfar Cemetery was well attended by the good and the great of Scottish football. He was survived by his wife.

December 22 2020

This is the pandemic Christmas, and there can be little doubt that the coronavirus outbreak, although minimal and close to non-existent in Forfar at the moment, has nevertheless caused a great deal of hardship for a great deal of families.

But it is for this reason that it is all the more heart warming and gratifying to record how two local businesses have teamed up together with a local Church to ensure that needy families got a turkey for Christmas.

Scott Ferrier of VIP taxis and Allan Rennie of Rennie the Butchers combined with Reverend Karen Fenwick of the Lowson Memorial Church to ensure that 50 turkeys were delivered to 50 needy families.

Mrs Fenwick said they would work with the Social Services Department to ensure that they went to the families most in need.

This was a magnificent Forfar gesture and had to be seen in the context of 2020 when Manchester United's Marcus Rashford and others had highlighted the problem of poor families.

The events of 2020 had hit many people hard. Many jobs had been lost, and the pandemic had hit many people notably in the hospitality industry.

It was a fine Forfar gesture, in some ways typical of the town tradition of looking out for each other. No doubt there was the other side as well of "Ah dunnae see hoo she gets it fan I dunnae...", but then again, Forfar people can be like that as well!

No doubt vegetarians and animal welfare people had something to say about it as well!

December 23 1833

Today, gas was introduced to the town of Forfar. Forfar was one of the first towns in Scotland to avail itself of this fascinating and indeed rather dangerous discovery.

This interesting fact was discovered by Councillor Whitson when delving into the archives one hundred years later. It would be a mistake to assume that gas was used in any widespread or general sense in 1833, but it was at least a start.

The 1830s were a great decade of progress with a start being made to other things as well like the reform of Parliament, the abolition of slavery and the idea that the Government was responsible for education.

At first it was only for the purpose of illumination, taking the place of the old foul smelling whale oil lamps. The cost was given at 13 shillings four pence per thousand feet (sic) so one would imagine that it would be looked upon as a luxury and indeed a status symbol.

The installation of this new illuminant was the result of some Forfar people blessed with foresight, in the same way that the railway came to Forfar a few years later, away ahead of most places in Scotland.

In 1866 the gas works in North Street were taken over by the burgh and run with crisp and homely efficiency, so that once again visitors to the town remarked on how well the place was lit at night and how many homes had gas light in their houses.

Gas light in the streets and homes lasted well into the 1950s before eventually conceding gracefully to electricity.

December 24 1920

It may be Christmas, but there is not very much cheer in the jute industry at the moment.

The trade had suffered a great deal since the War, particularly with the collapse of the German and the Russian markets, and the military orders from the British Army for jute to cover guns while being transported also drying up.

Today some of the Forfar factories — with the exception of Lowson's and Don's — are closing down until January 11. There will be no pay for the workers, but they will be able to claim unemployment benefit for two weeks.

Lowson's apparently are able to keep going until Hogmanay but then will close down until January 11, whereas Don's are "offering" their workers short time of a three day week of 20 hours, but will not close.

The long term prospects are far from encouraging, but the good thing seems to be that workers and owners are at least working together on this issue, unlike in the 1880s and 1890s when they didn't.

There is therefore a unity of purpose, and it is shared by the rest of the town because all this means less money in the town to spend in shops and on services.

There is of course no easy answer to the poverty of 1920, although the war profiteers are still doing well, and if you are rich, you are very rich.

Forfar people are aware that things are a great deal worse in big cities like Dundee, but they do also feel entitled to ask of Prime Minister David Lloyd George, "Whatever happened to the land that was going to be fit for heroes to live in?"

December 25 1958

It was an odd Christmas in Forfar today, for it was the first time ever in Scotland that there was a Public Holiday for Christmas Day.

The granting of a Public Holiday was nothing other than an acknowledgment of the reality of the situation; increasingly in previous years there had been a noticeable increase in absenteeism or failing to return after dinner time on Christmas Day.

A walk down the High Street today however revealed that there were still many shops open, usually family businesses or those who were prepared to pay their workers double time for coming in to work on what was now a holiday.

But the social life of the town was surely greatly enhanced by mothers and fathers both being at home to see children opening their presents as they prepared for a Family Christmas Dinner.

At least, that was the ideal. The pubs were open today, so there was the usual amount of drink consumed and no doubt the odd argument or two in Forfar houses!

But it was a step forward for most people and an indication that the bad old days of the Victorian era were being left behind. Incredibly — but this is Forfar after all! — there were those opposed to Christmas Day being a holiday

"They've goat ower muckle bloody holidays nooadays! Ah mind fan I wis young...!"

There usually followed a diatribe along the lines of only getting an apple and an orange for Christmas — and "we were a damned sicht happier" — a somewhat questionable statement, one feels!

December 26 1904

It is difficult to keep Bailie Lamb out of the news for very long!

The Forfar Herald renews its love affair with the admirable Bailie for his conducting of the South United Free Kirk Orchestra at a wonderful concert at the Reid Hall this Boxing Day evening.

Other editions of the paper have him dealing with drunks and vagrants at the Police Court (usually tempering justice with mercy and common sense) and making his contribution to the sometimes rather boring Council meeting.

Tonight, however, before the largest crowd ever assembled to see this Orchestra, which has improved steadily over the past few years, the Bailie provided marvellous entertainment.

His Orchestra tackled difficult pieces from Dalbey, Donizetti, Ricci, Volti and Hawkins — names possibly not immediately recognised by the Forfar audience, but certainly enjoyed by them.

In addition there were vocalist pieces from Mrs Bissett of Perth, Mr Stuart of Perth and Mr Hamilton of Dundee. Miss Gray was a delightful accompanist on the piano as was Mr Neill at the harmonium.

The pick of the singers was the tenor Mr Hamilton who increased his popularity with Forfar audiences with his "Come Into the Garden, Maud" "O A' The Airts" and "Afton Water", while Mrs Bissett sang "Golden Summer" and local favourite "The Bonnie Braes O' Airlie".

A young Forfar man called Mr Young, who was playing in the orchestra, did a fine flute and piccolo solo as well. The loud and prolonged applause paid eloquent testimony to the quality of the entertainment.

December 27 1976

An extremely rare event in Forfar today this Holiday Monday, as Forfar Athletic finished 1976 on a high note with their second home win of the calendar year.

This was a reward for their new management team and their ground staff who had worked hard to get the game on when lesser people might not have bothered.

Considerably fewer than 300 saw a good 4-1 victory over East Stirlingshire. Tribute must be paid to those who did turn up, because the form of the last few years, arguably the worst ever (and that is an ambitious claim!) would have tried the patience of a saint.

Not only that, but the temperature today was round about zero, and Station Park is one of the coldest grounds in Christendom. Mark Law, Sandy Whyte, Charlie Guthrie and an own goal gave Forfar a victory and this time, at least, the support stayed to the end, instead of the trickle home soon after half time.

The hard core support at last came down North Street with something approaching a smile on their faces, but even in this hour of triumph they had to endure the jeers of the cynics.

"They goat clappit aff the park" we chortled. "Clappit aff the park? They shud have been clappit ee jile!" said the disillusioned.

The trouble was that Forfar people were not used to success and could not cope with it.

Fortunately, the next few years would give them an opportunity to adapt to happier days. With Sam Smith as Chairman and Archie Knox as Manager, not to mention David McGregor as Programme Editor and general administrator, things were about to happen.

Jerry Kerr with what is generally regarded as being Forfar Athletic's worst ever team in 1975

December 28 1892

The weather has been exceptionally hard this winter but *The Forfar Herald* thinks that this is a good thing, for the "auld saw" of "a green Christmas and a fu kirkyaird" i.e. that more people die off in a mild winter will not apply this year.

Nights in particular have been beautiful with loads of moonlight and stars and an absence of any kind of dull cloudy weather.

Evidence of the hard winter appeared on the Loch today as the Angus Curling Club had its annual Forfarshire bonspiel. It took place on the Forfar Loch on "admirable ice".

There were an amazing number of 34 rinks (teams) taking part. The winner was Cortachy Number One, skipped by Mr Carnegie, while the runner up was Evenie Water. Glamis got a consolation prize. The trophies were presented by Mr Fothringham of Fothringham Estate.

The event attracted a great deal of attention with quite a few horse and traps being seen at the edge of the Loch.

It was as well however that the bonspiel took place when it did because a thaw set in that night and the Forfar v Kirriemuir game scheduled for the following day was still able to go ahead but on "dull ice" with a lot of water, and the longer the game continued conditions became more dangerous with one or two ominous creaks being heard from the ice.

Nevertheless the bonspiel was reckoned to be one of the better ones, and Forfar generally now looked forward to the New Year with prospects for improvement in the jute trade, and manufacturers promising full employment for the factories.

December 29 1942

One of the major problems about wars is that one doesn't really know what is going on.

The Second World War had now been going on for three years and a bit, and although everyone knew that there was had been a great advance in Africa, everyone also knew that there was still a long way to go.

More pertinently for Forfar mothers and wives, although mail arrived from their loved ones, it was always heavily censored and in any case several weeks late.

People had learned early in the war not to trust what the newspapers told them, and the news on the radio was usually so bland and generalised as not to be a great deal of value.

Thus when the momentous year of 1942 came to an end, people shared what news they had and enjoyed as far as they could their rations while wondering how the servicemen were doing in their distant theatres of war.

It was the same with those who were abroad. Advances to Libya and Tripoli or wherever meant very little. What mattered was "we nightly pitch our moving tent a day's march nearer home", and the advance that everyone really craved was the sight of the Zoar Bridge as the train taking them home pulled into the station.

For many of them, it would be another three years away, and some would never make it, but even for those who saw places like Rome, Paris, Singapore, Cairo or Naples would look forward to arriving home and saying "This is a bra' place, min!"

December 30 1782

Tonight the Forfar Town Council met in emergency session to discuss a plea from the Reverend John Bruce of the Parish Church to provide food for the people who had suffered from a succession of bad harvests.

With an angry mob gathering outside the Town House, the magistrates of the town and the deacon of the Trades were appointed along with Reverend Bruce to take any steps "that they might think necessary" to provide meal, oats and grain for the starving inhabitants, and they were empowered to borrow £500 from the Dundee Banking Company to spend on food.

This had followed several days and nights of severe unrest in the town. On one night, a starving mob had marched on the Manse in Manor Street of the fairly recently appointed Minister Reverend Bruce.

While singing revolutionary (and even old Jacobite) songs, they threatened violence by putting on a pike a loaf of bread steeped in blood, which seemed to be saying to Reverend Bruce that "You had better get us food...or else".

The weather had been bitterly cold as well, and the whole country was struggling economically from the disastrous and prolonged war in the Americas, as well as the periodic wars against the French.

The measures taken by the council and implemented by Reverend Bruce and his helpers took the sting out of the situation for a spell.

Although poverty was a feature of Forfar life for many years to come, there was usually enough food grown in the surrounding countryside to feed the population. On occasion, however, the townsfolk were known to march into the country and steal the corn or even slaughter some livestock.

December 31 1960

"The times they are a' changin'".

For the first time in many years, the crowd assembled at the Cross to see in the New Year was noticeably smaller than previously.

It used to be that hundreds (some would claim thousands, but that would be an exaggeration, although possibly one thousand wasn't!) would gather at the Cross to see in the New Year as the Steeple chimed.

Some were already in a considerable state of intoxication, others soon became so when bottles were passed around indiscriminately, an inordinate amount of pre-marital and extra-marital kissing took place (with the occasional hand straying to where it shouldn't) and generally speaking a good time was had by all.

There were of course casualties — a police van was usually on stand-by to take away the horizontal cases, and there was usually a huge reckoning the following morning in terms of illness.

But by about 12.30 am most of the crowd had dispersed to "first foot". The night was just beginning, and it was generally good natured stuff with any excesses usually explained away and excused by it being "the New Year".

There was often an excellent example of the typical Forfar habit of saying the opposite of what you mean in "Ah dinnae like the New Year!" said by someone who nevertheless always enjoyed it!

But was all this beginning to disappear?

Many Forfar houses now had a box called a television, and this meant that Cliff Richard and Elvis Presley, not to mention a fellow from Arbroath called Andy Stewart, were beginning to play a part in New Year festivities as well.

Rev Ian Pitt-Watson, St James's Kirk

ALEX.  BENNETT,

HORSE HIRER,

24, CASTLE STREET, FORFAR,

Livery Stables and Posting Establishment.

JOB AND SADDLE HORSES.

BRAKE FOR PIC-NIC PARTIES.

Flys, Landaus, Dog Carts, Phaetons, Waggonettes, &c., on the shortest notice.

Alex. Bennett, Advertisement from 1877

HENRY H. FENTON'S

Drapery, Millinery, & Dressmaking Warehouse,

170 & 172 EAST HIGH STREET, (East Port).

The Millinery Department, conducted as formerly by Mrs FENTON, but now assisted by Miss BETSY FENTON, after a course of training in one of the leading Wholesale Millinery Warehouses in Glasgow.

Miss FENTON (Certificated Teacher of Dress-Cutting), is now in charge of the Dressmaking Department, which is being very successfully carried on by the new Cosmopolitan system, whereby all waste of time and material is avoided, and no fitting on is required. A trial solicited.

Ladies can have their measures taken and paper patterns cut, if wishing to make up their own Dresses. Price 2/ each.

SHOP ADDRESS, **| EAST HIGH STREET, |** HOUSE ADDRESS,
170. | **Forfar.** | **172.**

Henry Fenton, Advertisement from 1891

484

1938

In This Year
Traders in Forfar

David Callander Ltd.

Directors—
D. Callander, A. Callander, W. F. Callander.

Motor Engineers
and Haulage Contractors.

Specialties.

DENNIS
COMMERCIAL VEHICLES
REPAIRS.

Office---Roberts Street, Forfar.

Telephone Nos. 140 and 141.

H

CAMPBELL & CO.'S
TABLE WATERS
ARE UNSURPASSED FOR PURITY AND FLAVOUR
—— IN SYPHON OR BOTTLE ——

ccxix

ccxxiii

ESSON & NAPIER,

MEN'S OUTFITTERS,

162 East High Street, Forfar.

OUR AIM—Satisfied Customers.
First-Class Tailoring. Personal Service given.

TELEPHONE No. **292**.

LIDDLE & CALDER,

Building Contractors,

FORFAR.

House Address:
67 QUEEN STREET,
FORFAR.

Yard:
QUEEN'S WELL LANE.
CASTLE STREET.

BEST BUTCHER MEAT. **Telephone 312.**

ROBERT F. CRAIK,

FAMILY BUTCHER,

5½ GLAMIS ROAD, FORFAR.

Orders called for and promptly delivered.

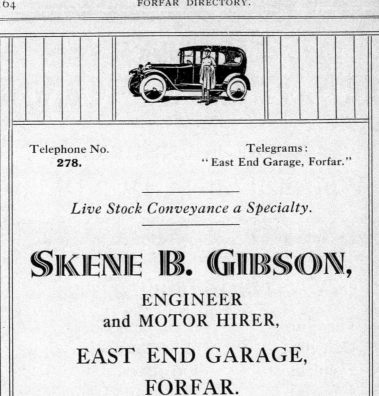

Telephone No.   Telegrams:
      278.   "East End Garage, Forfar."

Live Stock Conveyance a Specialty.

SKENE B. GIBSON,

ENGINEER
and MOTOR HIRER,

EAST END GARAGE,
FORFAR.

*Landaulettes and Touring Cars for Hire
at Moderate Charges.*
Oils and Petrol.
Funerals conducted in Town and Country.

THOMAS
JUSTICE & SONS
LIMITED,
HOUSE FURNISHERS,
Whitehall Street, DUNDEE.

Workshops and Depository—SOUTH WARD ROAD.

Departments.

Furniture.	Prams and Cots,
Carpets.	Mantelpieces.
Linoleums.	Fireplaces.
Curtains.	Household Ironmongery.
Soft Furnishings.	Gardening Tools.
Household Linens.	Cutlery.
Bedsteads.	Glass and China.
Bedding.	Pottery Wear.

Removals conducted by Road, Rail or Sea

TELEPHONE No. 4141.   TELEGRAMS: "Furniture, Dundee."

Telephone No. 97 KIRRIEMUIR.

JAMES KERR & SONS,

Slaters & Contractors,

KIRRIEMUIR and FORFAR.

All Orders punctually attended to.

Telephone No. **6.**   Telegrams: "Cumming, Hirer, Forfar."

C. CUMMING,

RAILWAY HOTEL, FORFAR.

First-Class Motor Cars for Hire.

Orders left at RAILWAY HOTEL GARAGE will have prompt and particular attention.

Funerals conducted in Town and Country.

GEORGE KYDD,

Jobbing Gardener,

100 WEST HIGH STREET, FORFAR.

Bouquets, Wreaths, and Sprays made to order.
Orders can also be left at A. TROUP, 26 Castle Street.

C. & D. LAIRD,

.⟨ BUILDERS, ⟩.

59 SOUTH STREET,

FORFAR.

Telephone No. 279 Forfar.

DON'T ASK FOR LEMONADE---
ASK FOR
" LAMB'S "

THE WATER USED IN THE MANUFACTURE OF
LAMB'S SPECIAL LEMONADE
IS DRAWN FROM OUR OWN ARTESIAN WELL,
THE EXCELLENT PURITY OF WHICH IS PROVED BY
ANALYST'S REPORT.

FOR YOUR HEALTH'S SAKE ALWAYS SPECIFY

LAMB'S, Strathmore Springs, Forfar.

H. Wright Macneill

High-Class
Fruiterer & Confectioner,

56 CASTLE STREET,

FORFAR.

Telephone No. 440.

Lyons' Ice Cream Puddings & Fancy Ices.

Wreaths, Sprays, and Bouquets.

Orders called for and delivered.

ITALIAN WAREHOUSE

Telegrams: "Melvin, Forfar."   Telephone No. 12.

B. & M. MELVIN,

Sole Partner: A. W. ORMISTON

FAMILY GROCERS,
WINE & BRANDY IMPORTERS,
WHISKY BLENDERS,

17, 19, & 21 CASTLE STREET,

FORFAR.

ESTABLISHED OVER A CENTURY.

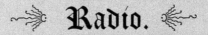

M. MILNE,
STATIONER,
NEWSAGENT and CONFECTIONER,

WEST PORT POST OFFICE, FORFAR.

General Fancy Ware in Great Variety.
LENDING LIBRARY.

TELEPHONE
No. 314.

WILLIAM BIRNIE,
Fishmonger, Poulterer, and
Game Dealer,
8 EAST HIGH STREET,
FORFAR.

FERGUS HUNTER,
Baker and Confectioner,

11 SOUTH STREET, FORFAR.

FANCY CAKES of all kinds.   CREAM GOODS.
FORFAR BRIDIES a Specialty.

L

GEORGE NEAVE,

Gent.'s Hairdresser,

163 EAST HIGH STREET, FORFAR.

Razor Blades and other Accessories stocked.

PARKER QUINK

WRITING INK

Quink

Prices---9d, 1/3, 2/3, 4/6, 7/6 per Bottle.
Colours---Black, Blue-Black, Blue, Green, Purple, Scarlet.

W. SHEPHERD, Stationer,

39 CASTLE STREET, FORFAR.

HIGH CLASS FISHMONGERS and POULTERERS.
Fresh Supplies Daily.

DIRECT FISH SUPPLY,

124 East High Street, Forfar.

Large variety of Tinned Meats.   Fresh Fruit in Season.   Country Eggs direct from Farm.
Regular supplies of Rabbits in season.   Orders called for and delivered.

ccxliii

A few of the many Trophies PATTERSON BROTHERS, for their Famous Bread. awarded to Messrs 48 WEST HIGH STREET, FORFAR, GIVE IT A TRIAL.

ROBBIE & NICOLL,

Seedsmen, Florists, and Potato Merchants,

Phone No.
152.
37 Castle Street, Forfar.
Nurseries,
Bankhead.

Farm and Garden Seeds of the highest quality.
Wreaths, Crosses, Sprays, Bouquets, or any other design made on the
shortest notice.   Cut Flowers in their Season.

Headquarters of the A.A. & R.S.A.C.

. . THE . .

ROYAL
HOTEL
FORFAR

Telephone No. 21.   J. P. MANN,
Proprietor.

Telephone No. 59.

D. PHILIPS,

FAMILY GROCER, TEA and PROVISION MERCHANT,
FRUITERER and CONFECTIONER,

11-13 WEST HIGH STREET, FORFAR.

High-Class GROCERIES and PROVISIONS.
Finest FRUITS in their Season.   CONFECTIONERY in great variety.

W. ROBERTS & SON,

Drapers and Clothiers,

170 East High Street, Forfar.

**Seasonable Goods in every Department all the year round.
Letter Orders carefully attended to.**

Telephone No. 75.

HENRY W. CAIRD,

CHEMIST,

69 EAST HIGH STREET,

FORFAR.

*Prescriptions compounded with Finest Ingredients.
Kodak and Cine Photographic Supplies.
A good Selection of Perfumes
and Toilet Requisites always in stock.*

Telephone No. 225.

ADAMS & RUSSELL,

PLASTERERS & CEMENT WORKERS.

— Orders can be left as usual at —

28 SOUTH STREET, FORFAR.

**Estimates Given.   Jobbing Promptly attended to.
Tile Laying neatly executed.**

TELEPHONE No. 180.

David Rodger

Painters and & Son,

Decorators,

13 East High Street, Forfar.

ccl

BOY WITH RABBIT.

Reproductions

FROM PICTURES, DRAWINGS, SKETCHES, OR PHOTOS,
SUITABLE FOR CATALOGUES, BOOKS, &c., SUPPLIED
AND PRINTED IN LINE, HALF-TONE, AND 4-COLOUR
PROCESS . . . . . . SPECIMENS AND PRICES FROM

W. SHEPHERD, 39 CASTLE STREET, FORFAR.

TELEPHONE No. 108.

Printing

in some form or other, constitutes an important part of every progres= sive business.

To be worth while, and to do credit to the business concerned, it must be Good Printing. . . . . . .

Good Printing costs relatively little more than the inferior article, but how vast the difference in appearance and how much greater the appeal to the reader. . . . . .

Why not call, 'phone, or write us about that piece of Printing you are thinking of having done. .

'Phone number one=o=eight will find us. . . . .

W. Shepherd,
39 Castle Street, Forfar

Sturrock & Son

Bakers & Confectioners,

50 East High Street,
10 West High Street,

Forfar.

'Phone No. 123.

Index to Tradesmen's Advertisements

William Dick, Clothier and Hatter	1890	xxiv
Direct Fish Supply, Fishmongers and Poulterers	1938	ccxli
John Doig, Plain & Ornamental Plastererer	1890	xxi
Thomas Doig, Auctioneer and Valuator	1910	clxxi
W. L. Doig, Draper and Ladies' Outfitter	1904	lxviii
W. L. Doig, Tailoring, Dressmaking, Millinery, Linens	1910	cxxxiii
W. L. Doig & Son, Ready-to-Wear Garments for Ladies	1938	ccxx-
George Donald, Slater	1890	xxii
Henry Donald, Family Grocer, Tea, Wine, & Spirit Merchant	1904	xciv
M. M. Donald, Tobacconist	1890	xxiii
George H. Douglas, Cycle Agent	1890	xxiv
Miss E. K. Duncan, Confectioner and Tobacconist	1910	cxxxiv
J. L. Duncan, General Drapery and Furnishing	1904	cxiii
J. L. Duncan, General Draper and Outfitter	1910	cxxxv
J. L. Duncan, General and Fancy Draper	1938	ccxxii
Dundee & District Hygienic Institute Ltd., Artificial Teeth, Extractions, Fillings &c.	1910	ccviii
John A. Dunn's Boot Warehouse	1890	lvi
Eaton & Fyfe, Butchers	1938	ccxlvi
Ednie & Kininmonth, General Furnishing and Builder's Ironmongers	1900	119
Ednie & Kininmonth, Furnishing Ironmongers	1938	ccxxiii
William Edward, Family, Bread, and Biscuit Baker	1890	xxvi
Charles Edwards, Family Butcher	1910	cxli
Mrs Edwards, Family Butcher	1938	ccxliii
Thomas Elder, Baker, Family Grocer & Provision Merchant	1904	lxix
Thomas Elder, Baker, Grocer, & Provision Merchant	1910	clxxiv
A. Esplin, Fruiterer and Confectioner	1910	cxciii
John Esplin, Tobacconist, Musicseller, and Stationer	1910	clxxiv
William Esplin, Boot and Shoemaker	1910	clxiv
Wm. F. S. Esson, Grocer and Wine Merchant	1938	ccxxxiv
Esson & Napier, Men's Outfitters	1938	ccxxiv
James Ewen, Wood and Coal Merchant	1890	xxvii
Adam Farquharson, Cloth Merchant	1890	xxv
Adam Farquharson, Tailoring, Dressmaking, Millinery, Drapery	1904	lxx
Adam Farquharson's, Drapery Goods	1910	ccix
J. Farquharson, Joiner	1938	ccxvi
James Fearn, Cycle Manufacturer and Motor Agent	1938	ccxxxviii
Henry H. Fenton, Dressmaking, Millinery and Drapery	1890	xxviii
Harry H. Fenton's Drapery, Millinery & Dressmaking	1891	484
John M. Fenton, Fenton's Restaurant	1904	lxxi
Mrs John M. Fenton, Fenton's Restaurant	1910	cxxxvi

Alexr. Hay & Co., Joiners and Funeral Undertakers	1938	ccxv
Hebenton's, Ironmonger	1890	liii
W. Hebington, Boots and Shoes	1890	xli
W. Hebington, Boots and Shoes	1904	cxi
Andrew Henderson, Painter and Decorator	1904	lxxv
Andrew Henderson, Painter and Decorator	1910	cxliii
Andrew Henderson & Son, Painters and Decorators	1938	cclvii
Hendry & Warden's General Drapery Warehouse	1890	xxxiii
The Herald Office, Letterpress Printing	1890	xxi
"Herald Office" Printing	1890	xxxvii
Hood's Boots & Shoes	1890	xxxiv
Hood's Boots	1904	cxiv
Hood's Boots	1910	cxlv
Wm. A. Horsburgh, The Central Bar	1910	clxi
J. Hosie, Radio and Electrical Engineer	1938	cclviii
Fergus Hunter, Baker and Confectioner	1938	ccxxxvii
Hutchison, Agent for A. & I. MacNab, Dyers and Cleaners	1900	cxxxvi
J. Hutchison, Prudential Assurance Company Limited	1890	xix
W. Hutchison, Draper, Clothier & Outfitter	1904	lxxiv
David Irons, Hardware and Seed Merchant	1890	xxvi
David Irons & Sons, House Furnishing Department	1904	cxv
D. Iron & Sons, Agricultural Implement Department	1904	cxvi
D. Irons & Sons, Furnishing and General Ironmongers	1910	cxlvi
R. D. Jack's, Liquors, Teas, Groceries and Provisions	1904	lxxv
R. D. Jack's, Liquors, Teas, Groceries and Provisions	1910	cxlvii
John Jamieson & Co., Clothiers	1890	xxxv
John Jamieson & Co., Clothiers and Outfitters	1910	clvii
Jarman's Hotel	1910	cxlviii
Jarman's Hotel	1938	ccxxxix
Jarvis Brothers, Drapers	1890	xlv
Jarvis Brothers, Ladies' and Gentlemen's Tailoring	1904	lxxvi
Jarvis Bros., Curtain hanging	1938	ccxxvii
D. Johnston, Grocer, Wine and Spirit Merchant	1904	lxxvii
D. Johnston, Wholesale and Family Grocer	1910	cliv
John Johnston, Chemist	1910	clxvii
Thomas Justice & Sons Limited, House Furnishers, Removals	1938	ccxxvi
R. D. Keiller, Upholsterer	1904	lix
R. D. Keiller, Upholsterer	1910	cxxxiv
Charles Kerr, Sculptor & Stone Carver	1904	lxxvii
James Kerr, Slater	1890	xxi
James Kerr, Slater	1904	lxi
James Kerr & Son, Slaters & Contractors	1910	cxxx
James Kerr & Sons, Slaters & Contractors	1938	ccxxviii

John Killacky, Kalac Cycles and Motor Repairs	1900	294
John Killacky, Cycles, Motor Cycles and Cars	1904	lxxviii
James T. Kinloch, Family Butcher	1910	clxxxi
David I Kydd, Tailor and Clothier	1910	cxlix
George Kydd, Jobbing Gardener	1938	ccxxviii
John S. Laing, Bookseller, Stationer, and News Agent	1938	cclx
C. & D. Laird, Builders	1938	ccxxix
Lakie, John, Coal Merchant	1890	liv
John Lamb, The Strathmore Aerated Water Works	1910	cl
Lamb's Special Lemonade	1938	ccxxx
David Langlands, Sanitary Plumber, Gas and Electric Bell Fitter	1910	cxliii
John Leith, Registered Sanitary Plumber	1904	ciii
John Leith, Registered Sanitary Plumber	1910	cxxix
J. & W. Lindsay, Drapers, Clothiers, Dressmakers and General Outfitters	1910	cci
Liddle & Calder, Building Contractors	1938	ccxxiv
Low & Company, Bakers and Grocers	1890	xxxvi
William Low & Co., Bread & Biscuits Bakers	1904	cxii
Wm. Low & Co., Bread and Biscuit Bakers	1910	ccv
William Lowden, Plumber, Tinsmith, and Gasfitter	1904	lxix
Willam Lowden, Plumber, Tinsmith, and Gasfitter	1910	clxxxi
A. Lowson & Co., Dress Materials, Millinery	1904	lxxx
W. Lowson, Horses, Carriages and Motor Cars for Hire	1910	cliii
M'Beth & Milne, Plumbers	1890	liii
James M'Dougall, Boots, Shoes and Slippers	1890	xx
James M'Dougall, Boots and Shoes	1904	lxi
D. B. M'Gibbons, Baker, Pastrycook, & Confectioner	1910	clix
Miss N. D. M'Gregor, Tobacconist and Confectioner	1910	clx
Alex. McKay, The Central Boot Shop	1904	cvii
A. M'Kay & Son, Bootmaker	1910	clviii
McKay & Son, The Footwear Specialists	1938	cclix
J. McKenzie, Painter and Decorator	1938	cclix
John M'Kinnon, Ladies' and Gent.'s Tailor	1900	cxxx
A. M'Laren & Son, Plumbers, Sanitary and Heating Engineers, &c.	1904	lxxxiii
Alex. M'Laren & Sons, Plumbers, Gasfitters, Sanitary and Heating Engineers	1910	clx
James M'Laren, Baker and Confectioner	1904	xciv
James M'Laren & Son, Bakers and Confectioners	1910	cxxviii
M'Laren & Fyfe, Painters, Decorators & Glass Embossers	1890	xxxvii
William McLaren, Painter, Paperhanger, Gilder, & Decorator	1904	xcix
William M'Laren, Painter, Paperhanger, Gilder, & Decorator	1910	cxix

William Roberts, Draper and Clothier	1910	clxxv
W. Roberts & Son, Drapers and Clothiers	1938	ccxlviii
Alex. Robertson, Osnaburgh Bar. Wine Merchant	1890	xliv
Archie Robertson Limited, Motor Engineers and Hirers	1938	ccxlix
David Robertson, Boot and Shoemaker	1900	212
David Robertson, Boot and Shoe Merchant	1904	lviii
Jas. W. Robertson, Painter, Paperhanger and Decorator	1890	xxxi
Wm. C. Roberston, Joiner & Cabinetmaker, Shop Fitter, Undertaker	1938	ccxlii
David Rodger & Son, Painters, Decorators, and Artists' Colourmen	1904	cvi
David Rodger & Son, Painters and Decorators, Artists' Colourmen	1910	cxxxiv
David Rodger & Son, Painters and Decorators	1938	ccl
Alex. Ross, Sculptor, Forfar Monumental Works	1910	clxxxix
Wm. Ross, Wholesale & Family Grocer, Wine, & Spirit Merchant	1890	xlvi
The Royal Hotel	1890	xlvii
The Royal Hotel	1904	xcv
The Royal Hotel	1910	cc
The Royal Hotel	1938	ccxlvii
Saddler's, Tea-Bread, Shortbread & Cakes	1890	xl
Saddler's, Tea-Bread, Shortbread & Cakes	1904	lxxiv
James Saddler, Baker	1910	ccx
William Saddler, Pastry Baker & Confectioner	1938	ccli
Salutation Hotel	1938	ccxlvi
James Samson, Joiner and Cabinetmaker, Glazier, Undertaker	1938	cclv
John Samson, Ladies' and Gent.'s Tailor	1904	xcvi
John Samson, Ladies' and Gent.'s Tailor	1910	cxlii
Scott & Coull, Wholesale and Retail Fish Merchants	1910	clxxxvii
Andrew F. Scott, Family Butcher	1910	ccix
George Scott, Boot and Shoe Warehouse	1910	clxxviii
James Scott, Watchmaker, Jeweller, and Optician	1910	cxcviii
William Scott, Joiner, Cabinetmaker, and Glazier	1890	xxiv
William Scott, Coal and Lime Merchant	1910	cxliii
Sharp, W. W., Coal Merchant	1890	xlix
Sharp & Co., Music and Musical Instrument Dealers	1904	lxxiv
A. & C. Shepherd, Slaters	1890	l
A. & C. Shepherd, Slaters	1904	xcii
A. & C. Shepherd, Slaters	1910	cciii
Andrew Shepherd, Baker and Confectioner	1890	l
Charles Shepherd, Tailor	1890	xxx
James Shepherd, Jun., China Merchant	1890	xlix
James Shepherd, China Merchant	1904	lxv

James Shepherd, China Merchant   1910   cxviii
W. Shepherd, Bookseller, Stationer, and Bookbinder   1847   viii
W. Shepherd, Printer   1904   xcvii
W. Shepherd, Stationer   1938   ccxli
W. Shepherd, Reproductions   1938   cclii
W. Shepherd, Printing   1938   ccliii
A. Simpson & Son, Cycles, Motor Cycles and Motor Cars   1910   clxxix
Charles Simpson, Bookseller, Stationer, Emigration
        and Shipping Agent   1938   ccxliii
Simpson, Charles O., Baker and Confectioner   1910   cci
Peter Small, Engineer, Horseshoer and Blacksmith   1900   413
Peter Small, Engineer and Blacksmith   1904   xcviii
Peter Small, Engineer, Blacksmith, and Horseshoer   1910   clxxx
Peter Small, Engineers   1938   ccliv
Allan Smart, Plumber and Sanitary Engineer   1938   cclv
George Smith, Drapery and Outfitting   1904   c
George Smith, The People's Draper   1910   cxxxix
Miss Smith, Shoe Seller   1890   li
Miss Smith, Boot and Shoe Specialist   1904   xcix
Miss Smith, Boot and Shoemaker   1910   ccx
Mrs Lewis Smith, Family Grocer & Wine Merchant   1904   cvi
Mrs Lewis Smith, Family Grocer & Wine Merchant   1910   clxxxi
Smith, Hood, & Co., Ltd, Coal Merchants and Colliery Agents   1904   cv
Smith, Hood, & Co., Ltd, Colliery Agents   1910   clxxxii
Spark Brothers, Artistic Photographers   1890   lii
Wm. Spark, Artistic Photographer   1904   ci
W. Spark, Artistic Photographer   1910   clxxxiii
The Station Hotel   1910   clxxxiv
Stewart's, Drapers   1890   xxii
Alex. Stewart, Cabinetmaker, Joiner, Upholsterer and
        Funeral Undertaker   1910   clxxxv
Andrew Stewart, Boot and Shoe Merchant   1904   cii
Andrew Stewart, Boot and Shoe Merchant   1910   cxxix
David Stewart, House Furnisher   1910   clxxxvi
J. & M. Stewart, Boot and Shoe Merchants   1938   ccxxi
William Stewart, Drapery & Millinery   1904   lix
William Stewart, Drapery and Millinery Warehouse   1910   ccvii
A. D. Strachan, Wood & Coal Merchant   1904   civ
Alex. D. Strachan, Wood and Coal Merchant   ·   1910   clxxxvii
Alex D. Strachan, Wood and Coal Merchant   1938   cclv
John Strachan, Jeweller and Silversmith, Watch and
        Clockmaker   1904   ciii
John Strachan, Jeweller and Silversmith, Watch and

Alexander Whyte, Fish, Game & Poultry Dealer	1910	clv
Alexander Whyte, Plumbers, Gasfitters, Sanitary and Heating Engineers	1938	cclviii
David Whyte, Potato Merchant	1904	cx
David Whyte, Potato Merchant	1910	clxvii
Henry Whyte, Fish, Game, and Poultry Dealer	1904	lx
Henry Whyte, Fish, Game, and Poultry Dealer	1911	16
Wilkie's Emporium, Lunanhead, Groceries, Drapery, Ironmongery, Boots and Shoes &c.	1890	xxxiii
J. F. Wilson, Auctioneer, Valuator, and Land Surveyor	1910	cxciii
James Wilson, Family Grocer, Tea, Wine, & Spirit Merchant	1904	cxi
James Wilson, Family Grocer & Wine Merchant	1910	cxciv
W. Wishart, Cycle Agent	1938	cclix
Robert Wood, Family Butcher	1910	cxcv
Miss Wood, Milliner	1904	cxiii
Miss Wood, Milliner	1910	clxviii

Index

10 Platoon "C" Company 50
3rd Lanarkshire Rifle Volunteers *see*
   Third Lanark

A

Aberdeen 169, 209, 215, 223, 243,
   245, 283, 287, 299, 326, 330, 335,
   359, 403, 447, 460
Aberdeen Press and Journal 223
Aberlemno 12, 446
Academy Street 17, 50, 124, 194, 220,
   273, 362, 394
Adam, Constable 300
Adam, Isabella Thomson 438
Adam, James, golfer 1932
Adamson, Harold 84, 146, 195
Adamson, JS 465
Adamson, Provost 105, 271, 303, 410
Afrika Korps 42
Agnew, Willie, footballer 51
Airdrieonians 279
Airlie 175, 256, 347, 476
Albert Street 346, 447
Alexander, James Lowson 234, 454
Alexander, Mr (Glamis) 219
Allahakbarries 218
Allan, James, musician 114, 217, 315
Allardice, JT 167, 232, 239
Anderson, Bill 223
Anderson, Brother 129
Anderson, James 138
Anderson, May 195
Anderson, Miss 65
Anderson, Provost 97
Anderson, Robert 284
Angus Athletic 185
Angus Curling Club 479
Angus Cycling Club 264
Angus District Council 223

Angus Spitfire Fund 363
Angus, Alexander 247
Angus, Cita 84
anthrax 75
Anti-Corn Law League 20, 243
Applegarth 280
Arbroath 3, 5, 12, 17, 23, 29, 34, 40,
   48, 73, 83, 89, 92, 101, 116, 129,
   136, 142, 148, 152, 161, 166, 215,
   219, 253, 256, 260, 261, 263, 269,
   283, 285, 287, 299, 326, 376, 396,
   398, 432, 440, 446, 482
Arbroath to Forfar Railway 5
armistice 423
Auldbar Road 5
Austin, Cecil 401
Avery, Captain 171
Ayr 240, 336, 347

B

Bachelors Dance 466
Baggerton 370, 432
Bain, joiner 160
Baird, John, railway contractor 59
Balfour, Davie 157, 329
Balfour, Ernie 157, 329
Balfour, Stewart 17
Balgavies Convalescent Home 83
Ballingall Cup 171
Balmashanner 35, 69, 99, 103, 243,
   328, 343, 453
Balmoral 28, 196
Balmuckety 281
Balnabooth 196
Bankhead 69, 464
Baptist Church 376
Barclay, A (artist) 189
Barclay, James 217 463
Barclay, Thomas (musician) 468

Barnhill 307
Barrie, JM 218
Barrie, William 434
Barron, Tom, Labour candidate 396
Barry, Agnes (later Lowson) 113
Batternach Burn 432
Baxter Bridie vii
Baxter, James 74
Baxter, William 89
Beechhill 182, 359
Beeching, Dr Richard 335
Bell Place 31, 43
Bell, Dave, golfer 200
Bell, David, RAF 440
Bell, Rev DM 17, 174, 334, 440
Bell, West School 171
Bernard, William, musician 110, 174, 262, 263, 440
Bervie 89
Beveridge Park 8
Beveridge, entertainer, 449
Bigwood, butler 358
Birse, George 167
Black, Bob 250
Black, Douglas 232
Black, James 65, 185, 234 267, 279, 284, 326, 379, 380
Blair, Ernie 405
Blairgowrie 206, 256, 291
Bloemfontein 81
Blyth, footballer 92
Boath, farmer 437
Boath, jute baron 196, 384, 435
Boath, Lieutenant 50
Boer War 2, 210, 264
bombs 106, 328
Boniface, St Curitan 229
bonspiel 479
Bowes-Lyon, Lady Elizabeth 416, 456
Bowman, footballer 51
Boyle JS 340, 341
Boyle, dressmakers 196
Boyle, Walter (hawker) 333

Boys' Brigade 349, 350
Brady, James, comedian 123
Brailsford, HN, Labour Candidate 458
Brechin ix, 3, 8, 23, 34, 48, 89, 101, 102, 136, 142, 166, 176, 177, 186, 190, 194, 206, 209, 215, 222, 226, 233, 266, 269, 271, 330, 338, 363, 376, 402, 406, 446, 447, 460, 466, 467
Brechin Road 3, 176, 190, 206, 271, 330, 467
Briar Cottage 115, 364
Brigton 264
British Expeditionary Force 175
Brittle, Willie, referee 26
Broughty Ferry 166
Broughty Junction 307
Brown, Colin 351
Brown, Eric 200
Brown, Isaac 169
Brown, John 235
Brown, Patrick 302
Brown, Peter 336
Brown, William 463
Brownlie, Jimmie, footballer 65
Bruce-Gardyne, Jock 382, 387
Bruce, football player 51, 250
Bruce, James 84
Bruce, James (gravel merchant) 333
Bruce, Lyndsay 423
Bruce, Rev John 481
Buffalo Bill's Wild West Show 321
Bummie v, 179, 210, 235, 286
Burgh Tribunal on conscription 70
Burial Ground 20, 378
Burns Night 30
Burns Supper 30
Burnside Farm 358
Busby, Matt, football manager 48
Butter's potato merchant 370

C

Cable, Dr Ewen 37, 87, 145
Caie, Rev George 38, 213, 247, 251, 376, 390
Caird, tradesman 345
Calder, Peter Ritchie 103
Caledonian Mercury 22, 302, 460
Caledonian Railway Company 60, 198, 225, 307, 446
California Cotton Mills 203
Callander 195, 311
Cameron, Donald 424
Cameron, Stuart 420
Canada 38, 62, 200, 275, 354, 448
canal 161
Canmore 174, 229
Canmore Bowling Green 147
Canmore Linen Works 360
Canmore Street 181
Cant, Janet 115, 364
Cardenden 146
Careston 209, 465
Cargill, Christina 181
Carnegie, Andrew 371
Carnegie, curler 479
Carseburn Road 112, 353
Carver, HC, pianist 84
Castle Street 3, 20, 25, 35, 69, 92, 99, 104, 122, 190, 208, 235, 275, 284, 296, 316, 325, 353, 355, 366, 414, 434
Castleton Farm 11
Cathkin Park 18, 313
Cattle Market 168, 266
Caw, National Gallery 114
Centre Arch 346
Chalmers, Sidney 167
Chamberlain, Neville 175, 334, 368
Chapel Street 66, 148, 266, 374
Chapelpark Primary School 362
Chapelpark School 336
Chapman DH, cricketer 157

Chapman, Councillor 274
Chapman, footballer 51
Charles Street 295
Charlton, CH 123
Chief Inspector of Constabulary 317
Children's Act of 1908 308
Chirnside 263
Choral Union 454
Christie, A and W, school footballers 171
Christie, James 29, 71
Christmas 342, 442, 466, 468, 472, 474, 475, 479
Chronicles of Mary-Ann 102
Church of Rome 89
Church of Scotland Training College 49
Churchill, Winston 42, 44, 175, 221, 255, 363
Clark, JD 210
Clark, John 2̶1̶1̶
Clark, John, footballer 13̶4̶
Clark, Miss, singer 384
Clark, Mrs, Model Lodging house keeper 22̶7̶
Clayton, Elgar, conductor 405
Clementson, John, hotel keeper 417
Clocksbriggs 5
Clocksbriggs Station 55
Clova 141, 196, 256, 281
Clugston, Rev William 188, 217
Collie, Sergeant George 257
Colliston 73
Commercial Hotel 92
Connell, Willie, Chief Booking Clerk 198
Convalescent Ward of Forfar Infirmary 20
Cook, footballer 171
Cook, William 101, 405
Cooper, Superintendent of Forfar Police, 266
Cooper, Miss, singer 384
Copland, Margaret 195, 448

561

Hogmanay 2, 474
Hollingworth, Catherin 146
Home Guard 50, 328
Hong Kong Telegraph 100
Hope Trust 441
Horsewater Wynd 164
Horticultural Society 274, 454
Hosie, JR, tradesman 388
Houston, Doug, footballer 131
Howie, JD, cricketer 157
Hume, Joseph 89
Hunter, John 134
Hunter, William 392
Hutchison, agricultural instruments
    396
Hutchison, Robert MP 13, 325
Hutton, JT 441
Hutton, Len 282, 469

I

Iannerelli, Sandy 221, 345
illegitimacy 126
India 23, 107, 179, 282, 298, 394
Inglis, Dr, Vet inspector 75
Inverarity 159, 228, 250
Ireland 65, 195, 211, 254, 283, 359,
    372, 378, 444, 452
Irons, stationmaster 465

J

Jarman's public house 131, 189, 410
Jarvis Brothers 196
John Street 363, 462
Johnston, Charles 383
Johnstone, "Sweddie" 327
Jolly Jesters Road Show 365
Jolly, David 84
Justinhaugh 102, 209
Juteopolis 185, 384

K

Kennedy, Tom, Labour candidate 246
Kerr, Col Charles 246
Kerr, Jerry, football manager 478
Kerr, R, Boer war veteran 210
Killacky, John v, 60, 69, 101, 149, 292,
    293, 317, 364
Kingennie 307
Kingsmuir 93, 307, 390
Kinnaber 215, 335
Kinnettles 138, 159
Kinnettles United Free Church 138
Kinninmonth 345
Kinnordy Estate 436
Kirk, Rev John F, 148, 174
Kirkbuddo 102, 307
Kirkcaldy 8, 13, 62, 132, 246, 293,
    396, 402
Kirking of the Council 172, 174
Kirkton 113, 118, 394
Kirriemuir 23, 40, 44, 48, 49, 69, 101,
    138, 166, 177, 213, 215, 218, 250,
    277, 281, 300, 363, 364, 376, 398,
    402, 479
Kirriemuir Harriers 69
Knox, Archie, footballer 477
Kruger, Paul, Boer 51, 393
Kunkel, Bruno 195
Kydd, David "Dancie" 171, 342

L

Ladies Missionary Work Society 160
Ladysmith 81
Laing, DM, photographer 182
Laird Bowl 383
Laird, footballer 171
Laird, Private J 81
Laird's 220, 360
Lamb, Bailie John, band conductor
    106, 108, 114, 147, 171, 189, 190,
    234, 284, 347, 410, 476

N

National Health Service 83, 312
National Union of Women's Suffrage 44
National Women's Social and Political Union 44
Nectan 229
Neill, AS 390
Neill, James "Dancie" 104, 342
Neill, musisian 476
Neill, Wilkie 34
Nether Bow Farm 75
New Road 97, 188
Newmanhill 337
Newmonthill 20, 124, 149, 186, 231, 235, 247, 380, 454
Newmonthill Cemetery 149, 380, 454
Newton, footballer 184, 250
Newtonbank 189
Newtyle 228
Nichol, Willie, footballer 51
Nicholl, footballer 184
Nicol, John, lamplighter 71
Nicol, William, Boys Brigade, 349
Nicoll Lieutenant A 50
Nicoll, Ian, boxer 457
Nicolson, James, Motor Transport Corps 257
No Change 411
Noble, Rev Douglas 406
Noran Burn 432
North Burgh School 31, 353
North Lone 113
North Mains 97, 284
North School 43, 248, 349, 353, 405, 406
North Street 31, 74, 81, 87, 92, 112, 124, 169, 225, 264, 299, 309, 346, 347, 353, 380, 473, 477
North Whitehills 112
Nursery Feus 71
Nursery Street 346

O

Oathlaw 40, 159
Ogilvie, I and D, footballers 184
Ogilvy, Bruce 457
Ogilvy, Lord 143
Ogilvy, Sir John 89
Old Forfar Library 137
Old Kirk 10, 73, 96, 110, 189, 247, 262, 334, 376, 380, 390, 399, 423, 438, 440, 454
Old Montrose Bothy 217
Old Parish Church 22, 110, 174, 182, 188, 263, 343, 349, 352
Old Parish Church Choir 110
Operatic Society 454
Oram, Miss, tradesperson 196
Ormond, Isabella 309
Osnaburgh Church 206
Osnaburgh Hall 129
Osnaburgh Street 141, 264
Oswald, Billy, artiste 147
Overseas League Tobacco Fund 47

P

Padanaram 59, 364, 377
Page, Harry, cricketer 287
Panmure, Lord 118
Parish Church Choir 98, 110
Paterson, Bill 51
Paterson, Isabella 121
Paterson, Rev 338
Patronage Act of 1875 251
Patterson, J, radio ham 211
Pattillo, Johnny, football manager 26
Patullo, Mary, actor 146
Pavilion 48, 76, 98, 107, 123, 147, 175, 210, 216, 277, 283, 340, 346, 412, 414, 443, 449
Pearson, Christen 64
Pearson, Private 433
Peel Monument 20, 165, 309

Z

Zeppelins 165, 378
Zoar 81, 190, 225, 281, 364, 480

Years:
710 229
1661 337
1662 64, 228, 426
1665 83, 174, 200
1745 54, 460
1746 143, 460
1782 481
1784 324
1785 99
1814 22, 302
1818 54, 161
1833 113, 473
1836 148
1837 28, 233
1839 5, 215
1845 463
1846 219, 378
1848 59, 115, 299
1851 20, 58, 113, 217, 378
1855 89, 126, 309
1856 12, 118, 315
1859 132, 266
1862 40
1864 138
1870 7, 307
1871 121, 177, 256, 468
1877 315, 366
1881 124, 268, 313
1885 30, 86, 112, 154, 185, 295, 386
1886 126, 381
1887 164, 225
1888 49, 417
1889 x, 15, 141, 261, 376, 402, 435,
  455
1890 69, 364, 398, 446
1891 15, 127, 285, 356
1892 55, 71, 100, 137, 220, 479

1893 196, 198, 273, 339, 398, 437
1894 115, 149, 254, 384, 424
1895 97, 209, 254, 309
1896 141, 198, 241, 242, 243, 244,
  298, 465
1897 20, 149, 235, 245, 259, 292,
  385, 448
1898 111, 125
1899 34, 317, 393
1900 2, 74, 81, 189, 338
1901 2, 27, 28, 100, 115, 160, 213,
  333, 351, 394, 425
1902 18, 264, 303, 351, 383
1903 169, 227, 240
1904 105, 263, 313, 321, 476
1905 100, 190, 271, 279, 313, 355,
  410, 441
1906 23, 92, 203, 247, 253, 470
1907 190, 332, 354, 434, 471
1908 7, 38, 132, 134, 298, 308, 313,
  399, 438, 444, 466
1909 44, 49, 51, 60, 134, 353, 471
1910 51, 52, 74, 98, 134, 147, 261,
  352, 374, 386, 412, 443, 444, 449,
  458
1911 10, 38, 51, 75, 120, 123, 181,
  236, 239, 320
1912 205, 380, 392, 406, 422, 462,
  471
1914 3, 31, 66, 67, 96, 180, 181, 182,
  198, 261, 286, 287, 296, 297, 298,
  323, 327, 438, 442
1915 14, 109, 114, 181, 253, 261,
  358, 391
1916 57, 98, 132, 165, 231, 257, 416,
  433
1917 29, 70, 313
1918 6, 14, 88, 104, 106, 109, 181,
  234, 261, 423, 450, 458, 459
1919 6, 11, 14, 25, 53, 106, 181, 253,
  284, 421
1920 10, 94, 104, 136, 238, 260, 265,
  279, 307, 326, 347, 372, 385, 411,

9 781849 212205